WITHDRAWN

THE CHICANO/HISPANIC IMAGE IN AMERICAN FILM

THE CHICANO/ HISPANIC IMAGE IN AMERICAN FILM

Frank Javier Garcia Berumen

VANTAGE PRESS
New York

To
Francisco R. Berumen (1916–92)
and Maria R. Berumen,
my parents,
who gave me love, faith,
and hope

Contents

Acknowledgments

I would like to express my thanks to all those who helped me in one way or another to write this book:

- Actress Rosaura Revueltas for her kind interview in Cuernavaca, Mexico, and her continued inspiration as a positive role model.
- Actress Pilar Pellicer (sister of the late Pina Pellicer) for her gracious interview in Mexico City.
- Actress Alma Martinez for her interview and indomitable spirit.
- Actress Silvana Gallardo for her interview and timely support.
- Producer Paul Jarrico for his rare stills of *Salt of the Earth*.
- Director Jesus Treviño for his stills of *Raices de Sangre* and consistent encouragement.
- Margarita Medina, Columbia Pictures, for photograph assistance.
- Jennifer Sebree at Universal Pictures for photograph assistance.
- Rebecca A. Herrera at 20th Century Fox for photograph assistance.
- Judith Singer at Warner Bros. for photograph assistance.
- Kathy Lendech at Turner Entertainment Co. for special use of the MGM stills.
- The staff at Academy of Motion Pictures Library.
- Larry Edmund's Bookstore for hard-to-find stills.

And last, but not least, thanks go to my students at Abraham Lincoln High School, who are all my beacons of hope for a future based on respect for cultural diversity and who will be the makers of that history.

Introduction

The purpose of this book is to chronicle the portrayal of the Chicano and Hispanic in American film. The word *Chicano* is a term coined in the 1960s by Hispanics in the U.S. Southwest (or Aztlan, the legendary origin of the Aztecs). The term denotes a person of Mexican descent, either born in or immigrated to the United States, who affirms cultural and ethnic pride as well as political consciousness. A general assessment of the Latin American is made as the Chicano/Hispanic generally underwent the same and identical fate of stereotyping.

The United States is essentially a nation of immigrants, and each group has contributed economically, politically, and culturally to enrich the progress and advancement of this most highly industrialized nation in the world. However, it must be recognized that historically the Chicano is not an immigrant but, in fact, native to this country and to this continent, as are the American Indians. In 1521, Cortez colonized Mexico and out of the blend of the Spanish conquistador and the Indian came forth the mestizos, who were to predominate in Latin America and the Southwest. During the 1520s, Alvar Nuñez Cabeza de Vaca explored Texas; during the 1540s, Francisco Vasquez de Coronado explored most of the Southwest; in 1598, Juan de Onate founded a colony in New Mexico; in the years 1687–1711, Father Kino established missions in Arizona and northwestern Mexico; in 1690, the first mission in Texas was established; in 1718, a *presidio* (a fortified settlement) was built in San Antonio, Texas. Some two thousand miles to the east, the first permanent English settlement took place at a place called Jamestown in 1607, almost a hundred years after the first Spanish settlements in the future continental United States.

The Southwest was administered as a unit of New Spain from the capital of Mexico City. Geographically, the Southwest and northern Mexico have always been one unit: arid and sparse of vegetation and of temperate climate. The economic foundations of these regions were established during the colonial period: cattle, mining, irrigation, farming. In 1821, Mexico became independent. Also, in that year, Mexico permitted Anglo colonists into Texas, provided that they obey all Mexican laws and that they not introduce the institution of slavery. The Anglo colonists proved to be less than law abiding. During 1835–36, the colonists rebelled against Mexico, and in 1845, Texas was annexed by the United States. The Mexican-American War of 1846–48 resulted in the loss of half of Mexico's territory, and in 1853, it lost more territory through the Gadsden Purchase. Thus, the Mexican-Americans, like the Indians, became a conquered people, and the United States achieved the goal of Manifest Destiny. Mexican-Americans were dispossessed of land, legal rights, and political power. Historian Rodolfo Acuña wrote about this period in his book *Occupied America: The Chicano's Struggle toward Liberation*:

> Most Anglo-Americans believed that, based on their right of conquest, they were entitled to special privileges and special citizenship status: this was reinforced by the belief in their cultural and racial superiority. The Chicano, in contrast, was a conquered person, an alien, and a half-breed. When a small number of Chicanos turned to highway banditry, Anglo-Americans did not bother to investigate why they committed anti-social acts or why the Chicano masses supported them. They merely stereotyped the entire group as criminal justifying further violence against the Mexican/American community. These factors created the colonization of the Chicano in California, with the Chicano becoming dependent on the Anglo-American majority, having no political or economic control, and being forced to adhere to an alien culture and government.[1]

U.S. hegemony in the American continent dawned in the latter part of the nineteenth century under the guise of the Monroe Doctrine and "gunboat diplomacy." Theodore Roosevelt, in his annual message to the Congress, added a corollary to that doctrine: "Chronic wrongdoing, or an impotence which results in a general loosening of the ties of civilized society, may in America, as elsewhere, ultimately require intervention by some civilized nation, and in the Western Hemisphere, the adherence of the United States to the Monroe Doctrine may force the United States, however reluctantly, in flagrant cases of such wrongdoing or impotence, to the exercise of an international police power." Indeed, the relationship between the United States and Latin America was one of continuous turbulence, intervention, and misunderstanding. The kernel of this imperial foreign policy was reflected in the race relations within the United States. In 1896, the U.S. Supreme Court ruled in *Plessy v. Ferguson* that the doctrine of "separate but equal" was constitutional. In essence, the court's decision espoused the superiority of the White race over people of darker skins. Within this legal context, racism and prejudice festered and flourished, and people of darker skins were the primary victims: Hispanics, Blacks, American Indians, Asians. The legal status of segregation was undermined with *Brown v. Board of Education* in 1954, but it took a civil rights movement as well as continuous federal legislation and enforcement to finally ensure its demise. However, de facto segregation would continue.

If art reflects life, then the American film reflected the prevailing images of people of color within the context of the times, periodically racist and frequently stereotypical. Thus, the Hispanic was inevitably portrayed as lazy, unintelligent, greasy, criminal, and "foreign." Their contributions culturally, economically, and historically were never properly documented or appreciated.

History was revised to suit the public's conceptual whim and fancy with the minimum of historical accuracy. The films dealing with the Texas rebellion are a case in point (e.g., *Man of Conquest, Man from the Alamo, The Last Command, The Alamo*). The recently arrived slave-owning colonists are inevitably portrayed as brave and pious victims who are fighting a second Thermopylae, while the Mexicans are the "foreign aggressors." As John King Fairbank wrote in *The Great Chinese Revolution 1800–95*: "After all, history is in our minds. It is what we think happened. . . ." The issues or concerns of Hispanics in this country were not addressed, or the films dealt with them in only a handful of exceptions (e.g., *The Lawless*, *Salt of the Earth*). According to Hollywood legend, when movie mogul Samuel Goldwyn was asked whether he ever considered the social message in his films, he is said to have replied, "When I want to send a message, I use Western Union."

While the discredited practice of Anglos portraying Asians and Blacks (e.g., *The Birth of a Nation*) had disappeared with the dawning of talking pictures, that practice, with regard to Hispanics, continued unabated to the contemporary era. Incoherent, mispronounced, and heavily accented Spanish was enunciated by these players in order to Latin-flavor the proceedings. Unfortunately for all concerned, these players' enthusiasm could not compensate for their malnourished thespian skills. Such films—acted, written, and directed by people who did not know, did not care, or were motivated by personal prejudices—created a screen world of cultural inaccuracies and stereotypes: sombrero and serape-draped Mexicans taking siestas on sidewalks; Mexicans consuming the only three diet staples of chile, tacos, and liquor; the Hispanic inevitably seeking political and social guidance, acceptance, and "enlightenment" of the Anglo (e.g., *The Magnificent Seven*).

Finally, the stereotype of the Hispanic provided no role models for youth who aspired to the fulfillment of the elusive American dream. Hispanics were never portrayed as teachers, doctors, engineers, or as leaders, but, predictably and permanently, as waiters, bandits, Latin lovers, prostitutes, and currently as gang members (e.g., *Walk Proud*) and drug dealers. The Hispanic who could not think for himself (e.g., *A Message to Garcia* and in *Two Mules for Sister Sara*) was a common type of character, which perhaps reflected only too closely American policy in relation to Latin America.

This, then, is the story of the Chicano/Hispanic in reel life and how it was once upon a time in a place called Hollywood.

Note

1. Rodolfo Acuña, *Occupied America: The Chicano's Struggle toward Liberation* (New York: Harper & Row, 1988).

THE CHICANO/HISPANIC IMAGE IN AMERICAN FILM

CHAPTER ONE
In the Beginning

The stereotyping of Hispanic men and women on film is a cumulative perception evolving and emanating out of several historical and political events: the Black Legend, Manifest Destiny, the Monroe Doctrine, the mythology of the Alamo, the Mexican-American War, and the racism implicit in the institutions of slavery and segregation.

The Black Legend was a propaganda campaign launched in the 1500s by England to discredit its archrival Spain in its methods of colonizing Latin America, attributing to it innate characteristics of violence, brutality, and treachery. History reveals, however, that all of the colonizers—England, France, Portugal, and/or Spain—were equally adept at the wholesale and systematic extermination of the American Indian and the dispossession of their land. Manifest Destiny was a symptom of the transformation of a mercantile appendage into an industrial nation. Acuña notes ". . . many citizens believed that God had destined them to own and occupy all of the land from ocean to ocean and pole to pole. Their mission, their destiny made manifest, was to spread the principles of democracy and Christianity to the unfortunates of the hemisphere."[1]

The Monroe Doctrine of the 1820s, which proclaimed that the American hemisphere was no longer open to European colonization, was a dubious policy of pan-Americanism but one that was designed to maintain the hegemony of England and the United States, backed up by the formidable British navy. The mythology of the Alamo was a wishful fulfillment of glorifying the transparent efforts of a motley assortment of filibusters to export the institution of slavery into Texas. The Mexican-American War (1846–48) and the forced incorporation of more than

1

half of the Mexican territory was a desperate attempt to maintain the precarious balance between free states and slave states that would ultimately result in the Civil War, with some one million casualties, more than all other military conflicts engaged in by this nation before or since. Despite this tragedy, the superiority of one race over another was upheld in *Plessy v. Ferguson* (1896) and de jure segregation was sanctioned and protected by the federal government, Social Darwinists, and misguided nativists. The federal government's belated break with such a racial fantasy in *Brown v. Board of Education of Topeka* (1954) and the multiracial civil rights movement was a historic turning point to establish a truly "color-blind society."

The film industry flourished in Hollywood, California, significantly by 1910, enhanced by the pleasant Mediterranean year-round weather; the diversity of coast line, desert, mountains, and snow; and its proximity to the sizeable Latin American market. Racism was in evidence in the popular literature of the 1800s and stereotypes developed specifically of Mexicans, Blacks, Indians, and Jews. Hollywood conveniently transplanted these stereotypes into film, usually in the guise of villains.

The first American film dealing with Hispanic culture was an obscure 1896 nickelodeon short by Enoch J. Rector about a bullfight in Mexico. The 1894 *Pedro Esquirel and Dionecio Gonzalez: Mexican Duel* introduced the first Mexican character reference. It was a distorted image that has remained static ever since: violent, treacherous, drunkard, crime oriented, and with the singular inability to control one's primitive passions. The stereotype of the grotesque Mexican bandit was thus given its cinematic birth. The epithetic titles of these films give an indication of their dubious accuracy and motivation: *Tony the Greaser* (1911), *Bronco Billy and the Greaser* (1914), *The Greaser's Revenge* (1914), *The Thread of Destiny*, *The Greaser's Gauntlet*, and *Guns and Greasers*, the latter was the last to use the epithet greaser in its title but not in its content. The epitome of yellow journalism, William Randolph Hearst, partly financed a fifteen-part serial entitled *Patria* purporting to show a Mexican-Japanese invasion of the United States, thereby justifying intervention in the Mexican Revolution.

2

The aforementioned films, along with hundreds of others, as well as innumerable assembly-line westerns, developed the established formula for the stereotypical image of Chicanos and Hispanics forever after in American film. First, there were only two types of Hispanics: docile and/or violent. Second, neither could think for themselves. The docile ones could only be saved by a Yankee hero (*The Aztec Hero* [1914] and *The Magnificent Seven* [1960]), and the undomesticated ones met a necessary Darwinist extinction at the hands of the Great White Hope (*Why Worry?* [1923] and *The Three Amigos* [1986]). Third, the Yankee hero always proved himself superior to his Hispanic counterpart in both love and war. The virtuous señorita always discarded her Latino lover for the white tenderfoot and the Latino hero discarded his cantinera women only to fail in pursuit of the Anglo women (*In Old Arizona* [1929] and *100 Rifles* [1969]). Fourth, all Hispanics were played almost exclusively by Anglos, as were Blacks, as in *Birth of a Nation* (1915), and Asians, as in *Broken Blossoms* (1915). It was an established practice that would only begin to alter in the 1920s with the arrival of the first Hispanic film stars.

One of the few films to break from the proverbial trend of stereotyped films was *War in Mexico* (1913). Pancho Villa needed money for munitions and supplies. He signed a contract with the Mutual Film Corporation for $25,000, permitting the cameramen to film his exploits. Most of the footage was subsequently incorporated into a second Mutual feature, titled *The Life of Villa* (1915), contracted to be directed by D. W. Griffith, but which was ultimately assigned to Christy Cabanne. Future director Raoul Walsh shot some additional footage and then played the revolutionary hero, with Villa's own approval. Villa was presented in a positive light by the American press due to the fact that he had always been cordial and diplomatic with the U.S. government. It would all soon quickly change. The U.S. government recognized the corrupt and counterrevolutionary General Carranza and permitted his troops to cross the border and attack Villa's army from the back (the north) at the battle of Agua Prieta. In retaliation, Villa attacked Columbus, New Mexico. That act earned him the U.S. government's and Hollywood's eternal enmity.

The first period of Hispanic images ended with the coming of World War I (1914–18). Hollywood found new villains in the Germans and, as usual, proceeded to take it to excessive limits. The war severely limited the export of Hollywood films to Europe and, as such, served to encourage the U.S. film industry to make inroads into Latin America, which welcomed the disappearance of the greaser image. Each country was permitted to make their own subtitles, and a harmonious hemispheric relationship flourished with the substantial increase of box-office receipts of American films playing in Latin America.

However, the respite from stereotypes came to an end with the termination of World War I. If the greaser character did not return, an approximate facsimile, in the guise of the Mexican and Hispanic bandit and desperado, did so. Films like *The Americano* (1916) and *Why Worry?* (1923) celebrated, with relish, the age of imperialism and "gunboat diplomacy" as the nation became a world power.

As the 1920s dawned, the "Latin lover" was about to make his debut on cue. However, there would be no love lost between the Hispanic image and Hollywood.

Note

1. Rodolfo Acuña, *Occupied America: The Chicano's Struggle toward Liberation* (New York: Harper & Row, 1988).

4

CHAPTER TWO

The 1920s—the Latin Lover and Señoritas

The Nicaraguans are better fighters than the Haitians, being of Indian blood, and as warriors similar to the aborigines who resisted the advance of civilization in this country. . . . Men who could kill with the ferocity unknown to any white soldier.
> —Harold N. Denny, *New York Times*

. . . every Californian of noble blood stands with me!
> —*The Mark of Zorro* (1920)

Show no mercy, spare nobody!
> —*Why Worry?* (1923)

This Cisco Kid, they say he's a very bad egg.
   He's bad all right.
   And plenty dangerous too . . . Probably just a dirty greaser.
> —*In Old Arizona* (1929)

The Roaring Twenties was a decade of unparalleled prosperity for the United States. It was a multi-faceted decade of diverse vitality: the production of the assembly-line Model T, the Lindberg flight across the Atlantic, the controversial Sacco and Vanzetti case, the Red Scare, the lost generation of Fitzgerald and Hemingway, the proliferation of bootleggers and gangsters stimulated by Prohibition, Babe Ruth and Jack Dempsey, and the beginning of the Golden Era of American films (1920–50). The good times ended suddenly on "Black Tuesday," October 29, 1929, with the stock market crash, beginning the decade-long Depression.

Abroad, in Germany, an obscure corporal, after a failed putsch had been imprisoned where he wrote a book titled *Mein Kampf*; in Italy, Benito Mussolini and his brown shirts had come to power early in the decade; and in the 1921 Washington Conference, Japan was allowed three-fifths of naval tonnage of what the United States and Britain each had, thus arousing the wrath of ambitious militarists. In the American hemisphere, the Mexican Revolution had been institutionalized. The U.S. Marines had been withdrawn from Nicaragua in August 1925 but were returned within a year after a renewal of political upheaval. Augusto Cesar Sandino led a guerrilla army against the foreign occupation. The ubiquitous secretary of state Frank B. Kellog warned of a dangerous Mexican-Soviet-Nicaraguan conspiracy to violently establish a "Mexican-fostered Bolshevist hegemony" that threatened the Panama Canal.[1]

At home, the restrictive immigration acts of 1917, 1921, and 1924 and World War I drastically limited European immigration. This, in turn, caused a demand for cheap Mexican labor. Additionally, a large number of Mexican workers emigrated due to the unstable economic and political conditions in their homeland. They formed mutual-aid societies like LULAC (League of United Latin American Citizens) to confront racial segregation and the ire of nativist animosity. For example, Representative Nance Garner of Texas cautioned: "In our country, they do not cause any trouble, unless they stay there a long time and become Americanized: but they are a docile people. They can be imposed on; the sheriff can go out and make them do anything."[2]

It was ironic, then, that for the Hispanic on American film, this would be the decade of the "Latin lover."

The Films

In the 1920s, the motion picture industry was the fifth largest industry in the United States. The twin foundations of Hollywood were the studios and their star systems. The autocratic movie moguls wielded their power with a paternalistic hand. They kept their stars under long-term contracts that even included "morality clauses."

Celluloid idols were considered demigods by their adoring public, permitting no discernable mortal flaws in their conduct, public or private. In 1918, when a divorce decree revealed that matinee idol Francis X. Bushman had been married, his career ended overnight. Popular stars Mabel Normand and Roscoe "Fatty" Arbuckle, when tarnished by scandal, met with similar fates. Hollywood movie fare of the 1920s perfected a craftsmanship and style that would become enviable and inimitable. However, it was the legendary stars who made it all memorable: Charlie Chaplin, Douglas Fairbanks, Mary Pickford, Buster Keaton, Harold Lloyd, John Barrymore, John Gilbert, Lon Chaney, Rudolph Valentino, Pola Negri, Clara Bow, and among them, the first quartet of Hispanic film stars, Ramon Novarro, Dolores Del Rio, Lupe Velez, and Gilbert Roland.

The films of the decade bent strongly toward the escapist and romantic. Romantic costume films became a popular staple. They contained the ingredients of adventure: the exotic, action, and, above all, the passionate love story. Male stars aspired to be great film lovers, as female stars desired to be sex symbols. Since the exotic and the faraway became synonymous with passion, it seemed inevitable that the ambiguous myth of the Latin lover developed.

A close analysis of the Latin-lover film image reveals that the word *Latin* was not synonymous with Latin American or Chicano. In the 1920s, the Latin lover was usually of Italian origin and, infrequently, Spanish or Latin American. The Latin-lover films began with *The Four Horsemen of the Apocalypse* (1921, Metro), an adaptation of the Vicente Blasco Ibañez novel set in pre–World War I Argentina. It starred the Italian-born newcomer Rudolph Valentino, whose sensual underplaying and tango dancing catapulted him as the cinema's leading heartthrob. Jet-black hair, dark complexion, half-lid eyes with smoldering passion became the physical characteristics of the Latin lover.

Hollywood studios quickly developed stories of the prototype character, and the rush was on to find male actors to fit the roles. Valentino quickly consolidated his stardom with *The Sheik* (1921, Paramount) and another Ibañez adaptation, *Blood and*

7

Sand (1922, Paramount), in which he played a Spanish bull-fighter. He continued in the forefront with such successes as *The Cobra* (1925, Paramount), *The Eagle* (1925, United Artists), and *The Son of the Sheik* (1925, Paramount). Valentino's career, however, was short-lived. A perforated ulcer, resulting in inoperable peritonitis, ended his life at the age of only thirty-one in 1926. Hollywood understandably tried to fill the profitable void with more incarnations.

Director Rex Ingram, who had discovered Valentino, had boasted he could discover another star, and he did with Ramon Novarro. Novarro shot to stardom in the swashbuckler, *The Prisoner of Zenda* (1923), and immediately became Valentino's main rival with the female audiences. While Novarro played the occasional Latin-lover variation, as in *The Arab* (1924, Metro), his range was much more versatile than Valentino's. Part of the reason is that he simply took himself much less seriously. Without such a handicap, he could aspire to be a more serious actor, such as in *Ben Hur* (1926, Metro).

Other rivals emerged to challenge Valentino and Novarro for the Latin-lover mantle, such as the Spanish-born Antonio Moreno, who starred with the popular Pola Negri in *Spanish Dancer* (1923, Paramount); the Mexican-American, Don Alvarado, in the Crimean costumer, *Drums of Love* (1928, United Artists), and *The Bridge of San Luis Rey* (1929, MGM), with Raquel Torres; the Mexican-born Gilbert Roland, in *The Blonde Saint* (1926), *Camille* (1927), and *The Dove* (1927), the latter two with Norma Talmadge. Some of the Latin lovers who passed themselves off as actually Latin Americans were not so in fact. Ricardo Cortez was a case in point. He was born Jacob Krantz of Hungarian and Austrian parents in Vienna, Austria. Nevertheless, he essayed Latin-lover-type roles in *The Spaniard* (1925, Paramount) and in Ibañez's *The Torrent* (1926, MGM), with Greta Garbo.

Other non-Hispanic stars by birth who played Latin-lover-type roles included John Gilbert, in *The Merry Widow* (1925) and in the films with Garbo such as *Love* (1925), *Flesh and the Devil* (1928), and *A Woman of Affairs* (1928). Another was John Barrymore, the greatest Shakespearean actor of his generation, in *Beau Brummel* (1924) and *Don Juan* (1926), about the legendary Spanish lover.

The Latin lovers were, for the most part, one-dimensional characters. Typically, these films had three key scenes: the meeting of the lovers, the seduction, and the inevitable duel to placate the aggrieved honor of the cuckolded husband and/or the dashing rescue of the lover of his beloved. Usually, the Latin lover seduced a woman who was already betrothed or otherwise engaged. They were thus illicit encounters, which only added spice to the passionate proceedings.

The vogue of the Latin lover ended with the coming of sound and the Depression. Several of the great screen lovers failed to make a successful transition into talking films, such as John Gilbert, Ricardo Cortez, Antonio Moreno, and Don Alvarado. Second, the anxious and financially strapped studios who were making the technological transition of the early talkies amid the Depression could not afford the big budgets for these costume melodramas. Third, the public taste underwent a change with the Depression, which aroused jingoism. Thousands of Mexicans were being deported as scapegoats of the economic crisis, and foreign-looking people, whether Latin lovers or not, were not too popular. The Latin-lover characters that did survive were reduced to small roles in which they inevitably lost the woman to a sterling Anglo hero. The Latin lover would make a brief comeback in the 1940s, and at that stage, the Latin lover took on an exclusively Latin American nationality.

Another type of Hispanic image in the 1920s was the caballero, the light-skinned, Spanish origin hero of the colonial Southwest and/or Latin America. His nemeses were inevitably the dark and cruel mestizos and Indians. These Robin Hood–like characters went forth fighting for the wretched of the earth, who were mestizos and Indians, against the recently empowered mestizo, who was oppressive and evil. Occasionally, the villain would be a renegade caballero. These films had begun with *The Caballero's Way* (1914), of which Zorro and, later, the Cisco Kid were a variation.

In reality, however, these romanticized incarnations of knight errants were bastardizations of the historical Joaquin

Murietta and Tiburcio Vasquez, who fought against Anglo injustices after the Mexican-American War. The key caballero films of the decade were Douglas Fairbanks's *The Mark of Zorro* (1921, United Artists) and its subsequent sequel, *Don Q., Son of Zorro* (1925, United Artists). Set in Spanish California, the masked avenger swashbuckled his way, athletically fighting the villains and making love to beautiful señoritas. Arthur Carew and Allen Sears played quarreling caballero siblings in *Rio Grande* (1920, Path). Rudolph Valentino played a caballero, in *A Sainted Devil* (1924, Paramount), in love with a cantinera (Nita Naldi); Johnny Walker played another in *Captain Fly-by-Night* (1924, FBO); Douglas Fairbanks, in *The Gaucho* (1927, United Artists), which introduced Lupe Velez; the stalwart Richard Dix, in *The Gay Defender* (1927, Paramount); and Gilbert Roland, in *Rose of the Golden West* (1927), with Mary Astor, and in *The Love Mart* (1928, First National), with Bessie Love. The best-known novel dealing with that historical period was Mary Hunt Jackson's *Ramona* (1928, Fox). It was, by far, the best film version and the only time the title role was played by an Hispanic actress, Dolores Del Rio. The caballero films were spoofed by Wallace Reid in *The Dictator* (1922, Paramount) and by Bebe Daniels and William Powell in *Señorita* (1927, Paramount). The Cisco Kid himself made his film debut in *In Old Arizona* (1929, Fox), winning Warner Baxter an Academy Award as Best Actor of the Year. In Allan Dwan's *Tide of Empire* (1929, MGM), the incorporation of California into the union is shown, predictably, as a time when an Anglo tenderfoot (George Duryea) could take a señorita (Renee Adoree) easily from her Mexican boyfriend. Similar geography was covered in *Wolf Song* (1929, Paramount), with Gary Cooper and Lupe Velez.

Apart from the Latin-lover and caballero films, there were the usual assortment of stereotypes familiar on film before. Mexican bandits ran amok in the Western: *The Bad Men* (1923, First National); in the George S. Kaufman-Marc Connelly play adaptation, *Merton of the Movies* (1924, Paramount); in *Mademoiselle Midnight* (1924, MGM), in which Mae Murray inherits a Mexican ranch. In *The Fighting Edge* (1926, Warner Brothers), a U.S. Secret Service agent (Kenneth Harlan) single-handedly wages a war against a gang who smuggles passports from Mexico for hordes of undocumented Mexican workers. In Harold Lloyd's *Why Worry?* (1923), all Mexicans are portrayed as having two pastimes: sleeping and killing. In *From Headquarters* (1929, Warner Brothers), Monte Blue leads a squad of invincible U.S. Marines in a Central America populated only by two types of people: docile and/or violent. In *Beyond the Sierras* (1928, MGM), the indomitable Tim McCoy plays a masked Californian bandit, and in *The Desert Rider* (1929, MGM), he plays a tenderfoot who wins the hand of the most beautiful señorita (Raquel Torres) away from her Mexican lover.

Hispanic women were portrayed in the 1920s essentially either as virtuous señoritas or as cantineras of easy virtue. In the caballero films, despite their virtue, they inevitably abandoned their possessive Hispanic lover for the Yankee tenderfoot. The cantineras took on all comers, but they ultimately ended up with the mestizo villain or lowly peon.

The decade and silent films ended with the advent of sound. The first talking film, *The Jazz Singer* (1927, Warner Brothers), had some prophetic dialogue, "You ain't seen nothing yet!" For the image of the Chicano and Hispanic, it would be true; it would get worse.

The following are representative films of the Chicano and Hispanic image in American film in the 1920s.

The Americano (1916)

Douglas Fairbanks, film pioneer and superstar, cheerfully exuberant and physically agile, was the prototype of the idealized American male during the silent film era. Beginning in films in 1915, he personified a carefree pursuit and attainment of the American dream that was elusive to some ethnic minorities, in such films as *Wild and Woolly* (1916), *Heading South* (1917), *His Majesty the American* (1918), and *The Americano*. Franklin notes:

His films were frankly escapist, yet didn't appear to be. They told every man in the audience that he could be this successful if he'd just stop worrying and tackle life with a smile. Nobody seemed to worry that it was never explained just how to go about this.

11

After all, what did it matter? It was a healthy and constructive philosophy, and it was no wonder that Doug was everybody's idol.[3]

It was, however, an image that celebrated Teddy Roosevelt's imperialist "gunboat diplomacy."

The Americano, scripted by Anita Loos, chronicled the adventures of the idealized Anglo hero (Douglas Fairbanks) in the politically unstable Latin American country of Paragonia. The hero is a mining engineer who is requested to come to the aid of the mining industry by President Valdes: "Without American capital and engineers, our mines are helpless." The admiration of the hero by the president's beautiful daughter, Juana (Alma Rubens), propels the hero into action.

Upon his arrival in Paragonia, Valdes has been overthrown by Generals Sanchez and Garcia in a military coup. The generals express their nationalist tendencies by being uncaring of U.S. interests. The hero, thus rebuffed, busies himself by helping the deposed and imprisoned Valdes. He is ordered to appear before Garcia and Sanchez, and, much to the hero's amazement, they seek his help in order to reopen the mines. Otherwise, they may be themselves overthrown by the wrath of the unemployed. He pretends to aid them but secretly plots their demise. The populace ultimately does rebel but is unsuccessful until the hero intervenes, freeing Valdes, and then all by himself, beats to a bloody pulp Sanchez and Garcia. Acclaimed by the masses, the impudent Americano boasts: "I am here to assure you that the mines will be opened and that the nation will be governed honestly." The idyllic scenario ends with his marriage to Juana, and he is made the commander in chief of the armed forces.

The villains are greasy and treacherous mestizos, unlike Valdes, who is a genteel and refined caballero of pure Spanish blood. The film perpetuates the image of the hopeless Latin American who cannot control his excesses of violence and greed. In this Darwinist scenario, the inevitable is the civilizing, firm hand of the neighbor to the north. It was a simplistic and chauvinistic rationale for the frequent U.S. armed interventions in Latin America.

The Mark of Zorro (1921, United Artists)

Douglas Fairbanks's thirtieth film, *The Mark of Zorro*, came about as a result of the complaints from exhibitors about the "failure to develop sufficient love interest" in his films and the inability to attract more female fans. Although Fairbanks was desirous of becoming a romantic star, costume films were considered poison. The disastrous failure of Griffith's *Intolerance* (1917) was still well remembered.

His brother Robert told him of a story, entitled "The Curse of Capistrano," by Johnson McCully, that had appeared August 9, 1919, in an issue of the pulp magazine, *All-Story Weekly*. The resultant film typecast him in the role of the swashbuckler for which he is now best remembered, which he played in *The Three Musketeers* (1920), *Robin Hood* (1921), *The Thief of Baghdad* (1922), and *The Black Pirate* (1925). The film transformed him into a phallic symbol, with his fulfillment as a lover (he had just married "America's sweetheart," Mary Pickford).

The film is set in California in the early 1800s, just before Mexican independence. Recently arrived from Spain, Don Diego discovers that his noble-born caballero father has been replaced by the evil Captain Ramon (Robert McKim). Dismayed at the injustice committed, he passes himself off both as foppish and effeminate Don Diego and as a disguised Zorro avenging the wrongs of the land. Encouraged by his father to court Lolita (Marguerite de la Motte), he alienates her, but she falls in love with him as the heroic Zorro. A progression of unjust acts—the jailing of his father for treason, the whipping of a Franciscan monk, the imprisonment of Lolita, and Captain Ramon's increasing vanity—propels Zorro to lead the noble-born caballeros to overthrow the corrupt governor and his henchman, Ramon. The film is replete with stunts, leaps, climbs, and sword duels that enhance the film and stamp it with the authoritative Fairbanks persona.

The film repeated many of the staples of the proverbial caballero films. All the villains are mestizos, who invariably and inevitably are corrupted when given a position of responsibility. Unable to regulate their own political morality, a noble-born caballero comes forth as an avenger to recover the position of his social class, much to the delight of the cowardly and simple-minded mestizo and Indian masses. The triumph of an authentic mestizo in American films would not come until *Juarez* (1939, Warner Brothers).

The Mark of Zorro was hugely successful, restoring the costume film to public favor and paving the way for more lavish, later Fairbanks swashbucklers. It spawned one sequel starring Fairbanks, *Don Q., Son of Zorro* (1925, United Artists), and many other films using the character of Zorro: *The Bold Caballero* (1937), *Zorro Rides Again* (1940, 20th Century), *Zorro's Black Whip* (1944), *The Ghost of Zorro* (1949), *The Sign of Zorro* (1960), *Zorro and the Three Musketeers* (1962), *The Erotic Adventures of Zorro* (1972), *Zorro* (1975, made for television), *Zorro, the Gay Blade* (1978), and two television series, "Zorro" (1957–59) and "Zorro" (1990). Despite the fact that the character is one of the few Hispanic film heroes, it has never been played by an Hispanic actor.

Why Worry? (1923)

This two-reeler comedy centers around a wealthy young clubman, Harold Van Pelham (Harold Lloyd), vacationing in the tropical country of Paradiso (really Latin America), in order to recover his health, as a result of his excessive vices of drinking and womanizing. The subtitle describes the country: "Paradiso—A drowsy city in a dreamy land. Rip Van Winkle's twenty-year sleep would be considered a nap down here."

Jim Blake, an American renegade, has a ragtag army which is in control of part of the island. His right-hand man is a native called Herculo the Mighty. Van Pelham is mistaken for a representative of World Allied Bankers, an American company that has been complaining about constant interference. Predictably, Van Pelham is imprisoned. There he meets the physical giant, Colosso, a wild hermit who has been finally subdued because he is suffering from a terrible toothache. Van Pelham and Colosso break out of prison and proceed to beat to a pulp the entire armies of both factions all by themselves, belatedly assisted by Van Pelham's pretty nurse. Returning to the United States, Van Pelham and his nurse settle into domestic tranquility.

Harold Lloyd's "Everyman," wearing a pair of oversized, black, horn-rimmed glasses and panama hat was eternally optimistic, persistent, and lucky in overcoming adversity. Lloyd's character was a slightly more sedate counterpart of Fairbanks's pre-*Mark of Zorro*, smiling and exuberant, an idealized American hero, with similar athletic prowess. Lloyd, groomed and trained in Hal Roach and Mack Sennett comedies, had catapulted to film prominence as early as 1916, with another character, Lonesome Luke. Lloyd's "Everyman," like Fairbanks' ones, personified and perpetuated a latent Social Darwinist bent in films chronicling the adventures of their heroes in Latin America. *Why Worry?*, like Fairbanks's *The Americano*, emphasized the superiority of Anglo resourcefulness, intelligence, and morality.

The opening scene, set in Paradiso, immediately conveys the old greaser and racist stereotypes. A sleeping native (clearly Mexican) maneuvers his donkey-pulled wagon down the street of the town. When the donkey stops, the driver gets off and the donkey falls asleep. Dozens of Hispanics are shown sleeping, some in rocking chairs, balconies, and benches, some with cobwebs in their heads that are attached to the walls. They are all mestizo, unkempt, greasy, menacing, and violent. They beat up old, defenseless women and men. Two of them, upon seeing the nurse, would rape her, but for the fortuitous interference of Jim Blake, the American renegade. Effortlessly, both Jim Blake and Van Pelham assert their leadership over the excessively violent natives. "Show no mercy, spare nobody," exhorts one native. It is a statement that perfectly illustrates this film's treatment of all Hispanics.

In Old Arizona (1929, Fox)

In Old Arizona was based on "The Caballero's Way" by O. Henry (pen name of William Sidney Porter), written in 1907. The writer spent several years in prison for embezzlement in a bank in Austin, Texas. His short stories were extremely popular early in the century, because of their formula premises and enlivenment with their inevitable twist endings. His Mexican character was blatantly stereotypical. In reality, the Cisco Kid character was a composite of Joaquin Murietta and Tiburcio Vasquez, Mexican rebels who became outlaws fighting the dispossession of Mexican land in California after its forced incorporation into the United States. The fictional Cisco Kid is a pureblooded bandit hero. The romantic side was an integral part of this caballero character: gentlemanly, witty, and charming. Not unlike other contemporary matinee cowboy heroes, the Kid would ride into a town, right a wrong, and, that done, would ride away into the mystic sunset to live to fight evil another day somewhere else. Invariably, the Mexican heroine was either a cantinera or a virtuous señorita. If it was the former, the Kid would discard or only flirt with her and go on to court the Anglo heroine, and if the latter, she would discard him for a Yankee tenderfoot.

No explanation was ever given for the Kid's banditry. Without the enigma explained, it would be logical to assume that his banditry was inherent in his culture. This notwithstanding, the Cisco Kid and Zorro were the only Hispanic characters who exemplified tenacity and resistance to the typical uniformed standard of Hispanic characters. They were not killed off in the last reel, and although they did not always get the girl and live the proverbial Hollywood "happily ever after" ending, they offered the hope that maybe down the road, one day they would. In the first three Cisco Kid entries, the Kid worked alone, and it was not until the fourth film, *The Return of the Cisco Kid* (1939, 20th Century), that he acquired a sidekick.

In Old Arizona's plot revolved around the efforts of Sergeant Dunne (Edmund Lowe) to trap the Kid (Warner Baxter), using the duplicity of the Kid's cantinera girlfriend, Tania (Dorothy Burgess). The resourceful Kid, however, turns the tables at the last moment, and it is Tania who falls victim to the sergeant's anxious bullets. The Kid sardonically remarks, "Her flirting days are over and she's ready to settle down," and then rides out unscathed.

The film was the first sound Western and brought the genre back to favor. Additionally, it is credited with making innovative use of exterior sound and photography. The film possesses a rustic and natural beauty comparable to *Shane* (1953, Paramount). Some of O. Henry's jingoism seeps through the dialogue.

For example, one of the troopers warns the lovelorn sergeant, "He better look out for those foreigners, they do things differently." The sergeant retorts, "The old sarge has a new girl and she's a pepper." One of the Anglo townspeople, upon hearing of the Kid's exploits, comments that he's "probably just a dirty greaser."

Director Raoul Walsh was originally slated to play the Cisco Kid, but an accident causing the loss of one eye resulted in his being replaced by the established star Warner Baxter. Irving Cummings finished the directorial task and got codirecting credit. Baxter was fresh from his success in *Ramona* (1928, Fox), opposite Dolores Del Rio. Although the film was nominated for six Academy Awards, only Baxter won, for Best Actor of the Year. An able actor, Baxter was successful at playing the Kid, limiting the usually outlandish physical flurries and quirky vocal gymnastics common among non-Hispanic actors playing Hispanics. Edmund Lowe, fresh from his biggest career hit, *What Price Glory?* (1926), injected some underplaying into the overly confident Sergeant Dunne. Dorothy Burgess, in her film debut, was less successful in her portrayal of Tania, some of her posturing bordering on the caricature.

Warner Baxter repeated the Cisco Kid role in *The Arizona Kid* (1930, Fox), *The Cisco Kid* (1931, Fox), and *The Return of the Cisco Kid* (1939, 20th Century). He was replaced by Cesar Romero, 1939–41 (six films), Duncan Renaldo, 1945–50 (eight films and a television series in the 1950s), and Gilbert Roland, 1946–47 (six films).

The Players

The 1920s saw the arrival of the first quartet of Hispanic stars to Hollywood: Ramon Novarro, Dolores Del Rio, Lupe Velez, and Gilbert Roland. Each, in turn, encountered, in varying degrees, the obstacles of stereotyping, prejudice, and typecasting in real and reel life.

Ramon Novarro catapulted to stardom in 1923, with a series of romantic and swashbuckling roles, reaching his pinnacle in *Ben Hur*. By 1937, he was reduced to rehashing familiar and worn-out tales of the Latin lover, as in *The Sheik Steps Out*, and left Hollywood a very disappointed man. Dolores Del Rio rose to stardom in 1925's *What Price Glory?* and, thereafter, only infrequently obtained real opportunities to develop her considerable dramatic talents. Typically, she was typecast as a native exotic girl and later as a sophisticate. According to Cortes, "Her claim to screen fame was sensuality, consistently restrained and ladylike."[4] She left Hollywood in 1942, after a series of unworthy films, and moved back to Mexico, where she helped to bring international acclaim to Mexican cinema. She returned to Hollywood for infrequent film appearances. Lupe Velez acquired her film stardom in *The Gaucho* (1927, United Artists) and developed into a versatile star in comedy and drama. Like Del Rio, she was typecast early in her career in exotic native roles, before becoming a considerable comedienne in the Mexican Spitfire films, beginning with *The Girl from Mexico* (1939, RKO), in which she played a strong-willed and independent woman. She committed suicide in 1944, after a series of romantic disappointments. The fourth Hispanic star was Gilbert Roland, who came to prominence in *Camilla* (1927) and was popular in a series of Latin-lover roles. With the arrival of sound films, he was demoted to supporting roles in A-films and leads in low-budget ones and earned admiration as a journeyman actor in more serious roles in the 1950s. Roland would later recollect, "The Mexican, even the lowliest peon, has a sense of dignity, a remarkable sense of stoicism. That's what I always fought for in Mexican characterizations, trying to correct misrepresentations that cause misunderstandings only because some writer or some producer was too lazy to learn his subject matter."[5]

Other Hispanic film stars gained prominence but met with less durable and popular success. Among these were a pair of matinee idol leading men. The Spanish-born Antonio Moreno and the Mexican-American Don Alvarado had similar trajectories. Both became popular during the vogue of the Latin lover, playing romantic leads, and were rivals to the Valentino and Novarro mantle. However, the arrival of talkies quickly relegated them to second leads in the 1930s and character roles in the 1940s. Similarly, Hollywood hoped to duplicate the Del Rio and Velez success. Hispanic actresses, like their Hispanic male counterparts, met with success on a temporary basis. Among these was Lupita Tovar, who debuted in *Veiled Women* (1929). She was quickly relegated to low-budget films, usually Westerns, although she played leads in Spanish-language films produced in Hollywood. Her Hollywood career came to an end with *Crime Doctor's Courage* (1945). Another promising actress was the Mexican-born Raquel Torres, who made an impressive debut in *White Shadows of the South Seas* (1928). Typecast in exotic roles in routine films, she retired permanently in 1933.

Notes

1. George Black, *The Good Neighbor*. (New York: Pantheon Books, 1988).
2. U.S. Congress, *Seasonal Agricultural Laborers*, p. 190.
3. Joe Franklin, *Classics of the Silent Screen* (New York: Cadillac Pub., 1959).
4. Carlos E. Cortes, "Chicanas in Film," in Gary D. Keller (ed.), *Chicano Cinema* (New York: Bilingual Press, 1985).
5. Oscar Rimoldi, "The Amazing Gilbert Roland," *Hollywood Studio Magazine*, July 1987.

CHAPTER THREE
The 1930s—Bandidos and Spitfires

I remember somebody asked the dialogue director what kind of accent we were supposed to simulate for our characters and he said, "Standard Hollywood-Mexican—nobody will know the difference!" I guess maybe he was a better critic than dialogue coach since I don't believe too many people saw the picture.
> —Rita Hayworth about *Under the Pampas Moon* (1935, Fox)

We aren't in the same tribe, savage!
> —Margaret Lindsay to Johnny Ramirez (Paul Muni)
> in *Bordertown* (1935, Warner Brothers)

. . . though she does a rumba for us
And calls herself Dolores,
She was in a Broadway chorus
Known as Susie Donahue.
> —The song "She's a Latin from Manhattan,"
> in *Go into Your Dance* (1935, Warner Brothers*)

The 1930s were the apex of Hollywood's Golden Era (1920–50). The early part of the decade was also a period of great change: in the technical sense, in popular tastes and trends, and in the personnel in front and behind the camera. For the Hispanic, the general image went from that of the exotic Latin lover to that of unscrupulous bandits and hot-tempered spitfires.

In general, the Hollywood of the 1930s provided escapism and reflected little of the great political and social issues of the day in a serious way. In Nicaragua, U.S. Marines were fighting a guerrilla war against a rebel named Augusto Sandino, and the occupation forces would be there until January 1933. Closer to home, in Mexico, the first revolution (1910–20) of the twentieth century had taken place, and had now been institutionalized. One of Mexico's greatest presidents, Lazaro Cardenas, conducted the most widespread agrarian reform, and in 1938, expropriated the U.S.- and British-owned oil fields, arousing the wrath of both countries. Elsewhere, three dictators had begun their long reign with U.S. sponsorship and support: Fulgencio Batista in Cuba, Anastazio Somoza in Nicaragua, and Rafael Leonidas Trujillo in the Dominican Republic. When Somoza visited Washington, D.C., in May of 1939, President Roosevelt is said to have asked his secretary of state, Cordell Hull, "Somoza? Isn't that fellow supposed to be a son-of-a-bitch?" Hull replied, "Yes, but he's our son-of-a-bitch."

Internationally, militarism and fascism were on the rise. Japan invaded Manchuria. Adolf Hitler became chancellor in Germany, and General Francisco Franco usurped the fragile democracy in the Spanish Republic.

Finally, here at home, the Depression had begun with the Wall Street Crash of 1929, and by 1933, one-third of the labor force was unemployed (some fifteen million), some of which lived in dilapidated, makeshift communities called "Hoovervilles." Others, like the Okies of Oklahoma, because of natural disaster, became perpetual migrants in a devastated land. Prohibition was finally repealed by Congress with the Twenty-First Amendment in December 1933. The American labor movement continued to organize and press for the right to unionize (National Relations Act) and the eight-hour day (Fair Labor Standards Act). Segregation was the rule of the land, de jure in the South and de facto in the North.

The American film only infrequently dealt with these issues. The Spanish Civil War was dealt with, albeit superficially and vaguely, in *The Last Train from Madrid* (1937, Paramount) and *Blockade*. The Depression and its consequences were dramatized in *Heroes for Sale* (1933, Warner Brothers), *Wild Boys on the Road* (1933, Warner Brothers), and *Our Daily Bread* (1934, United Artists). The treatment of Prohibition began the cycle of gangster films: *The Public Enemy* (1931, Warner Brothers), *Little Caesar* (1931, Warner Brothers), and *Scarface* (1931, Warner Brothers). Racial hatred and the Ku Klux Klan were dealt with in *Black Legion* (1937, Warner Brothers); bigotry in the South, in *They Won't Forget* (1937, Warner Brothers); prison conditions, in *I Am a Fugitive from a Chain Gang* (1932, Warner Brothers) and *20,000 Years in Sing-Sing* (1932, Warner Brothers). The emergence and threat of fascism was singularly effective in Charlie Chaplin's *The Great Dictator*. Ethnic minorities continued, however, to elude treatment. The American Indian had, for the first time, been treated sympathetically in *The Vanishing American* (1925, Paramount), and it would be another quarter of a century for another sympathetic treatment, in *Broken Arrow* (1950, Universal). Blacks were stereotyped as slow witted and shiftless people in mainstream films or segregated into low-budget, all-Black films (e.g., *Green Pastures* [1936, Warner Brothers]).

During the 1930s, the foundations of the status quo rested on the studio system and its star system. Nine major studios functioned: Columbia, 20th Century Fox, Metro-Goldwyn-Mayer, Paramount, RKO, United Artists, Universal, Warner Brothers (combined with First National), and Republic. Together with independent productions and important films, the number of features released from 1930 to 1939 combined for a grand total of 7,017 films (or an average of 500 per year).[1] Average weekly attendance at movie theaters totalled eighty million in 1930. Studios meticulously groomed their future stars through bit parts, supporting roles, and eventually leads. Thus, a full stock company of players were employed at each studio. American film during the 1930s, in output, craftsmanship, and quality, dominated world cinema. Film exercised great social and cultural influence. It represented the United States in a generally favorable light: democratic, pluralistic, just, free, and as a land of equal opportunity. Its flaws, especially those of bigotry and prejudice toward ethnic minorities, were conspicuously absent.

The Films

The great technical change that Hollywood underwent in the late 1920s was the advent of the talking picture. By 1930, talking films were firmly established. As a result, however, Hollywood was still trying to come to grips with the potential loss of the sizeable market of Latin America as a result of the introduction of sound. Furthermore, although Latin American audiences had become accustomed to American films and movie stars, nationalists warned of the pervasive penetration of the English language. The use of subtitles was inadequate because a significant amount of the Latin American audience was illiterate.

Ultimately, Hollywood opted for the making of Spanish-language versions of American films. Between the years 1930 and 1938, some 113 of these films were made by both major studios and independents: MGM, Warner Brothers, 20th Century Fox, Columbia, Universal, Sona-Art-World Wide, Chris Phillips Productions, Hollywood Spanish Pictures Company, Ci-Ti-Go, Exito Corporation, Inc., RNS Ltd., and Metropolitan Pictures Corporation. The films were low budget and quickly produced. Occasionally, they were shot at night on the set of an English-language film that was being filmed during the day.

Perhaps because of the deficient budgets of these films, Hollywood did not employ its only trio of Hispanic "stars": Dolores Del Rio, Lupe Velez, and Ramon Novarro. It would be only toward the end of the decade that Novarro, his career waning, would undertake two of these films. Utilized were Hispanic players already employed in Hollywood (Gilbert Roland, Lupita Tovar, Mona Maris, Conchita Montenegro, Antonio Moreno). Other leading players were brought from other Latin American countries, particularly Mexico. Twentieth Century Fox, for example, brought back the very popular Mexican tenor, Jose Mojica, for six films between 1933 and 1934.

However, several factors contributed to the decline and, ultimately, the failure of these films. First, Hollywood failed to understand that, although many things united Latin America, there were subtle geographical, cultural, social, and linguistic variations. Thus, the variety of accents, Mexican, Cuban, Argentine, and so forth, gave these films a certain lack of conviction and empathy. Second, audiences, notwithstanding the ideology and nationality, preferred seeing their favorite Hollywood stars to stand-ins. Ironically, these films were a premature attempt to find a market among Hispanics in the United States. The great influxes of Puerto Ricans (in the 1940s and 1950s) and Cubans (in the 1960s) were in the future, but the largest Hispanic group, Mexican-Americans, then as now, could have constituted a viable market. However, these films were primarily for export, and they received only limited runs and poor marketing in predominantly Hispanic neighborhoods. Additionally, many of these films were bland remakes of Hollywood films, without any of the gloss, and did not deal with any of the issues relevant to Hispanics in this country.

The image of Hispanics once more emerged as one of dubious accuracy. Popular tastes in the midst of the Depression changed from tales of foreign and exotic-looking Latin lovers, sentimental melodramas, and romantic costume dramas of the silent screen to urban tales populated by abrasive and streetwise tough guys (Cagney, Muni, Raft, Gable, Bogart, Robinson, Garfield). Their female counterparts were wisecracking dames (Carole Lombard, Claudette Colbert, Bette Davis, Constance Bennett, Miriam Hopkins, Ann Sheridan, Priscilla Lane) and newly arrived career women (Katherine Hepburn, Joan Crawford, Irene Dunne, Barbara Stanwyck). Staples of the decade included musicals (with Fred Astaire, Ginger Rogers, and Jeannette MacDonald), screwball comedies (with Cary Grant, John Barrymore, Jean Arthur, Wayne Morris, and Joel McCrea), scores of A- and B-Westerns (with Gary Cooper and John Wayne), and the return of the swashbucklers (Errol Flynn, Ronald Colman, and Douglas Fairbanks, Jr.). The Latin lover became an anachronism. Additionally, the emphasis was on youth, as virtually the entire galaxy of silent stars was replaced by the new young stars. Inevitably then, Hispanic players were deemed too exotic to play leads in big-budget films and only serviceable to portray Hollywood's latest conception of what Hispanics were: bandits and hot-tempered spitfires.

In general, all films dealing with Hispanic settings had certain characteristics. First, all titles employed inflammatory titles of ill-controlled passions (i.e., *The Mexican Spitfire, Call of the Flesh, In Caliente, Hot Pepper*) or violence and banditry (*The Arizona Wildcat, The Bad Man, Gay Caballero, Rebellion, Gay Desperado*). Thus, there was the implication that Hispanics were incapable of controlling themselves, either their sexuality or lawlessness. The films suggested further that these deplorable characteristics were innate and normal conduct of all Hispanics.

Second, the main characteristic of Hispanic males was lawlessness and banditry. As they were bandits, they were more likely than not the villains in films: cruel, unrepentive, violent, drunken, treacherous, inevitably involved in illicit activities like gambling, murder, or other rackets. Leo Carrillo, for example, made a career of portraying dozens of rogues in the 1930s, all of whom had an illegitimate source of income. Romantically, with the demise of the Latin-lover vogue, they usually lost the girl to their Anglo rivals. Finally, by the last reel, they were either apprehended and imprisoned or killed off. The Cisco Kid was the sole exception to this predictable scenario, although the source or reason of his banditry was never explained, as it was once again implied that Hispanics could not help themselves.

The proliferation of Hispanic bandits, the majority of them Mexican, began with the first Cisco Kid entry, *In Old Arizona* (1929, Fox), and five subsequent entries. Mexican and Hispanic bandits were portrayed in *The Bad Man* (1930, First National), by Walter Huston; in *Under a Texas Moon* (1930, Warner Brothers), by Frank Fay vying for Raquel Torres' affections; in *Captain Thunder* (1930, Warner Brothers), by Victor Varconi; in *The Lash* (1930, Warner Brothers), by Richard Barthelmess; in *Beau Bandit* (1930, RKO), by Rod La Roque; in *Girl of the Rio* (1932, RKO), by Leo Carrillo; in *The Gay Caballero* (1932, 20th Century), by C. Henry Gordon; in *The Man from Monterey* (1933, Warner Brothers), by Donald Reed; in *Hi, Gaucho* (1935, RKO), by John Carroll; in *Under the Pampas Moon* (1935, Fox), by Warner Baxter; in *The Gay Desperado* (1936, United Artists), by Leo Carrillo; in *The Californians* (1937, 20th Century), by Ricardo Cortez; in *Zorro Rides Again* (1937), by John Carroll; in *The Arizona Wildcat* (1938, 20th Century), by Leo Carrillo; in the Hopalong Cassidy Western, *In Old Mexico* (1938, Paramount), by Paul Sutton; in *Rebellion* (1938, Crescent), by numerous actors; in *The Llano Kid* (1939, Paramount), by Tito Guizar. In addition to these, numerous obscure B-Westerns perpetuated the image of the Mexican and Hispanic bandit.

Another prevalent type of Hispanic was the one who was incapable of determining his own life or destiny without the condescending guidance and civilizing influence of an Anglo. This was especially a common motif in period or historical films such as *The Man from Monterey* (1933, Warner Brothers) and *Rebellion*, in which the helpless Mexican, whose land is being taken away, requires the services of some solitary and brave Anglo hero (John Wayne and Tom Keene, respectively). It would be a recurring theme that would continue to be present as late as the 1960s in *The Magnificent Seven* (1961, United Artists) and the spaghetti Westerns and as late as the 1980s in *The Three Amigos* (1986, Orion). The historical film, *A Message to Garcia* (1936, 20th Century), set in the 1890s, revolves around an obscure incident in which President McKinley sends a message to the leaders of the Cuban independence movement with the news that the United States will back them in their desire to rid the island of Spaniards. The implication was that Cubans, who had been fighting under competent leaders like Marti and Cespedes, were not motivated to fight for their national independence without U.S. prodding.

Hispanics, with the sole exception of Dolores Del Rio, were generally stereotyped as sexual objects who inevitably leave their bandit lover for the Anglo tenderfoot (e.g., as in *In Old Arizona*). Hispanic women were usually portrayed as scheming saloon or dance hall vamps solely motivated by sex and money. This theme was played out in *Call of the Flesh* (1930, MGM), with Ramon Novarro and Renee Adoree; in *Hot Pepper* (1933, Fox) and *Rose of the Rancho* (1936, Paramount), the former with Lupe Velez; and in *Cuban Love Song* (1931, MGM), another Lupe Velez starrer. The few Hispanic actresses on screen, like Lupita Tovar, Conchita Montenegro, Raquel Torres, and Mona Maris, languished almost their entire film careers in such roles. A teenager named Rita Casino (later, Rita Hayworth) was typecast early for similar roles and appeared destined for a similar future in *Under the Pampas Moon* as a cantina girl, in *Charlie in Egypt* (1936, 20th Century) as an exotic vamp, in *Human Cargo* (1936, 20th Century) as a sultry undocumented worker, and in *Rebellion* as a victim of a stolen land grant. Faced with the impediment of prejudice in the film industry, Rita's first husband and agent, Edward C. Judson, changed his wife's name to Hayworth after *Hit the Saddle* (1937, Republic), a B-Western. Soon thereafter, "all connotations of Rita's partially Latin heritage slowly started disappearing although in her first film under her new Columbia contract, *Criminals of the Air*, she played a Mexican nightclub dancer in a below-the-border dive! After this film, her hair was restored to its natural shade of brown and she underwent long and painful electrolysis treatments in order to broaden her forehead and temporarily accentuate a widow's peak. . . ."[2]

Hollywood stereotyping of Hispanics resulted in some of the most blatant and ludicrous of these vehicles to be handed outright. In his work, Allen L. Woll notes that "all of Latin America was still depicted as a cultural backwater, populated by evil bandits and dancing maidens. Again, government embargoes and official censorship was brought into action in the face of an influx of American films which insulted the integrity of the Latin American countries. . . ."[3]

By the end of the decade and the beginning of World War II, Hollywood, with government prodding, harnessed its considerable resources to put consciously into effect the "Good Neighbor Policy" on behalf of hemispheric unity.

The following are representative films of the 1930s with examples of the images of Chicanos and Hispanics.

The Arizona Kid (1930, Fox)

This film was an unremarkable sequel to the first Cisco Kid film, *In Old Arizona* (1929), which had earned its star, Warner Baxter, an Academy Award as Best Actor. Having consolidated his stardom in talking films, the popular star turned out four films in 1930 alone, *The Arizona Kid* being one of them. Although rather undistinguished, the film had sufficient commercial success to keep the series alive. Assets in the cast included the Argentine Mona Maris as a discarded dance hall girl and the fast-rising Carole Lombard as the treacherous Virginia Hoyt.

The plot revolves around the Cisco Kid hiding out in Rockville, Arizona, and living off the earnings of his private gold mine. The sheriff, however, suspects him of robbing a stagecoach. Having discarded a dance hall girl, the Kid takes up with a vamp (Lombard), only to later learn of her treachery to dispose him of the mine in conspiracy with her husband, Nick Hoyt (Theodore Von Eltz). He prevails upon the villainous pair and rides away with the dance hall girl.

Although the Cisco Kid is presented as brave and astute and winning the day as a hero, he is nevertheless still a "bandit," and no explanation is attempted of what are the racial and political factors that would make such an individual an outlaw.

Cisco Kid (1931, Fox)

The third Cisco Kid film was directed by veteran director Irving Cummings (*My Gal Sal*, 1942, 20th Century), who had codirected *In Old Arizona*. Warner Baxter returned to essay the role for the third time, and he was reunited with Edmund Lowe, who again played the pursuing Sergeant Dunne (although he had presumably died in the first entry). Mexican actress Conchita Montenegro added some authentic Hispanic flavor to the proceedings, and Charles Stevens, the grandson of the great Apache chief, Geronimo, provided some historical ambience. Chicano actor Chris-Pin Martin was added as the Kid's sidekick, Gordito.

Fox Studios appeared not to put much care into the production, relying more on Baxter's marquee name (he was, at that time, one of the ten biggest draws at the box office). The threadbare story revolves around the Kid robbing a bank to save a widow's ranch and his affection for her children, while he is pursued by Sergeant Dunne. At the end, Dunne perceives the tarnished nobility of the Kid's act and lets him go free.

Viva Villa! (1934, MGM)

This was Hollywood's second and most costly attempt to deal with Mexican revolutionary Doroteo Arango (alias Pancho

Villa). However, this attempt, like subsequent ones dealing with Villa and the Mexican Revolution and its political and social complexities, would prove to be beyond the intellectual capacities of Hollywood: *Under Strange Flags* (1937, Crescent), *Pancho Villa Returns* (1950), *Villa!* (1958, 20th Century), *Villa Rides* (1968, 20th Century).

Although the film assembled some of the top talents in Hollywood, their finished product was unable to sustain any believability, realism, or historical accuracy. Wallace Beery, an actor of raw power when given an opportunity (he had been an Oscar winner for *The Champ* [1931, MGM]), was totally miscast in the title role, and ultimately what was conveyed was another stereotype of the unkempt, temperamental, violent, heavy-drinking Mexican bandit bordering on caricature. History records that, although Villa was flawed in many ways as a man, he was, in fact, neither a drinker of alcohol nor illiterate, as the film purports. Director Howard Hawks was a well-travelled man (he had been an ace pilot during World War I) and an extremely versatile Hollywood craftsman of every genre: gangster films such as *Scarface* (1932); screwball comedies such as *Twentieth Century* (1934) and *Bringing Up Baby* (1938); films noirs such as *The Big Sleep* (1946); Westerns like *Red River* (1948). He was, nevertheless, unable to imbue the film with more than superficial melodrama. Ben Hecht, a prolific screenwriter of many important films such as *Gone with the Wind* (1939) and *Notorious* (1946), could not begin to approach the historical complexities involved.

Hawks directed a substantial amount of the film on location in Mexico, until the advent of an international incident. Actor Lee Tracy, while in a highly intoxicated state, urinated from the balcony of the St. Regis Hotel on the Mexican Military Academy cadets who paraded on the street below. The Mexican government permit was predictably canceled quickly, and the studio, in turn, fired the actor. Tracy was temporarily arrested by the authorities, and Hawks refused to testify against him and was promptly fired, in turn, by the studio. Stuart Erwin was hired to replace Tracy, and director Jack Conway (*A Tale of Two Cities* [1935]) was hired to replace Hawks and was given sole directorial credit. All this notwithstanding, the film received a very negative reception in Mexico and was later banned.

The American newspaperman character, Johnny Syles, played by Erwin, was a vulgarization of progressive labor organizer and journalist John Reed. Reed, who had travelled with Villa for several months, went on to write the much-admired books *Insurgent Mexico* and *Ten Days That Shocked the World*, about the Russian Revolution. In this film, however, the Reed character was transformed into an indispensable confidant of military strategy and political affairs. Although Villa did have contingents of foreigners, including Anglo-Americans, fighting alongside his forces, they never served in leadership capacities.[4] Villa, who, along with Emiliano Zapata, was one of the two most important embodiments of the Mexican Revolution, is here reduced to ideological dependency on an American tenderfoot.

What appears to motivate this reel Villa is only revenge, even in the realm of love. At one point, he grabs the comely Fay Wray (*King Kong* [1933]) and growls, "You geev Pancho beeg kees, eh?," which she refuses to do and she is subsequently horsewhipped as a consequence. Villa is shown as nothing more than a plundering and murdering barbarian when his mentor, Francisco Madero (Henry B. Walthall) is not present or nearby. The usurper of Madero, General Huerta, is given the name of General Pascal and meets his death as a result of Villa burying him alive, pouring honey over him and then ants. This is historical revision, as the real Huerta went into exile after he was militarily defeated by Villa and Zapata. Villa's own death here is another gross historical deviation, as he is killed by a sniper who turns out to be the brother of Teresa (Wray). In fact, Villa was assassinated in a car by a group hired by the corrupt and ambitious Generals Obregon and Calles.

Only a handful of the cast was Hispanic. Leo Carrillo played Sierra (really General Fierro, one of Villa's generals). Chris-Pin Martin had a bit part as a peon.

In conclusion, one must look elsewhere than Hollywood fare for a perceptive view of Pancho Villa and the Mexican Revolution.

Bordertown (1935, Warner Brothers)

This movie was one of the series of socially conscious films produced at the most working class–oriented of all studios, Warner Brothers. It chronicled the story of Johnny Ramirez (Paul

Muni), a product of a Los Angeles barrio, who studies hard through law school at night and ultimately graduates at the head of his class. Nevertheless, in the most unconvincing part of the film, that of his first court appearance, he loses his temper and attacks a defendant. He is physically ejected and thereafter disbarred. Subsequently, he finds employment as a manager of a casino owned by Roark (Eugene Pallette). He is pursued by Roark's wife (Bette Davis), who is afflicted throughout with some incurable hysteria. He meets the society woman (Margaret Lindsay) who caused his downfall in court and somehow is attracted to her. After a short courtship, he proposes marriage, but a shocked and indignant woman spurns him and tells him, "We aren't of the same tribe, savage!" Soon thereafter, she is hit by a car and dies, and the event causes Johnny to leave the casino and return to the barrio. He states, "I know where I belong."

Despite its melodramatic inconsistencies, it attempted to recognize the dividing lines of bigotry which hampered the economic and political progress of Mexican-Americans. It was the first film to portray an Hispanic as an educated person with a desire of upward social mobility. However, the character traits of Johnny as being short tempered, passionate and uncontrollable were commonly attributed to Hispanics during the 1930s and undermine credulity. Paul Muni, a gifted actor (*Scarface, I'm a Fugitive, A Fugitive from a Chain Gang, The Life of Emile Zola*) and a product of the Yiddish Theatre, was one of the more progressive figures in Hollywood. Muni reportedly loitered in the barrios, where the exteriors were shot, to soak up the atmosphere. According to a well-researched biography, "wearing an old beat-up sweater and dark glasses, Muni travelled to Mexicali with Carroll Graham, the author of the novel on which the film was based, as his guide. Both men tried to act as non-touristy as possible, so they could explore the seamy side of the town, the saloons, the gambling casinos, the sagging shacks. When he got back to Los Angeles, Muni began taking private Spanish lessons. . . ."[5]

The voice model for Johnny Ramirez was supposed to have been a Mexican youth named Manuel that Muni had met at a street corner selling flowers. Muni subsequently offered and

31

gave him employment as a gardener at his ranch and then as a chauffeur, and both became long-time friends.

Muni, although well meaning, was made up with a dark shade of makeup (like Warner Baxter in *In Old Arizona*), which was not entirely convincing. Ramon Novarro, still potent at the box office, would have been well suited for the role. The exteriors in the barrios of northeast and east Los Angeles (among others, Olvera Street) went a long way toward adding some realism.

Although flawed, the film was a critical and commercial success. With *Bordertown,* Hollywood discovered and depicted the plight of Chicanos in the urban barrio.

Bold Caballero (1936, Republic)

Veteran Western film star Robert Livingston, star of the popular "Three Musketeers" series and the screen's second Lone Ranger in the Republic serial, *The Lone Ranger*, played the second Zorro in this programmer (assembly-line Western) film. Sig Rugman played an oppressive Spanish governor in southern California against which Zorro battles. Zorro is charged with murder by the newly arrived Robert Warwick, but by the film's end, Zorro gets the real culprit (Rugman).

This film, inferior to the Douglas Fairbanks and Tyrone Power versions, was strictly a nuts-and-bolts action Western disguised as a caballero film. It was one of Republic's efforts in color. No Hispanics were involved in front or in back of the camera. It was another example of Hollywood's insensitivity about taking a Hispanic hero (albeit a mythical one) and not bothering with more believable casting.

Ramona (1936, 20th Century)

The often-filmed Helen Hunt Jackson novel of Old California received its first and only talking screen adaptation. In cinematic history, its only importance is that it was 20th Century Fox's first film shot entirely in Technicolor.

Directed by veteran director Henry King (*Jesse James* [1938, 20th Century], *Song of Bernadette* [1943, 20th Century]), it was a perfect example of the whole artificiality of many films when non-Hispanics and non-Indians were cast in such roles. Originally, the relative unknown Rita Cansino (later Rita Hayworth) was given a Technicolor test with Gilbert Roland and another with newcomer Don Ameche. She spent considerable time in costume fittings and gallery portraits, but when Darryl F. Zanuck took over at the studio, he doubted her abilities and promptly failed to have her contract renewed. She would recollect later, "Zanuck just didn't have the time, or so he later said, to meet me face to face and tell me his decision. Naturally, I cried and I screamed and I vowed I would show those people they had made a terrible mistake. I was determined I would become successful and famous in films and they would be sorry."[6] Five years later, when she starred at the studio's *Blood and Sand* (1941) opposite Tyrone Power, on loan from Columbia at five times her salary, she was vindicated.

The plum role of Ramona went to one of the studio's leading stars, Loretta Young. Young had her hair dyed dark black to play the mestiza Ramona. A fine actress (she was an Oscar winner for *The Farmer's Daughter*), she was not physically convincing. The role of Alessandro went to newcomer Don Ameche, who had only three bits to his credit at that point and who was being groomed for stardom. Ameche would go on to become a fine light comedian (*Midnight* [1939]) and dramatic actor (*Heaven Can Wait* [1943]), but in this role, his cheerful urban personality was an example of miscasting. Again, one wonders why Roland, Novarro, or Renaldo could not have been cast as Alessandro or Del Rio, Velez, or Hayworth as Ramona.

The plot, set in Old California, revolved around a mestiza (half Spanish and Indian) who leaves her Spanish fiancé for a full-blooded Indian, Alessandro. She has been raised and sheltered by Spaniards and slowly becomes aware of the rampant racism in California. The story also presents greedy and unscrupulous Anglo settlers moving into California and dispossessing the Mexicans and Indians of their lands. Ramona's and Alessandro's marriage ends tragically. He is killed because he is thought to be stealing a horse, although he is actually attempting to get help for his sick daughter.

The picturesque Mesa Grande and San Diego Warner Brothers ranches were used for the numerous exteriors, and

Mesa Grande Indians were used as extras. The three-piece Technicolor lensing was impressive.

The play is performed annually in California with the same casting logic as this unremarkable film.

Sutter's Gold (1936, Universal)

Originally set to direct this film was famed Russian director Sergei Eisenstein, during his extended Hollywood visit some years before. Howard Hawks was hired to direct, and then when costs skyrocketed, he was replaced, in turn. James Cruze, the veteran and prolific director of romantic comedies with Wallace Reid, slapstick films with "Fatty" Arbuckle, and the Western epic *The Covered Wagon* (1923, Paramount), was employed to direct this sprawling biography of pioneer John Sutter, whose once-prosperous colony in California was ruined by the discovery of gold.

The film was an outright distortion of California during the 1840s. It depicted the historical myth that James Marshall was the first to discover gold in California along the American River. Historian Rodolfo Acuña offers historical evidence that gold was known to exist in Mexican California:

> Moreover, the discovery of gold by Francisco Lopez in 1842 at San Feliciano Canyon in Southern California focused attention on a fact already known by Mexicans: there was gold in California. The events prior to the 1840's left no doubt about the nefarious intentions of the Anglos. Since 1829, President Andrew Jackson and the U.S. Presidents who followed had attempted to coerce Mexico into selling California. . . .[7]

The mass immigration of foreigners (Sutter among them) only helped to further legalize the deprivation of Mexicans of their rights. A "foreign miner's tax" was instituted and required all "foreigners" to pay $4.00 a month to work in the gold fields. The "foreigners" deemed by this law were no less than the Mexicans, the actual natives, along with the Indians, in California. Forty-Niners felt a free rein to dislodge Mexican prospectors, while using the very mining techniques developed by Mexicans in Zacatecas and Sonora and brought to the Southwest.

Sutter's Gold did not deal with that part of history but instead attempted to validate the takeover at the expense of the Mexican. Without a single Hispanic cast member, the film portrayed Mexicans as childlike and in dire need of "civilizing." A captured Mexican general, portrayed by Billy Gilbert, was shown with as much dignity as a buffoon.

A later film, *Gold Is Where You Find It* (1938, Warner Brothers), sumptuously photographed in Technicolor and directed by Michael Curtis, dealt with the same period equally evasively.

The Robin Hood of El Dorado (1936, MGM)

The popular Warner Baxter was borrowed from his home studio, 20th Century Fox, to play Joaquin Murietta. This film was the first to deal with his story and the disenfranchisement of Mexicans after the Mexican-American War. Despite its flaws, the film was superior to the subsequent productions that were later to be produced about Murietta: *Firebrand* (1962, 20th Century), *Murietta* (1965, Warner Brothers), and *Joaquin Murietta* (1969, Warner Brothers). The pluses were ace director William Wellman, who had directed such films as *Wings* (1929), *The Public Enemy* (1931), *A Star Is Born* (1937), *Nothing Sacred* (1937), *The Ox-Bow Incident* (1943), and *Battleground* (1949). Wellman's fluid, invigorating style and humanist approach to the story enhanced its effectiveness.

Warner Baxter, reaching the end of top-flight stardom (he was the second highest paid star, after Claudette Colbert, that year at $280,000), was less restrained by melodramatic mannerisms than he was in *In Old Arizona*. Gone was the heavy-accented English, and in its place was some effective underplaying that captured some of the sensitive pathos of a man faced with a great injustice and an anger that propels him to take the law into his own hands. Margo turned in a sensitive portrayal as Murietta's girlfriend. The film was shot in extensive California locations where the real Murietta had travelled, among these the San Gabriel Mission, lending authenticity to the proceedings.

Under Strange Flags (1937, Crescent)

This routine B-Western served as the third Hollywood depiction of Pancho Villa. Needless to say, it featured a totally non-Hispanic cast. Maurice Black played an unconvincing Villa, and the hero was the veteran B-Western star Tom Keene.

The paper-thin plot dealt with Pancho Villa giving Keene a hand when his girlfriend's silver mine is threatened by some villainous Federales. They are assisted in their nefarious activities by no less than one of Villa's aides. Pooling their resources, Villa and Keene are triumphant.

Heroes of the Alamo (1938, Columbia)

The first talking film etc. to deal with the Alamo was a low-budget effort that preceded the big-budget treatment of *Man of Conquest* by a year. The lead role was played by veteran B-Western star Lane Chandler in his last starring role (as Davy Crockett) before his descent into character roles. It perpetuated all the myths about the Alamo, albeit very feebly (please see the entry on *Man of Conquest* for an elaboration of Alamo myths and legends).

It was a forgettable film in all respects, as reflected in the reviews. *Variety* noted (April 6, 1938):

"Heroes of the Alamo" is one of the most amateurish production efforts of the century. It is likely to get a first-class run around among exhibitors and a horse-laugh from audiences . . . although in Texas, where local sentiment and historical regard may figure, it may be received with some indulgence . . . The story of the massacre at the Alamo which highlighted early incidents in the fight for independence of Texas, is a sadly mediocre effort by Roby Wentz. . . .

It is interesting to note how pervasive the word "massacre" had become in association with the Alamo.

Return of the Cisco Kid (1939, 20th Century)

After an absence of eight years, Warner Baxter returned for the fourth and last time as the Cisco Kid. Baxter, at age forty-eight, was a little old for the derring-do of the Kid. His telling physical weariness added some conviction to the tongue-in-cheek heroics. Ironically, the actor who would replace him in the title role, Cesar Romero, portrayed his sidekick, Lopez.

Variety (April 26, 1939) noted, ". . . another light in set-up, it's a fast-paced western. . . . Warner Baxter again handles the title role of the border, whose gay banditry and romance is displayed with tongue-in-cheek attitude. . . . It's the Bad Man formula constructed on a slender story thread. . . . Baxter gives standard characterization of the Cisco Kid, with Romero and Martin his amiable pals and partners in crime. . . ."

As noted in the review, the emphasis again was on the Cisco Kid's illegal activities. The thin plot dealt with the Kid escaping from a firing squad and falling in love with Ann (Lynn Bari). He then proceeds to help her and her father retrieve some money that they were cheated out of. When her boyfriend returns, the Kid is out of a romance. Self-sacrificing by character, he nevertheless deals with the crooks and rides off to Mexico.

It was one of the better entries of the series and a commercial success. It would also be the last big-budget Cisco Kid film.

Man of Conquest (1939, Republic)

Republic Pictures, whose mainstays during the 1930s were low-budget, quickly made Westerns, augmented the budget for this film considerably to depict the story of Sam Houston and the birth of the state of Texas. The dramatic and action climax of the film, however, was the battle of the Alamo.

The film chronicled Houston's entry into Tennessee politics under the tutelage of Andrew Jackson, his two terms as governor, his adoption by Cherokee Indians, and his conspiratorial role in the tumultuous years of the Texas rebellion and subsequent statehood. Houston was portrayed impressively by the square-jawed, stalwart veteran Richard Dix, who had enjoyed considerable popularity in the 1920s and 1930s. Among his career highlights were the leads in DeMille's *The Ten Commandments* (1923), *The Vanishing American* (1925), and his Oscar-nominated role as Yancy in *Cimarron* (1930). The stoic Victor Jory played William Travis, Robert Barrat was Davy Crockett, and the embodiment of the fearless B-tough guy of the 1930s, Robert Armstrong (the hunter in *King Kong* [1933]), was Jim

Bowie. General Santa Ana was played as a predictable one-dimensional villain by C. Henry Gordon. There were no Hispanics in the large assembled cast.

Released only seventeen days before *Juarez*, the film was a blatant revision of history. It espoused a Social Darwinist view that "men of conquest" must exist to prevail over lesser civilizations. No effort was made to provide even the minimal Mexican view of the historic conflict. What Hollywood opted for was the filmic enhancement of a myth about the Alamo and the Mexican-American War.

The legend of the Alamo portrays the defenders of the Alamo as peace-loving Texans. In fact, of the 187 defenders, two-thirds were recent aliens, and only about a dozen of them had been there for less than six years. Their background and motivation were equally dubious. According to historian Trujillo Herrera, Travis had killed a man who had made advances to his wife, then let a slave be convicted of the crime, and subsequently abandoned his wife and two offspring. Bowie was a notorious thug from New Orleans who had become wealthy slave-running and was looking to expand the infamous trade in Texas. Crockett, a former Congressman from Tennessee, was a true zealot of Manifest Destiny.[8] As for the rest of the folklore, Acuña notes, "While the defenders only numbered about 180, they had twenty-one cannons to the Mexicans' eight or ten. The Anglo-Americans were expert marksmen and had rifles with a range of 200 yards; in contrast, the Mexicans were poorly equipped, inadequately trained, and were armed with smooth-bore muskets with a range of only 70 yards. . . ."[9]

Additionally, most of the Mexican population of some 5,000 did not join the uprising. Acuña writes that:

> the Mexican nation was divided, and the centers of power were thousands of miles away from Texas. From the interior of Mexico, Santa Ana led an army of about 6,000 conscripts, many of whom had been forced into the army and were then marched hundreds of miles over hot, arid, desert land. In addition, many were Mayan and did not speak Spanish. In February 1836, the majority arrived . . . sick and ill-prepared to fight. . . .[10]

Historically, the military victories of Indians against Anglo settlers were deemed "massacres" and those of the Mexicans were documented likewise. Thus, the battle of the Alamo and the subsequent conflicts stereotyped Mexicans as inferior, treacherous, and cruel and left a legacy of hate and mistrust. Notwithstanding the era of Roosevelt's "Good Neighbor Policy," *Man of Conquest* reverted to the old stereotypes and revisionary history for the sake of entertainment.

The Girl from Mexico (1939, RKO)

The film was Lupe Velez's first film after an absence of eighteen months. Her film career had been in decline for several years, but *The Girl from Mexico* would resuscitate it and initiate the Mexican Spitfire series of another eight films: *The Mexican Spitfire* (1939), *The Mexican Spitfire out West* (1940), *The Mexican Spitfire's Baby* (1941), *Six Lessons from Madame La Zonga* (1941), *The Mexican Spitfire at Sea* (1942), *The Mexican Spitfire Sees a Ghost* (1942), *The Mexican Spitfire's Elephant* (1942), and *The Mexican Spitfire's Blessed Event* (1943). All the films were consistent moneymakers for RKO.

In *The Girl from Mexico*, Lupe plays a fiery entertainer who turns Manhattan topsy-turvy with madcap activities. *Variety* (May 24, 1939) noted, "This Lupe Velez starrer, with a dandy cast, excellent direction and generally good production, will exceed its costs despite a mediocre story. It'll redeem, too, Miss Velez's earlier, less successful tries despite the fact that for her comeback she's been given a yarn right off the cob, with only slight variations. . . ."

Donald Woods (later replaced by Charles "Buddy" Rogers) played the bewildered ad man, and Leon Errol was the shiftless uncle in the series.

While the Spitfire films reinvigorated Lupe's career, they also typecast her as the temperamental Carmelita. The plots were thin (some would say to the point of caricature), but her versatile gifts of comic timing, singing, dancing, and mugging are the redeeming features of the films. To a degree, there is evidence to suggest that she was playing herself at this point, albeit profitably. One could only speculate on what direction her career might have turned beyond these films if she had lived.

The Spitfire was the first film series about an Hispanic character in which the star was Hispanic.

As for the immediate sequel, *The Mexican Spitfire* (1939, RKO), *Variety* (December 13, 1939) reviewed it as "a slick package of laugh entertainment, crammed with broad comedy and slapstick situations. . . ."

Juárez (1939, Warner Brothers)

The beginning of World War II at the end of 1939 heavily influenced United States concern for hemispheric unity, and Hollywood, in turn, obliged. The Hispanic on film went from derision to revergent concern.

Juárez had three interlinking stories: the intrigues relating to Napoleon III's attempt make Mexico part of the French Empire; the doomed romance between Maximilian (of the Hapsburgs), who was Napoléon's appointed Emperor of Mexico, and Carlota; and Benito Juárez's efforts to fight foreign rule and establish democracy. Juárez, a Zapotec Indian, had been the elected president of the Mexican Republic when the Hapsburg prince, a younger brother of Franz Joseph, invaded Mexico with French troops. Forced to leave the capital, Juárez launched a tenacious guerrilla war that forced France to begin evacuating French troops, leaving Maximilian to rely more on the collaborator army and mercenaries. Carlota returned to France to plead a change of policy. Juárez's army finally captured Maximilian, and he was executed as a warning to all foreigners with similar ambitions.

A variety of resources were used to fashion the story: Bertita Harding's *The Phantom Crown* and Franz Werfel's play, *Juárez and Maximilian*, and some other 357 sources of information. Unfortunately and ironically, the third story, that of Juárez, consists of the briefest part of the film. This factor is crucial as Juárez is the character who was meant to arouse sympathy, and his limited time on screen hampers the viewer's understanding of the great leader's political vision.

The studio furnished a lavish budget of $1,750,000, which, at that time, was the largest for a studio picture. For a change, a conscientious effort was made for historical accuracy. The studio research department amassed a vast amount of material about Juárez. It included, among other things, Juárez's private and official correspondence, contemporary newspapers, and congressional debates. Paul Muni, producer Hal Wallis, and director William Dieterle (*The Life of Emile Zola*) went to Mexico for further research, at the request of President Lazaro Cardenas, and spent six weeks there. Muni personally interviewed two aged survivors of the Juárista Army, General Velasquez and Colonel Gabriel Moreno, and inquired about every aspect of Juárez's personality: mannerisms, voice, physical features. Muni chose to underplay Juárez and captured the appearance of a great man, stoic and indomitable, and physical appearance was astonishing. The makeup included the high Indian cheekbones, the straight black hair, and body padding to give emphasis to the massive shoulders. Muni was effective, but the brevity of his scenes prevented him from giving a more dimensional portrayal. John Garfield, a powerful actor in urban roles, was terribly miscast as the future dictator Porfirio Diaz, his New York accent too incongruous for the role. Brian Aherne, who was nominated for Best Supporting Actor, made an impressive Maximilian, and Gilbert Roland, the only Mexican in a major role in the large cast, played well the traitor Colonel Miguel Lopez. Bette Davis's Carlota was played in typical hysterical fashion by the actress, which, for once, was appropriate. The studio arranged a special screening for President Cardenas, who was highly impressed, and as a consequence, the film premiered at Mexico's National Theater in Bellas Artes, the first time a film had been so honored. Mexican audiences responded enthusiastically.

Reviews of the film were glowing. *Variety* (April 26, 1939) commented:

To the list of distinguished characters whom he has created in films, Paul Muni now adds a portrait of Benito Pablo Juárez, Mexican patriot and liberator. With the aid of Bette Davis, co-starring in the tragic role of Carlota, of Brian Aherne giving an excellent performance as the ill-fated Maximilian, and a story

41

that points up the parallels of conflicting political thought of today and three-quarters of a century ago . . .

The *New York Times* was equally positive in its praise: "A distinguished, memorable, and socially valuable film."

The film, a well-meaning enterprise on behalf of hemispheric harmony, is a flawed epic. The film presented for the first time as its subject the first view of a Mexican person in a positive light and as a historical hero. However, as *Variety* noted, "There is frequent mention of the Monroe Doctrine, of one-man rule over the lives and destinies of millions, and of the rights of common man to possess land and work out his own salvation. . ." It is ironic that the Monroe Doctrine, the tool and rationalization of numerous military interventions in Latin America, should thus have been historically perceived. Comment was also made that the American Civil War was over and that it was somehow Washington's future course of action that would deter French intervention in Mexico and not the historical fact that Juárez's forces had inflicted numerous defeats on the foreign troops. This idea was pure myth, which has also been expounded in other Hollywood films dealing with the French Occupation, and denigrates Mexican patriotism and heroism. Like many historical films of the period, the speeches of patriotism had a double meaning, specifically in reference to European countries invading other countries. It was clear that Nazi Germany was a country to which these speeches could have applied.

Another production titled *The Mad Empress* (1939, Warner Brothers) was brought by the Warner Bros. studio to avoid competition. It was a lackluster affair, muddled and ineffective.

Juárez initiated an expectation that the Hispanic would be seen in a favorable light. It was an expectation that was only temporary and ultimately premature.

The Players

The 1930s saw the arrival of a new group of young Hispanic players: Mexican-born Anthony Quinn, Margo, Movita; the Cuban Cesar Romero; the Mexican-American Leo Carrillo; the Spanish-born Duncan Renaldo.

Quinn, the most durable and most famous of this group, began inconspicuously as an extra in *Parole* (1936, Universal) and then in a bit in *The Plainsmen* (1936, Paramount) and toiled in the salt mines of every studio, playing every type of role (as a Mexican, Indian, Filipino), in every type of film. Most of these were low-budget and routine fare like *King of Alcatraz* (1938, Paramount), with occasional roles in big-budget films such as *They Died with Their Boots On* (1941, Warner Brothers) and *The Black Swan* (1942, 20th Century). He met the similar fate of typecasting common to Hispanic actors. He went on to play hoods in *Sworn Enemy* (1936, MGM), *Night Waitress* (1936, RKO), *Partners in Crime* (1937, Paramount), *Daughter of Shanghai* (1937, Paramount), *Tip-Off Girls* (1938, Paramount), *Hunted Men* (1938, Paramount), *King of Chinatown* (1939, Paramount), *Union Pacific* (1939, Paramount), *Island of Lost Men* (1939, Paramount), and *Television Spy* (1939, Paramount), among others. The fact that he was director Cecil B. DeMille's son-in-law did not seem to help to consolidate his career. He would recollect later in his autobiography of his frustrations:

My career had been reduced to playing third-rate gangster parts, Mexican bandits and poor Indians who were always getting the shit kicked out of them by the big strong white man. I knew I was a long way from defeating the ghosts. One day, I walked into the office of the head of the studio and asked to be released from my contract. I told him I was unhappy with my roles. He must have sensed there was more to it than the usual actor complaining about his career. . . .[11]

It would not be until the 1950s that Anthony Quinn would find real stardom, at one point actually quitting films (1948–50) to return to the theater and acquire real recognition as an actor.

Both Margo and Movita would meet with much less success. Margo began with an enviable lead in Ben Hecht's fascinating *Crime without Passion* (1934, Paramount) but was rapidly relegated to low-budget leads in inconsequential films, one notable exception being Kazan's *Viva Zapata* (1952, 20th Century). Movita began as Clark Gable's Tahitian girlfriend in Milestone's *Mutiny on the Bounty* (1935, MGM) but was thereafter abruptly exiled to poverty row actioners.

The other male Hispanic stars were destined to meet with more long-term success. Both Renaldo and Carrillo began with bits in silents. Renaldo played leads mostly as a Mexican hero of low-budget Westerns (a lead in the classic *Trader Horn* [1931, MGM] being the exception), and Carrillo was usually stereotyped as a bandit or provided comic relief until the two were paired in "The Cisco Kid" television series in the 1950s. Romero, in turn, was typecast as amiable, charming Latin-lover types, usually in second leads (e.g., as in *Love before Breakfast* [1936, Universal]), and then became the second Cisco Kid, after the aging Warner Baxter, with *Viva Cisco Kid* (1940). Romero essayed the role in six entries.

Of the first wave of Hispanic players who had entered films in the 1920s, only three had become genuine stars: Dolores Del Rio, Lupe Velez, and Ramon Novarro. Del Rio played a wide variety of roles in a variety of films (musicals such as *Flying Down to Rio* [1933, RKO] and costume dramas such as *Madame Du Barry* [1934, Paramount]). Velez underwent a decline in popularity and then, toward the end of the decade, rocketed back to popularity with the Spitfire films. Novarro continued in top rank until he voluntarily retired at the end of the decade. He had successfully made the transition into talking films and flourished in a variety of roles such as the lovelorn Russian lieutenant in *Mata Hari* (1931, MGM) and the failed composer in *Cat and the Canary* (1934, MGM). Other luminaries such as Antonio Moreno and Don Alvarado rather quickly faded into character roles. The youngest of these, Gilbert Roland, was reduced to obscure leads in programmers such as *Mystery Women* (1935, Fox), with occasional second leads in big-budget films such as *Juarez* (1939, Warner Brothers).

Notes

1. Joel W. Finler, *The Hollywood Story* (New York: Crown Publishers, 1988).
2. Gene Ringgold, *Films of Rita Hayworth* (Secaucus, N.J.: Citadel Press, 1974).
3. Allen L. Woll, *The Latin Image in American Film* (Los Angeles: Latin American Center Publications, University of California, Los Angeles, 1977).
4. Jim Tuck, *Pancho Villa and John Reed: Two Faces of Romantic Revolution* (Tucson: University of Arizona Press, 1984).

5. Jerome Lawrence, *Actor: The Life and Times of Paul Muni* (New York: Samuel French, 1974).
6. Gene Ringgold, *The Films of Rita Hayworth* (Secaucus, N.J.: Citadel Press, 1974).
7. Rodolfo Acuña, *Occupied America* (San Francisco: Canfield Press, 1972).
8. Trujillo Herrera, *Olvidate de el Alamo* (Mexico City: La Prensa, D.F., 1965).
9. Rodolfo Acuña, *Occupied America* (San Francisco: Canfield Press, 1972).
10. Ibid.
11. Anthony Quinn, *The Original Sin* (Boston: Little, Brown and Company, 1972).

CHAPTER FOUR

The 1940s—Stinking Badges and the Return of the Latin Lover and the Cisco Kid

This spick speaks American.

Don't give him a knife, he uses a knife better than most men use a gun.

Who did the murder?

The Mexican did it. I saw him do it. I heard him talk about it in his speak.

—The Ox-Bow Incident (1943)

Who are you?

We're the mountain police.

If you're the mountain police, where are your badges?

Badges? We don't need any badges. We don't need any stinking badges.

—The Treasure of Sierra Madre (1948)

A great deal of the film fare produced in the 1940s was influenced by the United States' fight for survival in World War II and the subsequent cold war and McCarthy witchhunt. Within this context, there was a return to escapist films laced with patriotism during the war, and Hispanics on film were depicted as hard-working members of the American nation. After the war, a historical amnesia returned, and the Hispanic reverted to the old stereotypes of the bandit and a brief return to the Latin lover.

The 1940s can be divided into three periods: the U.S. prewar period of 1939–41, the war years, 1942–45, and postwar period, 1946–49. In the first period, films increasingly anti-Nazi in tone began to appear, such as *Confessions of a Nazi Spy* (1939, Warner Brothers), and then, gradually, films calling for assistance to beleaguered nations of the Nazi onslaught, such as *A Yank in the R.A.F.* (1942, 20th Century). With the advent of Pearl Harbor on December 7, 1941, films took a more strident and patriotic context. Even costume films such as *The Sea Hawk* (1940, Warner Brothers) made pointed reference to the Axis danger. Films made an effort to include minorities, including Hispanics, as loyal and patriotic citizens (with the exception of Japanese-Americans, who were being interned). Films such as *Gaudalcanal Diary* (1942, Paramount), *Air Force* (1943, Warner Brothers), and *The Human Comedy* (1943, MGM) depicted Mexican-Americans fighting and dying for their country. The fact that the armed forces remained segregated, however, was not documented. A great bulk of these war films, however, were light escapist fare with no pretensions of realism other than morale boosting.

The postwar period became a battleground for the cold war in which patriotic and propagandist features (e.g., *Iron Curtain* [1948, 20th Century]) became common staples. Ironically, at the point when Hollywood had begun to deal with serious social and political issues, the infamous House Un-American Activities Committee set out to investigate the alleged Communist influence in Hollywood. It gave the American film a crippling blow from which it never fully recovered. A blacklist emerged of "fellow travelers," "premature anti fascists," and the disloyal. Naming names and informing on past friends and associates made spectacular headlines but not substantial films. The "Hollywood Ten" were a group of film people who refused to be friendly witnesses and went on to serve prison terms as a result: producer-writer Adrian Scott (*Mr. Lucky*, 1943); director Edward Dmytryk (*Crossfire*, 1947); producer-director Herbert Biberman (*Salt of the Earth*, 1954); screenwriters Alvah Bessie (*Objective Burma*, 1945), Lester Cole and Ring Lardner, Jr. (*Woman of the Year*, 1942), John Howard Lawson (*Blockade*, 1938), Albert Maltz (*This Gun for Hire*, 1942), Samuel Ornitz and Dalton Trumbo (*Thirty Seconds over Tokyo*, 1944).

The hundreds of others who were blacklisted were usually done so based on vague links to aid to Republican Spain in the

1930s or mobilization for war ally Soviet Union or on personal vendettas. Among the players blacklisted were John Garfield, Charlie Chaplin (deported in 1952), Burgess Meredith, Melvyn Douglas, Jane Wyatt, Edward G. Robinson, Zero Mostel, Karen Morley (*Our Daily Bread*), Ann Revere, Gale Sondergaard, Howard Da Silva, Will Geer, Jeff Corey, Paul Robeson, and the impressive newcomer, Beatrice Pearson (*Force of Evil*). The victims among directors were Robert Rossen (*Body and Soul*), Abraham Polansky (*Body and Soul*), Jules Dassin (*The Naked City*), Joseph Losey (*The Boy with Green Hair*), and Carl Foreman (*The Champion*, screenplay only). Among screenwriters, the suspects included Lillian Hellman (*Dead End*), Dashiell Hammett (*Watch on the Rhine*), and Michael Wilson (*A Place in the Sun*). Even those who self-confessed some transgressions suffered career damage: Sterling Hayden, Larry Parks, Lloyd Bridges; playwright-screenwriter Clifford Odets (*None but the Lonely Heart*); director Frank Tuttle (*This Gun for Hire*). The political acrimony and social intolerance led to the exodus from Hollywood of two other major talents: Orson Welles and Ingrid Bergman, at the end of the decade. Another round of investigation in 1951 further decimated the film industry of its leading creative talents.

Toward the end of the 1940s, Hollywood had begun to deal with anti-Semitism, in *Gentlemen's Agreement* (1947, 20th Century) and *Crossfire* (1947, RKO); the plight of Blacks, in *Pinky* (1949, 20th Century) and *Lost Boundaries* (1949, De Roche); and Mexican undocumented workers, in *Border Incident* (1949, MGM). They were courageous and commending efforts to address bigotry, prejudice, and segregation but ultimately proved premature in the face of the McCarthy era.

Other changes were also evident in Hollywood in the 1940s. As a result of the loss of foreign markets during the war years, production declined to a grand total number of films for the decade of 5,023 films.[1] Technically, new, more effective lenses and sound recording and mixing devices were developed. Films in color rose some 14 percent. In 1948, the federal government's "consent decree" forced the studios to sell their film theaters, to end violation of antitrust legislation. While studio film craftsmanship was still at its height, the studio system began to disintegrate.

In 1945, Olivia De Haviland had won a landmark case against Warner Brothers establishing that "the severely restrictive and punitive provisions of the contract system were now outlawed by the courts."[2] The advent of television, the increasing independence of stars and directors, and the diminishing film receipts led the studios to begin dismantling their stock companies of players and craftsmen. The big stars began freelancing and demanding and obtaining a percentage of film profits.

By the end of the 1940s, Hollywood's Golden Era was coming to an end.

The Films

The expectations of a qualitative improvement of the image of Hispanics in American films were somewhat realized during the war years, because of the need for hemispheric unity and patriotic concerns. The postwar years, however, brought a return to old stereotypes of bandits and Latin lovers.

The Mexican Spitfire series came to an end with its eleventh entry, titled *The Mexican Spitfire's Blessed Event* (1943, RKO). The Cisco Kid mantle passed from Warner Baxter to Cesar Romero (six entries, 1940–41), Duncan Renaldo (eight entries, 1945–49), and Gilbert Roland (six entries, 1946–47). For the most part, with these exceptions, Hispanic players receded to small roles in films. Ramon Novarro retired in 1938, Dolores Del Rio left Hollywood in 1942, and Lupe Velez died in 1944. The only Hispanic players to rise to stardom during the decade were Rita Hayworth (formerly Rita Casino) and Maria Montez.

The Mexican bandit continued to be a convenient villain, in *Virginia City* (1940, Warner Brothers), played by a miscast Humphrey Bogart; in *Cisco Kid and the Angel* (1940, 20th Century), *Ride On, Vaquero* (1942, 20th Century), and *Romance of the Rio Grande* (1942, 20th Century), played by Cesar Romero; and in *Twenty Mule Team* (1940, MGM) and *The Bad Man* (1941, MGM), played by Leo Carrillo. Anthony Quinn played an innocent Mexican taken for a murderer and bandit and lynched in William Wellman's powerful *The Ox-Bow Incident* (1943, 20th Century). In *Moonlight and Cactus* (1944, Universal), the irrepressible Leo Carrillo played yet another bandit. After the war,

49

the Mexican bandit returned in the Cisco Kid series, with Gilbert Roland and Duncan Renaldo; in *The Pirates of Monterey* (1947, Universal), played by Gilbert Roland; in *The Kissing Bandit* (1948, MGM), played unconvincingly by Frank Sinatra; in John Ford's *The Three Godfathers* (1948, MGM), played by Pedro Armendariz; and in *The Treasure of Sierra Madre* (1948, Warner Brothers), played by Alfonso Bedoya. Hispanic women continued to be prominently portrayed as perpetually aroused and promiscuous, such as Chihuahua (Linda Darnell) in *My Darling Clementine* (1946, 20th Century) and Pearl Chavez (Jennifer Jones) in *Duel in the Sun* (1946, Selznick). On the contemporary scene, Steve Cochran played an incongruous Cuban gangster in *The Chase* (1946, United Artists). Cuba's Machado dictatorship was depicted in John Huston's offbeat but interesting *We Were Strangers* (1949, Columbia), with John Garfield, Jennifer Jones, Gilbert Roland, and Ramon Novarro (in a comeback role) as revolutionaries and Pedro Armendariz as a henchman.

An attempt was made to bring back the Latin lover in a spate of musicals, beginning with *Weekend in Havana* (1941, 20th Century), in which Cesar Romero discards his Latin girlfriend, Carmen Miranda, and makes a play for Alice Faye, believing she's a wealthy heiress. Argentine star Alberto Vila met with romantic failure when he tried to woo Maureen O'Hara in *They Met in Argentina* (1941, RKO), as did Cesar Romero, in *Carnival in Costa Rica* (1947, 20th Century). Failure was the inevitable fate of Latin lovers. Toward the end of the decade, MGM brought Ricardo Montalban from Mexico to groom him for the Latin lover mantle, in such efforts as *Fiesta* (1947, MGM), *On an Island with You* (1948, MGM), and *Neptune's Daughter* (1949, MGM), all opposite the studio's reigning musical star, Esther Williams. Other similar films included *Pan-Americana* (1945, RKO), *Moonlight in Havana* (1942, Universal), and the featurette, *Fiesta* (1941, United Artists), with future Mexican superstar Jorge Negrete.

Elsewhere, legend and myth passed for history in *Kit Carson* (1940, United Artists) and *California* (1946, Paramount), both dealing with dispossession through Manifest Destiny of half of the territory of Mexico. Rather unconvincing Latin American backgrounds for the films, studio sets crammed with donkeys and caricature peons, rather than actual on-site locations, included Cuba, in *Six Lessons from Madame La Zonga* (1941, Universal); Mexico, in Abbott and Costello's *Mexican Hayride* (1948, United Artists); Peru, in the feeble remake of *The Bridge of San Luis Rey* (1944, United Artists); Mexico, in the Errol Flynn–Alexis Smith films *San Antonio* (1945, Warner Brothers) and *Tampico* (1944, 20th Century); and Central America, in the James Cagney–Ann Sheridan film *Torrid Zone* (1940, Warner Brothers).

The only film to deal with the contributions of Mexican-Americans in World War II as its sole concern was *A Medal for Benny* (1945, Paramount). Another film, *Guadalcanal Diary*, had Anthony Quinn as a Mexican-American marine in a substantial role, but with these two exceptions, the much-decorated heroism of Hispanics in uniform went relatively unnoticed on film. The plight of undocumented Mexican workers was first dealt with in Anthony Mann's *Border Incident* (1949, MGM).

On-location shooting in Mexico enhanced the authenticity of *Captain of Castille* (1947, 20th Century) about the Cortez conquest of Mexico; *The Fugitive* (1947, RKO), based on a novel by Graham Greene; and John Huston's *The Treasure of Sierra Madre* (1948, Warner Brothers) and *The Big Steal* (1949, RKO), a film noir. Additionally, these films utilized Mexican film crews and players, which fostered more cultural understanding and lessened the likelihood of Hollywood inaccuracies. One Mexican film, *The Pearl* (1948, Aguila), based on John Steinbeck's story, was dubbed into English and met with considerable critical and commercial acclaim.

In conclusion, in the 1940s, the image of the Chicano/Hispanic went through a slight improvement over the previous decade, although some old stereotypes remained. The bandit, Latin lover, and female cantinera (saloon woman) diminished in sheer volume but continued to be the stereotype staples for the Chicano/Hispanic on film. Government concern for hemispheric unity in World War II and the cold war helped to remove the most blatant excesses. Ironically, the very cold war and the McCarthy inquisition prevented the exploration of the roots of bigotry and racism in American society.

The following are representative films of the decade.

Kit Carson (1940, United Artists)

The film *Kit Carson* was an aberration in the era of the Good Neighbor Policy, celebrating with brash bravado Manifest Destiny and Social Darwinism.

The film chronicles some dubious exploits of Christopher "Kit" Carson (1809–68), scout, Indian-killer, and conspirator to dispossess Mexico of half its territory. Here, Carson (Jon Hall) guides John C. Frémont (Dana Andrews), his troops, and a wagon train through a trek of Manifest Destiny and the takeover of California. Predictably, they encounter Indian attacks, and a love triangle ensues between Carson, Fremont, and a beautiful and genteel señorita, Dolores Murphy (Lynn Bari). Their arrival, or rather invasion, is met by Mexican generals Castro (C. Henry Gordon) and Vallejo (Lew Merrill), portrayed here as evil and treacherous. The Mexican forces defeat one group of filibusters, and then they are repulsed when Anglo reinforcements arrive. Dolores and Carson, according to the plausible scenario, live happily ever after.

The real, historical Frémont (on a secret U.S. government mission) had been permitted by Mexican authorities to quarter for the winter in 1845. He prematurely raised the U.S. flag at Hawk's Peak, near Monterey, on March 1846. A little later, Frémont was joined by Anglo-American immigrants (including Kit Carson) and, adopting the Bear Flag, declared war on Mexico. The invaders were then defeated on December 5, 1846, at San Pasquel Pass, northeast of San Diego, by a party of Mexicans led by Andres Pico. Overwhelmed by Anglo reinforcements, Pico and his forces were defeated and hostilities came to an end on January 10, 1847, with the Treaty of Cahuenga. Again, there was a significant amount of discrepancy between Hollywood and history.

Critical reviews abounded with historical amnesia. Columnist Louella O. Parsons stated, "Children will cheer for this picture and so will adults who still enjoy Indian fights because there's a scalping party to about every ten revolutions of the wagon wheels. . . . " *Variety* (August 28, 1940) commented, "In contrast with many of his contemporaries, the Carson saga is a matter of fairly accurate record, any biographer who would attempt a screening of his career should find it unnecessary to add much fiction to the facts. . . ."

The Mark of Zorro (1940, 20th Century)

Zorro, a combination of Robin Hood and Joaquin Murietta, made his fourth film appearance in this skillfully directed (Rouben Mamoulian) and sumptuously produced (Darryl F. Zanuck) film. Since the famous Douglas Fairbanks' *Mark of Zorro* (1920), the character had been played by Robert Livingston in the inferior *Bold Caballero* (1936) and by the famed stuntman-actor, Yakima Canutt in *Zorro Rides Again* (1937).

This film followed the Fairbanks version closely, but not identically. It is set in the early 1800s, in Los Angeles, California. It begins with Don Diego Vega (Tyrone Power) at the Royal Spanish Military Academy, where he is informed that he must return immediately to California. Upon his arrival, he becomes aware that his father (Montague Love) has been deposed as the *alcalde* (mayor) and the city is now under the corrupt rule of Don Luis Quintero (J. Edward Bromberg). He is bolstered in his tyranny by the arrogant and vain Captain Esteban Pasquale (Basil Rathbone). Don Diego upholds the people's cause of justice, masquerading as Zorro by night and as an effeminate dandy by day. He falls in love with Quintero's beautiful niece, Lolita (Linda Darnell), while he organizes the caballeros to overcome the alcalde.

Tyrone Power, at the height of his box-office power, was cast as Zorro in direct competition with Errol Flynn, his swashbuckling rival at Warner Brothers. Power was to prove to be a considerably serious actor, both on screen and stage, when he would finally begin to break the typecasting in the late 1940s. He would play the French architect De Lesseps in *Suez* (1938, 20th Century), the Indian Rama in *The Rains Came* (1939, 20th Century), the Spanish bullfighter Juan Gallardo in *Blood and Sand* (1940, 20th Century), the Spanish conquistador Pedro de Vargas in *Captain from Castille* (1947, 20th Century), and the Irish (his heritage) Marty Maher in *The Long Gray Line* (1955, Columbia). Basil Rathbone, well respected for his fencing expertise, was to state, "Power was the most agile man with a sword I've ever faced on the camera." Despite this, the film avoided the dazzling acrobatic display given by Douglas Fairbanks in his rendition of the role. Power, though, gave an interesting performance of a double life and climaxed it with one of the most memorable examples of swordplay on the screen with his nemesis, Rathbone.

Like previous versions, this film perpetuated the Darwinist concept that only the blue-blooded caballero class could run and administer political power and control the excesses of newly empowered mestizos. In casting, Hollywood played it safe, casting the title role with one of the biggest box-office draws, Tyrone Power. In retrospect, of the leading Hispanic male leads in the period, two could have been well cast: Ramon Novarro and Gilbert Roland. It would also have been possible for the studio to have taken a chance with a very promising newcomer, Anthony Quinn. As of this writing, the character of Zorro has yet to be portrayed by an Hispanic. The film also contains some disturbing scenes perpetuating some old stereotypes. When Zorro first rides into town, the whole town is shown in a prolonged siesta that is almost a caricature and that is reminiscent of *Why Worry?*

On the plus side, Hollywood craftsmanship is at its best, not the least in the memorable Alfred Newman film score. The reviews were generally excellent. Typical of the reviews was *Variety* (November 6, 1940):

> Power is no prototype of the original Fairbanks, but, fortunately, neither the script nor direction forces him to any close comparison. He's plenty heroic and sincere in his mission, and delays long enough en route for some romantic interludes with the beauteous Linda Darnell. But overall, it's a fanciful character done up in a neat enough package to hit public fancy for good biz.*

Needless to say, the film was a big success and remains the best known Zorro film.

---

*This and all other articles from *Variety* included in this book are used by permission.

Tortilla Flat (1942, MGM)

Tortilla Flat is an example of Hollywood film craftsmanship at its finest and condescension at its worst.

The film is based on a novel written by John Steinbeck in 1935. According to Arthur G. Pettit, the novel:

> is the clearest example of North American literature of the Mexican as a happy savage. For better or worse, the book is frequently cited as the "Anglo" prototype novel about Chicanos. . . . The portrayal by Steinbeck of the "paisano" universe is related to his profound disenchantment of the "Anglo" world corrupted and maddened by machines. The "paisanos" of Tortilla Flat, literally isolated ("marooned") in their fields, inhabit metaphorically the last redoubt of Paradise before the fall.[3]

On closer inspection, Steinbeck's paisanos, while described as being descendants of the Spanish and Indian, are never actually designated as mestizo or Mexican-American. They appear to live in a cultural vacuum like cultural eunuchs.

The plot revolves around the troubles that beset the prone-to-be-lazy Danny (John Garfield), when he inherits two houses in Tortilla Flat, and his manipulative wastrel friend, Pilon (Spencer Tracy) and assorted friends move in to show him how a man of wealth should live. Danny begins courting Dolores (Hedy Lamarr), while Pilon plans to steal an old man's (Frank Morgan) money. When one of Danny's houses burns down, he has a falling out with Pilon, who attempts to redeem himself by raising money to buy Danny a fishing boat. Danny and Dolores get married, and Pilon concludes that property was the cause of all the trouble and burns his friend's second house. He returns to the happy-go-lucky life of a wastrel.

Both Spencer Tracy and John Garfield, lifelong liberals (Garfield would later be blacklisted), are miscast, as is the Vienna-born Hedy Lamarr. Hispanic players appear in bit parts, and their absence deprives the film of any Chicano/Hispanic cultural ambience.

The critical response was enthusiastic and predictably condescending to the film's mistruths and romanticized myths. The *Hollywood Reporter* (April 22, 1942) noted:

Steinbeck wrote of the paisanos, those curiously childlike natives who loaf on the sunny hillside overlooking Monterey, California. Vagabonds and idlers of the land . . . they are lovable, winesoaked thieves who would rather hunger than work—gentle, almost poetic wastrels. They are descendants of a race who has lived where they are living for "a hundred or two years," and they sing of their lives with gusto and humor. . . .

Variety (April 22, 1942) commented, "*Tortilla Flat*, John Steinbeck's story of the simple, picturesque paisanos of Monterey, California, is brought to the screen in a production calculated to reap a rich box-office reward. . . ."

Mexican Spitfire's Blessed Event (1943, RKO)

The film was the eleventh and final feature of the Mexican Spitfire series.

Lupe Velez had made three films back-to-back in 1943 (the others were *Ladies Day* and *The Redhead from Manhattan*). *Mexican Spitfire's Blessed Event*, ironically, would prove to be her last film. Faced with a three-month pregnancy and a broken relationship, she committed suicide on December 14, 1944. It is uncertain whether she would have continued with the series had she lived. Despite her increasing enmity with critics, Lupe and her films continued to be big money-makers.

This film's thin plot revolves around Carmelita (Lupe) wiring Uncle Matt (Leon Errol) about the kitten her pet ocelot has had. A misunderstanding arises regarding the telegram that leads Lord Epping (Leon Errol in a dual role) to promise that he will sign an advertising contract with the baby's name as soon as he's seen the child. Carmelita borrows someone's baby, and the rest of the film involves her trying to keep Epping from learning the truth.

The critics were rather unkind to the film. The *Hollywood Reporter* (July 13, 1943) noted, "These 'Mexican Spitfire' pictures have reached the point of repeating themselves shamelessly. . . ." *Variety* (July 15, 1943) commented, "This is the last of the 'Spitfires' which have tarried around for several years.

Finals of series display the usual complications on light framework for display of broadcast farce and horseplay. . . ."

The Ox-Bow Incident (1943, 20th Century)

The novel, by Walter Van Tilburg Clark, on which the film is based has its basic antecedents in a true event that took place in 1885 in Nevada.

Selected to direct the film version was William Wellman, who had previously directed some powerful social dramas, including the gangster classic *Public Enemy* (1931, Warner Brothers), with James Cagney; the Depression tale *Heroes for Sale* (1933, Warner Brothers), with Richard Barthelmess; and the sensitive *Robin Hood of El Dorado* (1936, MGM), the best screen version of Joaquin Murietta.

This film depicts how, through the desire for revenge, a posse is organized after the supposed murder of a popular rancher, Larry Kinkaid. The posse is agitated by the rancher's best friend, Farnley (Marc Lawrence) and a vain ex-Confederate officer, Tetley (Frank Convoy), who takes charge wearing his Civil War uniform. Among the assorted group is the contradictory messenger, Poncho (Chris-Pin Martin), of the alleged murder. In the middle of the night, the motley crew of rogues comes across three men: a farmer, Martin (Dana Andrews), a bewildered old man (Francis Ford), and mysterious Mexican Juan Martinez (Anthony Quinn). When the old man is confronted about who committed the murder, he blurts out, "The Mexican did it. I saw him do it. I heard him talk about it in his sleep."

Anthony Quinn was cast in his first Mexican role in this film. As Martinez, he attempts to pass himself off as a Spanish-speaking cowboy and responds with a continuous "No sabe" to the persistent interrogation. He attempts to escape, is wounded in the leg, and then proceeds to fearlessly dig the bullet from his leg. When he drops his ruse and speaks English, one of the posse snaps, "This spick speaks American!" When Martinez is lent the knife to withdraw the bullet, another warns, "Don't give him a knife, he uses a knife better than most men use a gun."

Wishing to be expedient with the flimsy circumstantial evidence, the posse proceeds to hang the unfortunate trio, despite the protest of a few dissenters (Henry Fonda, Harry Morgan). Unlike the farmer, who breaks down, and the old man, who becomes incoherent, Martinez goes to his death bravely and defiantly, after confessing his sins to Poncho, who is to take them to a priest. Soon thereafter, the posse discovers that Kinkaid is not dead and that his attempted murderer has been apprehended.

The film powerfully conveys the hysteria of vigilante and mob violence and how, sometimes, decent men are engulfed in the psychology of a mob. An ensemble cast performed excellently in a gallery of deeply etched characters. Since its release, the film has rightly been elevated to a classic film status. Never before had the Old West looked so unglamorous and unheroic.

Quinn's portrayal of the doomed Martinez imbued him with dignity and humanism in the midst of social chaos and bigotry. It was an excellent performance for the newcomer, and one of those rarest of Hollywood events, a positive role of a Mexican (in a Western, of all places) on film without being condescending.

The Three Caballeros (1945, Disney/RKO)

The part live action and part animation in the Technicolored *The Three Caballeros* followed Walt Disney's *Saludos Amigos* (1943, RKO) as the U.S. government–sponsored goodwill gesture of Roosevelt's Good Neighbor Policy.

While the forty-three-minute *Saludos Amigos* had concentrated on South America, *The Three Caballeros* had Mexico as its emphasis. Walt Disney wisely employed prominent composers: the Brazilian Ary Barroso, and the Mexican Agustin Lara and Manuel Esperon. Lara's "You Belong to My Heart" and Barroso's "Baia," introduced in the film, became top songs in another film that year, *Song of Mexico*. A leading lady was the Brazilian Aurora Miranda (Carmen's sister).

The film was a dazzling display of brilliant animation and live action. Donald Duck is delivered three presents on his birthday, the first of which is a film projector which plunges the viewer into three segments. The first involves Pablo the Penguin, who becomes tired of the cold and travels to the tropics. The second chronicles the adventures of a little Mexican boy, who finds a flying donkey. Donald Duck opens another present, which is a book, from which pops up Joe Carioca (from *Saludos Amigos*), and the two travel to Brazil and then to Mexico. A brief history of the country is provided, along with the Christmas tradition of the piñata, and visits to Veracruz, Acapulco, and Patzcuaro.

Critically and commercially, the film was a huge success, specifically in Mexico and Brazil, the two most important American allies during World War II. Rivera noted, "what is appreciated in Disney is a visible interest in documentation: his Mexican postcards reflect the same popular places manipulated in Mexico by a complacent nationalism. . . ."[4] The *New Yorker* commented: ". . . a mixture of atrocious taste, bogus mysticism, and authentic fantasy, guaranteed to baffle any critic not hopelessly enchanted with the word 'Disney'. . . ."

While the film has some sexist suggestiveness, it is exceptional in its appreciation of Latin American customs and culture. In light of some of the patently racist stereotypes that abounded in the era's animation features, this film is refreshing.

A Medal for Benny (1945, Paramount)

Historically, Chicanos/Mexicanos have joined the U.S. armed forces in war and peace in large numbers, during war because of their patriotism and during peace because of their low economic status. Acuña notes that "25 percent of the U.S. military personnel on the infamous Bataan 'Death March' were Mexican-Americans and that, in World War II, Mexicans earned more medals of honor than any other ethnic or racial group. . . ."[5] Hollywood films have only rarely documented such historical facts.

Irving Pichel's *A Medal for Benny*, written by John Steinbeck, is one of only two films ever made by Hollywood to solely deal with Chicano/Hispanic heroism in war (the other is *Hell to Eternity* [1960, Allied Artists]). The film is set in a small northern seashore town that is predominantly Chicano/Mexicano. Joe Morales (Arturo De Cordova) is an amiable but useless young man who spends most of his time with Lolita (Dorothy Lamour), whose boyfriend, Benny Martin, had been run out of town a year ago by the police. The town is thrown into a consternation when it is learned that Benny has been awarded the Congressional Medal of Honor posthumously for killing one hundred Japanese soldiers in the Philippines.

The opportunistic city fathers become joyously imbued with civic pride. A general, reporters, and newsreel cameramen are expected the next day. The city fathers look forward to putting their town on the map and to making large profits. They attempt to find some credible background to Benny and his poor family. They finally find his hard-working father, Charley Martin (J. Carrol Naish), through Benny's jail record, who is expecting to get evicted. Joe has sunk Charley's boat, which Charley has used as collateral for a bank loan.

The suddenly socially indignant civic leaders move Charley to more dignified surroundings until after the ceremony takes place. When Joe is humiliated by a dance partner, Toodles Castro (Rosita Moreno), Lolita realizes that she loves him and not Benny. Joe convinces Lolita to keep their secret until after the ceremony. Charley returns home when he learns of plans to commercialize the event, where the medal is finally presented. Lolita, publicized as the hero's girlfriend, becomes engaged to Joe when he enlists, attempting to redeem himself.

The film received glowing reviews, especially Arturo De Cordova, who had been typecast as Latin lover, and Dorothy Lamour, previously admired only for her physical attributes. It is interesting to note, however, how reviewers described Chicanos/ Hispanics condescendingly. *Look* magazine (June 26, 1945) noted:

> Dorothy Lamour and Arturo De Cordova, Paramount's sexy stepchildren, get a long-deserved chance as Lolita Sierra and Joe Morales, the romantic team of Steinbeck's *A Medal for Benny*—to show they can really act. . . . Steinbeck tells a simple story of a group of paisanos (Spanish-Indian half-breeds) living in the "slough town" of a small California city. . . .

Time (September 28, 1945) commented, "*A Medal for Benny* rates a medal for Paramount. . . . It is a story about one of the minor U.S. minorities—California's Paisanos, the indigent descendants of the original Indians and Spanish settlers. . . ." The *Hollywood Reporter* (April 9, 1945) wrote that it had:

> a sensitively written screenplay, which vividly brings to life the characteristics of the easy-going but justifiably proud Mexican-Americans. . . . Miss Lamour, beautiful to look at, displays a quality of talent that surely will lessen her identification with the sarong. De Cordova manifests some of the promise that has been expected of this experienced, highly competent Mexican actor. Here he has a colorful role which he is able to interpret with convincing flourishes. . . . Rosita Moreno and Fernando Alvarado complete the small but unusually efficient acting company. . . .

Variety (April 11, 1945) noted, "Paramount not only has a real sleeper in 'A Medal for Benny,' but also a picture that lifts two players to new histrionic heights. . . . The performance of Arturo De Cordova is also one that will not pass unnoticed. . . ." The *Los Angeles Times* (June 29, 1945) commented, "It has strength and irony, and merits respect for its quality. . . . Miss Lamour puts sincerity into her excellent depiction of the Lolita, while De Cordova is pleasing in his quixotic interpretation. . . ."

It was a type of film that appeared few and far between.

Duel in the Sun (1946, Selznick)

The role of the mestiza Pearl Chavez in David O. Selznick's sprawling Western, *Duel in the Sun*, is the very epitome of accumulated stereotypes of a Latina woman.

Produced by David O. Selznick, who had produced *Gone with the Wind* (1939, MGM), the Western took some two years to complete and was the most expensive film ever made up to that time. For the central role of Pearl Chavez, he cast his then wife, Jennifer Jones, who had won an Academy Award in an entirely different role in *The Song of Bernadette* (1943). In the role of Pearl Chavez, she is entirely miscast, and the consequence is a blatantly stereotypical portrayal.

The film is set in 1880 in Texas. Gambler Scott Chavez (Herbert Marshall) is hanged for killing his faithless wife (Tilly

61

Losch), an Indian, and her lover. His daughter, "Pearl Chavez, the half-breed from along the border," is taken by the kindly distant relative of her father, Laura Belle McCanles (Lillian Gish). Her cattle baron husband, "who helped build Texas," Senator McCanles, is a bigot who treats Pearl with easy disdain. One of their sons, Jesse (Joseph Cotten), who is dispatched to pick her up at the stagecoach station, quips, "I'm sorry in not recognizing you. I guess they were the clothes." Upon seeing her, the Senator exclaims, "Girl, what are you doing in that get-up?" Her Mexican culture is constantly an object of derision.

Pearl becomes romantically involved with Jesse and Lewt (Gregory Peck), a vain, egotistical, and manipulative cowboy. When his father comments on his scorn for Pearl, Lewt states, "She looks like a pretty good tamale." To this, the Senator responds, "She wouldn't appeal to me." On another occasion, the Senator, disgusted with Lewt's continued involvement with her, says, "I haven't been working in this place to turn it into an Indian Reservation." To this, Lewt responds laughingly, "You want me to have a good time, don't you?" Both father and son are equally adept opportunists.

Jesse has a falling-out with his father over the conflict between the ranchers and the railroad. When he rejects Pearl because "like mother, like daughter," Pearl seeks solace with Sam Pierce (Charles Bickford), with whom she becomes engaged to marry. Lewt kills Pierce and seeks out Pearl for sexual gratification, although he refuses to marry her: "No woman can tie on to me, least of all a bobtail little half-breed like you." Lewt subsequently wounds his unarmed brother. His father continues to be blind to his son's evil ways and bigoted perception, "It's that Indian girl, if you hadn't brought her here." Finally, Pearl tracks Lewt to the desert where they kill each other in each other's loving arms!

Pearl Chavez personifies all the accumulated stereotypical characteristics of a Chicana/Mexicana woman in American film: governed by uncontrollable sexual urges, promiscuous, unredeemed, and ingrained with a sense of inferiority and the self-fulfilling prophecy of failure.

My Darling Clementine (1946, 20th Century)

The character of Chihuahua in *My Darling Clementine* is one of the key Chicana/Mexicana lead roles of the decade and one of the most fatalistic.

John Ford directed an evocative and lyrical film centering on the events that led to the legendary gunfight at the O.K. Corral. The story has been filmed countless times, but this remains the superior rendition. The film has gained the status of a film classic. Katz notes, "Ford may possibly be best described as a populist; emotionally as a sentimentalist. His films, particularly the Westerns, betray a deep sense of nostalgia for the American past and the spirit of the frontier. . . ."[6] It is, however, a romanticized past that never really existed. One of Ford's last films, *The Man Who Shot Liberty Valance* (1962, Paramount), carries an aphorism that accurately symbolizes Ford's Westerns: "When the legend becomes the fact, print the legend!"

Set in Tombstone, Arizona, in 1882, Wyatt Earp (Henry Fonda) and his brothers, Virgil (Tim Holt) and Morgan (Ward Bond), become marshals after one of their brothers is killed by Old Man Clanton (Walter Brennan) and his sons (John Ireland, Grant Withers). Earp first draws attention when he single-handedly subdues a drunken Indian (Charles Stevens, Geronimo's real life grandson), in disgust, "What kind of town is this, serving liquor to Indians?" Dragging and kicking the Indian, Earp threatens him, "Stay out of town, Indian!" The notorious gambler and gunfighter, Doc Holliday (Victor Mature), runs the town and establishes a sardonic accommodation with the Earps. He is loved by Chihuahua (Linda Darnell), a beautiful cantinera girl whom Holliday uses and maltreats frequently, in a similar way to how Lewt treats Pearl in *Duel in the Sun*. At one point, Holliday tells her, "Why don't you go away, squall your stupid little songs and leave me alone?"

Wyatt, from the beginning, treats Chihuahua with quiet contempt, as he did the Indian. He shuns her in the saloon and then dumps her in a drinking fountain and addresses her as "wild cat." His treatment contrasts dramatically with how he treats the very ordinary Clementine (Cathy Downs), Holliday's discarded childhood sweetheart who shows up. He treats her

63

like a lady, tipping his hat, and, with benign cordiality, calls her "Madam." His brother Morgan amuses himself by making horse laughs when Chihuahua passes by.

Loveless and the object of everyone's ridicule and disrespect, Chihuahua cavorts with Billy Clanton, who subsequently shoots her. Holliday attempts to save her by operating, and a glimmer of sincerity and respect finally shines through, "You're all right. You've been a brave girl." Her death motivates Holliday, at last, to try to redeem himself at the gunfight at the O.K. Corral.

Chihuahua's fate was representative of all the trials and tribulations of Chicanas/Mexicanas in real life and reel life.

The Treasure of Sierra Madre (1948, Warner Brothers)

John Huston's adaptation of B. Traven's *The Treasure of Sierra Madre* has one of the most famous of Mexican film bandits, that of Gold Hat.

The story is set in Tampico, Mexico, in the 1920s. Fred C. Dobbs (Humphrey Bogart) and Curtin (Tim Holt) are two down-and-out North Americans who join an old miner, Howard (Walter Huston), enticed by his tales of gold fields in the interior. Traveling to their destination by train, they are attacked by bandits on horseback led by Gold Hat (Alfonso Bedoya), which they successfully repulse. The trio ultimately finds a rich gold vein, but the men soon start fighting among themselves because of their increasing greed. They encounter Gold Hat and his men once more in the mountains. "Who are you?" asks Dobbs. "We're the mountain police," replies Gold Hat. "If you're the mountain police, where are your badges?" asks Dobbs. "Badges? We don't need any badges! We don't need any stinking badges!" exclaims Gold Hat.

When Howard departs to care for a sick boy in a nearby Indian village, Dobbs's increasing paranoia results in leaving Curtin for dead. Howard and the Indians rescue Curtin, but Dobbs is ultimately killed by Gold Hat and his men. They are subsequently apprehended and executed for their crimes. Curtin is dejected, but Howard makes him understand the ironies of life as the gold sacks blow in the wind.

The film was shot on location in Mexico, and almost the entire cast is authentically Mexican, except for the four leads. Additionally, Huston had Spanish spoken by the Mexican cast members, adding considerably to the realism. A vigilant Department of the Interior of Mexico confiscated footage that they felt was derogatory. Huston, who had been a cavalry officer in the Mexican Army in his youth and would later live there for several years, protested but complied. Huston's characters are dimensional and believable. There are no idealized characters; both Anglos and Mexicans are portrayed with tangible and discernable flaws of weakness, resourcefulness, greed, duplicity, and vigor. Within this realm, Gold Hat has proper context and validity.

The film went on to acquire a considerable and well-earned reputation. Among the honors were Academy Awards to John Huston for Best Director and to Walter Huston for Best Supporting Actor. Luis Valdez would later write a play entitled *Stinking Badges*, about a Chicano film actor and father who had been an extra in the film.

The Players

In the 1940s, Hollywood contracted three established Mexican actors: Pedro Armendariz, Arturo De Cordova, and Ricardo Montalban.

Armendariz would go on to star in seventeen American films, while alternating his career with notable Mexican films, usually directed by Emilio Fernandez, in such films as *Maria Candelaria* (1943) and *La Perla* (1945). In Hollywood, he proved himself an extremely versatile actor in a wide range of roles and was perhaps most memorable in a trio of John Ford films: *The Fugitive* (1947), *Three Godfathers* (1948), and *Fort Apache*.

De Cordova starred in nine films of mixed quality. An excellent actor and one of the authentic immortals of the Mexican screen, he was given mostly unsubstantial roles, with the exception of Irving Pichel's *A Medal for Benny* (1945), scripted by John Steinbeck, in which he played the friend of a Mexican-American war hero. De Cordova left Hollywood in 1948, disappointed, and returned to Mexico to star in more challenging films, such as Luis Buñuel's *El* (1951), among others.

Montalban debuted in Hollywood in an Esther Williams musical, *Fiesta* (1947), and, thereafter, was typecast as a Latin lover and a hero in inconsequential films. By demanding from his studio, MGM, more substantial roles, he made several films that explored the Chicano/Mexican experience in American society: *Mystery Street* (1949), *Battleground* (1949), *Right Cross* (1950), and *My Man and I* (1952). His career declined in the 1960s with a slew of mediocre films, until his success in television's "Fantasy Island."

Hispanic actresses, with the sole exception of Rita Hayworth (formerly Rita Cansino), met with less success. Hayworth had worked her way from extra, bit player, and supporting decorative beauty in scores of routine films, mostly Westerns, until scoring in Howard Hawks's *Only Angels Have Wings* (1939), opposite Richard Barthelmess, Jean Arthur, and Cary Grant, and, thereafter, became a sultry sex symbol with box-office power, in films such as *Blood and Sand* (1941, 20th Century), *Gilda* (1946, Columbia), and *The Lady from Shanghai* (1948, Columbia). With the death of Lupe Velez and the departure of Dolores Del Rio, Hayworth would become the dominant Hispanic female star. By the late 1950s, she would finally begin to obtain long-overdue critical acclaim as a fine dramatic actress.

Stella Inda, an established Mexican actress, played the fabled Aztec maiden Malinche impressively in the epic retelling of Cortez's Mexican conquest in Henry King's *Captain from Castille* (1947), but, thereafter, no further offers developed. She returned to Mexico for some memorable films, such as Buñuel's *Los Olvidados* (1950). Both Elena Verdugo and Estelita Rodriguez spent their entire careers in low-budget actioners, usually Westerns. Dominican Republic–born Maria Montez was the only other Hispanic actress to reach stardom, besides Hayworth, during the decade. Teamed with Jon Hall in some half a dozen, very popular, Technicolored costume actioners by Universal, she was typecast as the romantic, exotic, and alluring sexual goddess. Attempting to break the mold, she left for Europe at the end of the decade, where she died suddenly in 1951, at the age of only thirty-one.

Several other actors of Hispanic descent were introduced during the 1940s: Puerto Rican-born Jose Ferrer and Cuban-born Desi Arnaz, who played supporting roles in the 1940s, and went on to fame in the 1950s in the *I Love Lucy* television series with his wife, Lucille Ball. Bedoya made his impressive American film debut in *The Treasure of Sierra Madre* (1948, Warner Brothers) and uttered the memorable line, "Badges! We don't need any badges! We don't need any stinking badges!" Unfortunately, he was thereafter typecast as either a bandit or villain, usually one-dimensional in less distinguished films.

Notes

1. Joel L. Finler, *The Hollywood Story* (New York: Crown Publishers, 1988).
2. Robyn Karney, ed., *The Movie Stars Story* (New York: Crescent Books, 1984).
3. Arthur G. Pettit, *Images of the Mexican in Fiction and Film* (College Station: Texas A & M University Press, 1980).
4. Emilio Garcia Rivera, *Mexico Visto for el Cine Extrajero* (Guadalajara: Ediciones Era, 1988).
5. Rodolfo Acuña, *Occupied America* (San Francisco: Canfield Press, 1972).
6. Ephraim Katz, *The Film Encyclopedia* (New York: Perigree Books, 1979).

CHAPTER FIVE

The 1950s—the Premature Chicano Cinema and the Hollywood Inquisition

> Then I knew we had won something they could never take away—something I could leave to our children and they, the salt of the earth, would inherit it.
>
> —Esperanza (Rosaura Revveltas)
> in *Salt of the Earth* (1954)

American films of the 1950s were affected by the great events taking place in the world, but most of the time attempted to deal with them in a simplistic, jingoistic, and condescending manner. The decade witnessed the pervasive decline of Hollywood as the film capital of the world. Various factors contributed to this decline: television, declining audiences, the divestiture of the studio theaters, the demise of the studio, and the intimidating political climate created by the House Un-American Activities Committee (HUAC). Despite all this, a premature effort was made to document the sociohistorical experience of the indigenous Chicano in American film.

The postwar world was characterized by radical changes. The powerful force of nationalism manifested itself in the decline of old, decaying empires such as the British and French. Having survived World War II relatively unscathed, unlike its wartime allies, the United States became the Western guardian of the status quo. Postwar peace gave way to escalation of the cold war over the issues of nuclear weapons, territoriality and ideological self-interest. Inevitably, the rising Third World became the arenas of contention (e.g., Cuba and the Congo) by the two competing superpowers. A policy of nonalignment with neither was sufficient to arouse a retaliatory suspicion about the voluntary departure from the faithful flock of hegemony.

The cold war induced an intellectual rigor mortis in international and national leaders. On one occasion, President Kennedy would lucidly assess the era:

> The revolution of national independence is a fundamental fact of our era. This revolution will not be stopped and it is in our own national interest that this revolution of national independence succeed. . . . We must reject over-simplified theories of international life. The theory that American power is unlimited or that the American mission is to remake the world in the American image. We must seize the vision of a free and diverse world and shape our policy to speed progress toward a more flexible world order. . . .

Needless to say, such wise counsel of tolerance was not heeded in the overthrow or destablization of a series of regimes that attempted to determine their own political and economic destiny: Iran, Guatemala, Hungary, Vietnam, Cuba.

At home, the United States experienced unparalleled prosperity of material production and consumption under the resurgent Republican Party. But that national tranquility was deceptive. The contemporary civil rights movement was given impetus by the historical Brown decision in 1954. Segregationists used all means at their disposal to maintain the myth of the superiority of one race over another. Operation Wetback, a military-styled effort, deported more than one million Mexicans and Mexican-Americans, and the McCarren-Walter Act was another reflection of the attempt to maintain national purity. Senator Pat McCarren from Nevada justified it: "If we scrap the national origin formula we will, in the course of a generation or so, change the ethnic and cultural composition of this nation."[1]

The notorious Senator Joseph McCarthy from Wisconsin and the HUAC held an encore appearance in Hollywood in March of 1951. Some 212 people in film, theatre, and television were blacklisted. Still others, who were merely tainted by innocuous association of friendship or employment were on an alternative, unofficial "gray" list. A cowed Hollywood, out of self-interest, produced a spate of mediocre melodramas parroting the hysteria of the era: *My Son John* (1951), *Big Jim McLain* (1952), *I Was a Communist for the FBI* (1951), *I Married a Communist* (1949), and *The Trial* (1955) among others.

The HUAC retarded the efforts of the Hollywood film industry, which blossomed after the war, to explore serious social themes. Segregation, colonialism, nationalism, and racism were for the most part Hollywood taboos. Isolated attempts were made to improve the image of minorities. Delmer Daves' *Broken Arrow* (1950, 20th Century) was the first film to analyze Indian culture and its historical roots. The excesses of bigotry were dramatized in *No Way Out* (1950, 20th Century) and *The Defiant Ones* (1958, United Artists). Drug addiction was depicted in *The Man with the Golden Arm* (1955) and *A Hateful of Rain* (1957), and the ethos of young manhood were depicted powerfully in *East of Eden* (1955, Warner Brothers) and *Rebel without a Cause* (1955, Warner Brothers) by one of the more arresting icons of the 1950s, James Dean.

The proliferation of television severely undermined the film industry. Initially, the industry attempted to ignore the new medium. At the Warner Brothers studio, for example, mogul Jack Warner required that no television sets be exhibited in studio films. By middecade however, the studio had succumbed to produce a spate of lucrative television series, such as *Cheyenne* and *Sugarfoot*. Director Billy Wilder would be quoted as saying that "it used to be that films were the lowest form of art. Now we have something to look down on."[2] The film industry attempted to entice away audiences from television with a series of technological devices beginning in 1952 with *Bwana Devil* in "3D" and *This Is Cinerama*, providing audiences with an experience very much like riding a roller coaster. Then came 20th Century-Fox's Cinemascope in *The Robe* (1953), Paramount's VistaVision in *White Christmas* (1954) and United Artists' 70-mm Todd-AO process in *Around the World in Eighty Days* (1956).

Unfortunately, for Hollywood, bigger was not always better, and after temporary increase in film receipts early in the decade, they began to once more decline. The total number of releases (including an increased number of independents) for the decade totalled 5,050, actually more than the previous decade total of

5,023. However, by 1956, film audiences continued to erode year by year.

The divestiture of studio theatre became complete by the 1950s. As a result of the loss of its stable of directors and players, studios began to depend increasingly on package deals with independent producers and freelancing and percentage-taking stars. To help compensate for falling receipts, companies invested heavily in shooting abroad motivated by lower costs and colorful locales. Italy, Spain, and Mexico were the main beneficiaries of this trend.

The Films

The image of the Chicano and Hispanic in the 1950s was discernably derived from some staples of the past (bandits and latin lovers) as well as new staples directly influenced by the cold war.

The postwar era resurfaced some of the old stereotypes of prewar Hollywood. The U.S. film industry recovered the European film market. By 1949, the twenty Latin American nations made up almost one-fifth of the total market for Hollywood films. Previous Latin American displeasure over Hollywood products led to the establishment by the Motion Picture Association of America of an International Information Center located in Los Angeles to "affect the deletion from motion pictures of any elements which might reasonably be expected to offend the sensitivities of foreign peoples. . . ." Additionally, the increase of coproductions with Latin American countries, employing their locales, actors, and crews, did much to diminish ignorance and misunderstandings. Despite it all, some of the images persisted.

Blood-thirsty, hard-drinking Mexican bandits (Robert Taylor, Anthony Quinn) were on display in *Ride Vaquero* (1953, MGM) menacing peace-loving Anglo settlers (Ava Gardner, Howard Keel). The appropriately titled *Bandido* (1956, United Artists) cast Robert Mitchum and Gilbert Roland as unscrupulous gunrunners during the Mexican Revolution. In *The Naked Dawn* (1955, United Artists), Eugene Iglesias plays an ungrateful Mexican farmer who is hired by an Anglo (Arthur Kennedy) to collect money from a freight train holdup and who, unable to control himself, plans the murder of his benefactor. In *Border Incident* (1954, Universal), a virtuous Confederate Major (Joel McCrea) in the closing days of the Civil War steals $2,000,000 in gold bullion from a Union mint to augment the South's fortunes, and almost immediately, an attempt is made to dispossess him of his ill-gotten wealth by an evil renegade Mexican general (Pedro Armendariz). The general not only fails at his effort but also loses his beauteous girlfriend (Yvonne De Carlo) to the man from the South. In *The Wonderful Country* (1959, United Artists), Armendariz played yet another nefarious renegade Mexican general at odds with an Anglo mercenary (Robert Mitchum). In *Passion* (1954, RKO), endemic banditry seems to be the rule rather than the exception in Mexican California.

The Latin lover had a brief vogue early in the decade. It survived in such features as *Jivaro* (1954, Paramount), essayed by Fernando Lamas; in *Sombrero* (1953, MGM), by Ricardo Montalban and new Italian import Vittorio Gassman; in *Latin Lovers* (1953, MGM), by Ricardo Montalban; and in *Americano* (1955, RKO), with Cesar Romero as a mixture of bandit and Latin lover all rolled up into one.

A third type of image evolved for Hispanics during the decade, that of ideological and/or political disciples to Anglo character mentors. This image had been glimpsed at in *Juárez* (1939, Warner Brothers)—in every indoor scene, Benito Juárez had at his back the benevolent and guiding portrait of Abraham Lincoln. The ideological disciple image was magnified in the 1950s because of the cold war during which the United States was inevitably portrayed as the "arsenal of democracy" and the home of the brave and the land of the free. The role of the Anglo ideological missionary on film is that of the disseminator of a cultural and political morality not unlike the religious missionary of colonial times. The symbolism of the overthrow of the Arbenz duly elected government in Guatemala in 1954 by the Central Intelligence Agency was reflected in cinema.

In *Crisis* (1950, MGM), for example, a Latin American dictator (Jose Ferrer) is invariably lectured on the rudiments of Democracy by his Anglo brain surgeon (Cary Grant). In *Appointment in Honduras* (1953, RKO), an American adventurer (Glenn Ford) is employed by outside (presumably American) democratic forces to trek through the jungle to deliver money to an ousted *presidente* which is crucial to the seizure of power. In *Tropic Zone* (1953, Paramount), Ronald Reagan played a man on the run in Central America because of his involvement in an underground political movement. Ending up on a banana plantation, he becomes a latter-day messiah, leading the peasantry against a caudillo who tries to monopolize all the banana trade. In *Vera Cruz* (1954, United Artists), a dozen former Confederate soldiers, led by Gary Cooper and Burt Lancaster, fight against the French intervention in Mexico, albeit well-paid for their efforts, deciminating more of the occupying forces than the entire Juárista army put together. Similarly, "decisive material and physical aid" is given by American gunrunners, led by Alan Ladd, to the Cuban Independence movement against the Spanish in *Santiago* (1956, Warner Brothers). In *The Trial* (1955, MGM), a Chicano youth (Rafael Campos), who is charged with murder, is severely beaten by his attorney (Glenn Ford) under the assumption that he is guilty. The preposterous story goes on to depict the attempted martyrdom of the youth by the Communist Party despite his innocence. The attorney ultimately shows the youth and his sister (Katy Jurado) just how gullible they are, while soft-pedaling the greater dangers of bigotry and racism in the town where the youth will be tried. The image of the Hispanic as an ideological disciple would transcend the 1950s as U.S. foreign policy in Latin America continued to defend the status quo. The Hispanic and Latino image of being unable to think and act alone politically was one personified in U.S. foreign policy and mirrored in American cinema.

The fourth type of film that complemented that ideological disciple film was the historical film in which revisionism of history buttressed U.S. national values in the context of the McCarthy era and the cold war. Such films would document myths and legends taken for historical fact. Four films within the decade recycled one of the most blatant distortions of all, that of the Alamo: *Man from the Alamo* (1953, Universal), *The Last Command* (1955, Republic), *Davy Crockett: King of the Wild Frontier* (1955, Disney), and *First Texan* (1956, Allied Artists). A fifth film, *Lone Star,* glorified Texas in the aftermath of the Alamo battle (1951, MGM). The conquest of California as depicted in

73

California Conquest (1952, Columbia) reflected the cold-war syndrome. The preposterous plot centered on the attempts of one caballero's (Cornel Wilde) attempt to fight for U.S. statehood rather than have the Russians take over the state. Another film set in colonial California, titled *Mark of the Renegade* (1951, Universal), had a refreshingly different thrust. It chronicled the efforts of an undercover agent (Ricardo Montalban) for the Republic of Mexico to thwart the efforts of an unpatriotic caballero (Gilbert Roland) to create a separate Republic of California. It was enhanced by a predominantly Hispanic cast that included former silent matinee idol Antonio Moreno and newcomer Armando Silvestre.

The Mexican Revolution was used as a backdrop in several films of varying quality and accuracy. Pancho Villa was the subject of *Pancho Villa Returns* (1950, Hispanic Continental), in which he was portrayed as more like a human being than in the caricature of *Viva Villa* (1934, MGM). Villa was unseen, but he inspired gunrunners Gilbert Roland and Rory Calhoun in the actioner *The Treasure of Pancho Villa* (1955, RKO). He was also present but uninspiring in the programmer *Villa!* (1958, 20th Century). The Mexican coproduction *The Torch* (1950, El) chronicled the era more realistically. During the French intervention period, Mexico was depicted sympathetically, although melodramatically, in *Stronghold* (1952, Lippert) by a mostly Mexican cast, headed by Arturo De Cordova and Veronica Lake in their last Hollywood film, and by Rita Macedo in her only American film. The Spanish exploration of the U.S. Southwest was chronicled in *Seven Cities of Gold* (1955, 20th Century) and the demise of the gaucho in the Argentinean-lensed *Way of the Gaucho* (1952, 20th Century). Cuba was depicted in *Lady without a Passport* (1950, MGM) with Hedy Lamarr and John Hodiak, *Pier 5 Havana* (1959, United Artists), *Machete* (1959, United Artists), and in two of the last films made by Errol Flynn, *The Big Boodle* (1957, United Artists) and *Cuban Rebel Girls* (1959, Brenner). The four latter films were set in the ambiance of the Cuban Revolution and the second of the Flynn films was particularly partisan.

Finally, the fifth type of film that evolved in the decade was the premature attempt at a Chicano cinema and a series of films attempting to deal in a more serious way with the experience of Chicano and Mexican. The decade began with *The Lawless* (1950, Paramount), about the plight of undocumented Mexican farm workers and nativist mob violence directed by the soon-to-be blacklisted Joseph Losey. John Sturges' *Right Cross* (1950, MGM) dealt with prejudice in the boxing profession, as experienced by a promising Mexican-American boxer (Ricardo Montalban). William Wellman's *My Man and I* (1952, MGM) depicted the trials and tribulations of a Mexican farm worker (Ricardo Montalban) married to an Anglo wife (Shelley Winters). Kurt Neumann's *The Ring* (1952, United Artists) told the tale of a Chicano barrio youth's efforts to seek fame in the boxing ring, portrayed most convincingly by bright newcomer Lalo Rios. *The Fighter* (1952, United Artists), directed by blacklisted Herbert Kline, was a sensitive, true story of a Mexican boxer (Richard Conte) raising money for the Mexican Revolution by boxing. Elia Kazan's *Viva Zapata* (1952, 20th Century) was a flawed effort but caught some of the passion and power of the men and women who fought the Mexican Revolution. The apex of these efforts came with *The Salt of the Earth* (1954), a powerful, true story of a mining strike in New Mexico, starring Mexican actress Rosaura Revueltas, directed by Herbert J. Biberman, and written by Michael Wilson, all of who were hounded, harassed, and blacklisted by McCarthy inquisitors and their minions. The film, for the most part banned in the United States, garnered international awards and achieved the status of a milestone in the image of the Chicano/Hispanic in American film. Unfortunately, the politically charged climate of the times prevented the further development of such uncompromising independent and socially conscious films.

Elsewhere, George Stevens' sprawling *Giant* (1956, Warner Brothers) depicted racism against Mexicans in Texas. The prodigal and prodigious Orson Welles returned to Hollywood to make the powerful and impressive *Touch of Evil* (1957, Universal), in which a corrupted cop (Welles) is defeated by the efforts of a Mexican-American cop (Charlton Heston). Two maverick directors, Robert Rossen (blacklisted) and Budd Boetticher, directed a trio of evocative films about bullfighting that provided a realistic cultural milieu: *The Brave Bulls* (1951, Columbia), *The Bullfighter and the Lady* (1951, Republic), and *The Magnificent*

Matador (1955, 20th Century). Jack Arnold's *Man in the Shadow* (1958, Universal) was a well meaning but not entirely effective film that depicted the exploitation of undocumented workers by an unscrupulous grower (Orson Welles). In the offbeat *Man from Del Rio* (1956, United Artists), Anthony Quinn played the first Mexican gunfighter hero in a Western, as well as the first existential one. Blacklisted screenwriter Dalton Trumbo, under a pseudonym, won an Oscar for the refreshing Mexican-lensed *The Brave One* (1956, RKO), one of the few films dealing with the childhood of a Mexican boy.

Other films of the decade having Mexican characters or locales were *The Outriders* (1950, MGM), *One Way Street* (1950, Universal), *Dallas* (1950, Warner Brothers), *Blowing Wind* (1953, Warner Brothers), *Second Chance* (1953, RKO), *The Big Affair* (1955, United Artists), *The Tall Men* (1955, 20th Century), *Serenade* (1956, Warner Brothers), *The Big Country* (1958, United Artists), and *The Badlanders* (1958, MGM). The growing Puerto Rican community was portrayed in *Cry Tough* (1959, United Artists). Ernest Hemingway's *The Old Man and the Sea* (1958, Warner Brothers), set in Cuba, was a mixed success.

The following are representative films of the decade.

California Conquest (1952, Columbia)

One of the most historically revisionist films of the decade was *California Conquest*. It mixed cold-war propaganda and Manifest Destiny myths with reckless disregard for historical fact.

Don Arturo Bodega (Cornel Wilde), a pure Spanish-blooded caballero in Mexican California, is the leader of a group of caballeros that espouse U.S. annexation. Another caballero, Fredo Brios (John Dehner), accepts Russia's promise of influence and power if he works for Russian annexation of California. As part of his plan, he hires the mestizo bandit Jose Martinez (Alfonso Bedoya) to steal all the arms in a gun shop owned by Julia Lawrence (Teresa Wright) and her father. With her father dead, Julia joins Bodega to recover the weapons, frustrate the Russian takeover, and conspire for U.S. annexation. In the final fadeout,

Bodega comments to Julia, "You would give a lot to be an American, wouldn't you?"

It is a pathetic and racist film. The light-skinned caballeros are portrayed as the only characters able to exercise restraint and leadership, while the mestizos (especially Martinez) are unable to control their excesses of violence and destruction. It justifies the expropriation of California from Mexico on the historical fraud of Russian expansionism. Finally, it denigrates the patriotism and heroism of the Mexicans who died in the Mexican-American War fighting for their independence and self-determination.

The reviews were indicative of the McCarthy era's historical amnesia and jingoism. The *Hollywood Reporter* (June 4, 1952) commented:

> Using as a springboard the little-known Czarist Russian conspiracy to take over California, "California Conquest" is a fairly diverting film that falls halfway between swashbuckler and western.

Giant (1956, Warner Brothers)

George Stevens' sprawling film adaptation of Edna Ferber's popular novel *Giant* garnered its director an Oscar as Best Director and nine nominations, including a posthumous one for Best Actor (James Dean) and ones for Best Actress (Elizabeth Taylor), Best Actor (Rock Hudson), and Best Film. The film, both a critical and commercial success, deflated many of the pompous myths associated with the founding of the state of Texas.

Cattle rancher Bick Benedict (Rock Hudson) travels to Virginia to purchase a stud horse from the father of the headstrong and rich Leslie Benedict (Elizabeth Taylor). Over breakfast, she challenges his revisionist Texas history:

Leslie: We really stole Texas didn't we, Mr. Benedict? I mean, away from Mexico.

Bick: You're catching me a bit early to start joking, Miss Leslie.

Leslie:	But, I'm not joking, Jordan. Why it's all right there in the history books. This man Austin came down with about 300 families it says and then the next thing you know, they're up and claiming it from Mexico.

Later, married and living in his huge Texas ranch, Leslie finds her new community filled with bigotry and sexism. Among the disparate characters she encounters is Bick's truculent spinster sister Luz Benedict (Mercedes McCambridge) who resents Leslie's liberal views and her more respectful treatment of Mexican-Americans. Luz complains to Bick that Leslie doesn't speak Spanish:

Bick:	Oh, they speak plenty of English when they want to.
Luz:	I know how to handle Mexicans. I've been doing it all my life. They'd sit on their honkers all day if I didn't keep after them.

Leslie herself succumbs to some of the Texan myths until enlightened by the elusive and wayward cowhand Jett Rink (James Dean):

Leslie:	They bought this land long ago, the Benedicts. They purchased it years ago.
Jett:	They took it off a bunch of ignorant Mexicans.
Leslie:	That's not true, Jett. They bought and traded Spanish land grants.
Jett:	They paid for it, all right. They paid five cents an acre!

Jett is subsequently left a tract of land by the deceased Luz Benedict. His newfound status has a fatally corruptive influence. Visited on one occasion by Leslie, he is a changed man:

Leslie:	Jett, the other people around here, why don't they help themselves like you?
Jett:	Oh, those bunch of wetbacks. Well, I hope you don't start mixing me up with them. . . . I'm just as much Texas as Bick Benedict is. I'm no wetback.

Rink goes on to become a ruthless oil baron. Benedict's head wrangler, Angel Obregon II (Victor Millan), has a son, Angel Obregon III (Sal Mineo), who becomes the first casualty of the region in World War II. Bick's son, Jordan Benedict III (Dennis Hopper), refuses to take up his father's mantle, becomes a doctor, and marries a Chicana medical student, Juana Villalobos (Elsa Cardenas).

His sister, Luz Benedict II (Carroll Baker), becomes infatuated with Rink and is selected the queen of "Jett Rink Day," to which the Benedicts are invited. Juana is turned away from a local salon because she is Mexican, which leads to a confrontation between Jordan and Bick and subsequently with Rink. On their way home, the Benedicts stop at a diner, which refuses to serve a Mexican family, to which Bick takes issue. A fight ensues, which he loses, but which wins the respect of his family.

The film completed director George Stevens' trilogy on the pursuit and price of the American Dream. He had explored the idealism of youth and rural Americana in *Shane* (1953), the restlessness and disillusionment of the urban laboring class in *A Place in the Sun* (1951), and the corrupting influence of blind ambition and wealth in *Giant*.

The Last Command (1955, Republic)

The Last Command was the fourth of six films made during the decade dealing with the Texas rebellion and/or about the filibusters involved. *The Lone Star* (1951, MGM), with Clark Gable and Ava Gardner, concerned itself with the post–Mexican-American War period; *The Iron Mistress* (1952, Warner Brothers), with Alan Ladd as Jim Bowie, dealt with the prerising period; and *The Man from the Alamo* (1953, Universal), with Glenn Ford, covered the aftermath of the Alamo battle. Subsequent films included *Davy Crockett, King of the Wild Frontier* (1955, Disney), which chronicled the dubious exploits of Davy Crockett, and *The First Texan* (1956, Allied Artists), which dealt with the life of a romanticized Sam Houston (Joel McCrea). The revisionist histories portrayed were further distorted by the allegory to the cold war.

This film concentrated mostly on Jim Bowie, the notorious slaverunner, thug, and adventurer from New Orleans and his involvement in the Texas rebellion. The narrator introduces the history of the period innocuously, "From the north and east had come other settlers who took up land granted to them by the Mexican government in an effort to speed up the development of the new territory. But like to all new people in a new raw land problems arose." Returning to Mexico, Jim Bowie (Sterling Hayden) is told by his friend General Santa Ana (J. Carrol Naish) that his wife and two children have succumbed to an epidemic. Falling out with Santa Ana, he tells him, "People just don't take to one man rule anymore." Embittered and restless, Bowie drifts into friendship with the conspirators of the Texas rebellion: Stephen Austin (Otto Kruger) and William Travis (Richard Carlson). The recently released Austin asks him self-righteously, "Should a man live under a tyrant who makes laws filled with inequities, inhumanities and injustices?" No mention is made of the historical fact that the Mexican Republic had abolished slavery upon independence, an institution that Anglo Americans were attempting to introduce. Austin and Travis' tirades about "injustice" are obviously misdirected.

Bowie is pursued by Consuelo (Anna Maria Alberghetti), the daughter of Lorenzo de Quezada (Eduard Franz), a sympathetic Mexican caballero apparently based on the historical Juan Seguin. The conspirators are subsequently trapped in the Alamo, where they are joined by Davy Crockett (Arthur Hunnicutt) who states, "Hear there's a certain general called Santa Ana. Seems he wants to make it a game preserve for coyotes." The siege ends when the filibusters are defeated by Santa Ana.

The Last Command is a pure distortion of historical fact and well-made Hollywood filmic hokum. *Variety* (July 21, 1955) noted:

> "Command" is the story of events leading up to and including the Alamo, when Bowie, Crockett and a band of Texas and Tennessee volunteers sacrificed their lives to free Texas from Mexico's tyranny. It's the factual story. . . .

The *Hollywood Reporter* (July 21, 1955) commented:

80

J. Carrol Naish, with a superbly accurate makeup, gets the half-friendly arrogance of a Latin politician, with the half-sad pride of an Indian, into his role of Santa Ana. . . . Sterling Hayden is just about perfect as the morose Bowie, who turned to drink, but never lost his courage after his interest in life was taken from him. . . .

It is obvious that the true story according to historical fact is yet to be told.

The Magnificent Matador (1955, 20th Century)

The decade witnessed the release of a trio of bullfighting films that attempted to penetrate with human depth the romantic facade documented previously on film.

Robert Rossen's *The Brave Bulls* (1951, Columbia) with Mirosalava and Anthony Quinn was an evocative film marred by Rossen's subsequent McCarthy blacklisting. The two others were Budd Boetticher's autobiographical *The Bullfighter and the Lady* (1951, Republic), with Gilbert Roland and Katy Jurado, and *The Magnificent Matador* (1955, 20th Century), with Maureen O'Hara and Anthony Quinn. The three films were enhanced by on-site Mexican location shooting, impressive cinematography (by James Wong Howe, Floyd Crosby, Jack Draper, and Lucien Ballard, respectively) and authentic Mexican casts. What contributed to the telling ambiance of the last two films was director Boetticher's background. Boetticher had been a varsity boxer and football player, who had gone to Mexico to become a professional matador in the mid-1930s and had subsequently served as a technical advisor in *Blood and Sand* (1941, 20th Century). Beginning in 1960, he left once more for Mexico for seven years to make a documentary about the great matador Carlos Arruza, entitled *Arruza* (1968), narrated by Anthony Quinn.

The Magnificent Matador chronicles the twilight of the former great matador Luis Santos (Anthony Quinn), whose reputation is ruined when he takes flight from a bullfight that features his rival Rafael Reyes (Manuel Rojas), a professional bullfighter in real life. Santos seeks temporary solace with a rich American jet-setter, Karen Harrison (Maureen O'Hara). He overcomes his fear gradually and makes a comeback in the ring alongside Rojas. At the end, he, Santos, reveals that Rojas is his illegitimate son and that he could not face his son's confrontation with death.

Variety (May 18, 1955) stated:

"The Magnificent Matador" should be to the liking of aficionados of Mexico and bullfighting. . . . Miss O'Hara, the rich girl, and Quinn, in the title role, both give sympathetic handling to the characters. . . .

The *Hollywood Reporter* wrote:

Top quality is stamped all over "The Magnificent Matador," from its explicit and alluring title, sure-fire story and perfectly picked cast, to the understanding and judicious direction by Budd Boetticher. . . . Magnificent, too, is Anthony Quinn in the title role. He looks and acts the part, delivering a performance that really makes the title something to remember. . . . The picture was meticulously cast, every character looking as if he really belonged in his surroundings . . . a tribute to Boetticher's smoother direction and familiarity with his subject. . . .

The Magnificent Matador and the pair of two other bullfighting films brought some overdue maturity to the sport within a cultural context.

My Man and I (1952, MGM)

William Wellman's *My Man and I* is a sadly neglected film about the plight of Chicanos/Mexicanos, which was ahead of its time.

Much of veteran director William Wellman's body of work has a strong sense of social consciousness: the readjustment of a drug-addicted World War I veteran (Richard Barthelmess) in the Depression in the brilliantly stark *Heroes for Sale* (1933), the rovings of a group of poverty-stricken youth in *Wild Boys of the Road* (1933), the perceptive character study of the lynch mob in *The Ox-Bow Incident* (1943). In *My Man and I,* the social concern continued with the plight of Mexican migrant workers.

Anthony Mann's *Border Incident* (1949), also starring Ricardo Montalban, had been the first Hollywood film to concern itself with the plight and exploitation of Mexican migrant workers, and *My Man and I* was another contribution to that effort. That both films were made was primarily a result of Montalban's demands to MGM to let him discard his "Latin-lover" image and make more meaningful films.

The film is set in California's San Joaquin Valley. A Mexican farm worker, Chu Chu Ramirez (Ricardo Montalban), has recently acquired his U.S. citizenship and, as part of his efforts for self-improvement, spends much of his hard-earned money on an encyclopedia set. He falls in love with Nancy (Shelley Winters), an Anglo cantinera. He takes a job in a ranch owned by Ansel Ames (Wendell Corey), a bigot, and his wife (Claire Trevor). Ramirez is paid with a rubber check and returns to the ranch to collect. While he is doing so, the Ames couple has an argument in which Mr. Ames is shot. Both accuse Ramirez, and he is tried and sentenced to prison. It is not a predictable ideological mentor who helps Ramirez, but his friends (Jose Torvay, Pascual Garcia Peña) who induce the Ames' to drop the charges.

The film has been dismissed disparagingly in recent film history. Keller, for example, states, "later Montalban did another B-picture."[3] This was hardly a B-picture and the initial reviews reveal the progressive stance of the film. *Time* (September 15, 1952) commented:

> *My Man and I* is an oversimplified homily on the theme of good and evil. Good is personified by a pure-in-heart Mexican field worker (Ricardo Montalban) . . . he meets and proposes to embittered Shelley Winters (Evil), a California wino who has hit the bottom of the barrel. . . .

The *Motion Picture Herald* (August 23, 1952) noted, "Director William A. Wellman has obtained fine performances from his stars and character people and at the same time kept the story elements moving smoothly. . . ." The *Hollywood Reporter* (August 15, 1952) stated, "Montalban, in his most demanding role to date, turns in a warmly sincere performance, registering honest sentimentalism and decency. . . ." *Variety* wrote, "Montalban's role could almost have been tailored for him, and he gives it a fine performance. . . ."

My Man and I is a film that begins to explore the possibility that Mexicans can determine their own destiny and help others as well.

The Ring (1952, United Artists)

The first film to be shot almost entirely in the East Los Angeles barrio (Lincoln Heights and Chavez Ravine) with an almost all-Chicano cast and to view the rest of society from the confines of the barrio was *The Ring*.

Tommy (Lalo Rios) is a Chicano barrio youth whose father (Martin Garrologo) is laid off as his family (Julia Montoya, Lillian Molleri, Robert Atuna) anticipate the purchase of new furniture. Thwarted by prejudice and the lack of a college education, he finds temporary solace with his girlfriend, Lucy (Rita Moreno), and friends (Pepe Hern, Victor Millan, Tony Martinez). A seasoned fight manager (Gerald Mohr) enlists him after he sees him in a street brawl and, after several fights, he appears to have a promising future as Tommy Kansas, the "Kansas" added to de-Mexicanize him. The success imbues him with confidence and a sense of purpose.

One evening, Tommy takes his friends to a Beverly Hills restaurant where they are refused service, and a policeman is called. Noticing the bruises on Tommy's face, the cop says, "Look's like you've been in a little trouble." When informed that Tommy is professional boxer, the policeman recognizes him and is sympathetic to the group's predicament. The policeman orders the reluctant waitress to serve them. He stays on until the friends finish their meal and exits with them. When he asks them if they are going to the beach next, but finds they are returning home, he asks, "Are you superstitious?" "We're not superstitious, we're Mexicans," one of them responds.

On the way home, the friends reflect on the night's events. One of them says, "Just like Tommy said, being somebody means something, we found that out tonight." Tommy returns to the ring with renewed dedication, but his impetuosity leads him to fight a more seasoned pro (Art Aragan) when another boxer is unable to go on in the main event. He takes a beating. Retiring from the sport, he manages to have earned enough to buy his father a concession stand on Olvera Street, and his girlfriend makes him realize that there are other ways to make a successful life.

The reviews for the film were generally favorable, with some subtle displeasure at the film's exposé of prejudice in the United States. The *Hollywood Reporter* (August 20, 1952) wrote:

A depressing, rather pointless harangue on American discrimination against its Mexican minority group, "The Ring" is a lacklustre film that seems limited in interest to East Los Angeles, the Mexican-American population and those who love films depicting minorities as abused in America. . . . It emerges only as the type that does this country definite disservice abroad. . . . The fights are clumsily staged and Rios seems uncertain in the role. . . .

Variety (August 18, 1952) noted:

The film has a worthy aim but an indecisive presentation that lessens its significance. . . . Lalo Rios is likable as a youth who turns to the prize ring in the hope that he will gain respect and be able to aid his family. He's an unassuming, natural performer. Gerald Mohr is good as the fight manager who takes Rios under his wing, as is Rita Moreno as the fighter's girl who wants him to try other means to better himself. . . .

The main flaw of the film is its inconclusive ending and its inability to propose education as a viable option for self-improvement. The restaurant scene has been criticized as condescending in that Tommy and his friends need to be rescued from their distress by an Anglo policeman, similarly to the ideological disciples who were common staples in the decade. However, Tommy receives assistance only as the result of his hard-won status. The plot validates that "being somebody means something" within the context of the American dream. But, the film's perception of the outside, hostile world and the boxing world's sordid exploitation of Chicano and Black youths' aspirations for fame and glory is an overview of the postwar expectation and disillusionment of the Chicano community.

Salt of the Earth (1954, International Union of Mine, Mill & Smelter Workers)

In the history of the Chicano/Hispanic image in American film, *Salt of the Earth* was a landmark film. No film before or since that dealt with an ethnic minority's emancipation has become so controversial and such a cause celebre.

The film was directed by producer-director-screenwriter Herbert J. Biberman (1909–77). In 1947, when summoned before the notorious HUAC, he refused to testify about others or himself. Subsequently, in 1950 as one of the Hollywood Ten, he was convicted of contempt of Congress and imprisoned for six months. The film's screenwriter was Michael Wilson (1914–78), who had just won an Oscar for co-writing George Stevens' *A Place in the Sun* (1951). His refusal in the same year to testify about the HUAC led to his blacklisting in the industry. Wilson would later write:

> The film was made by blacklisted people. . . . They had formed an independent company on the theory that, though blacklisted, they were not going to stop making films. They would do a film outside the aegis of Hollywood and beyond its control . . . something that was an honest portrayal of working class life in America.[4]

Producer Paul Jarrico, who was the brother-in-law of Wilson, was a veteran screenwriter at the RKO studio, and had scripted films such as *Song of Russia* (1943) and *The Las Vegas Story* (1952). When he was subpoenaed by the HUAC, he refused to testify and was blacklisted.

The strike depicted in *Salt of the Earth* was based on one that took place in Hanover, New Mexico, in a mine owned by Empire Zinc, a subsidiary of New Jersey Zinc, and lasted from October 17, 1950, to January 24, 1952. The striking miners were predominantly Mexican-Americans and their demands were portal-to-portal pay and a parity of paid holidays with local mines in the area. Juan Chacon (who would play himself in the film) commented, "We had all the Anglos checking in on one side of the time clock and all the Mexican people on the other side. We had lines of pure Anglos, getting higher pay . . . and the change rooms were separated, the restrooms and everything, even the eating rooms. . . ."[5] The overriding issues were bigotry and racism. The union that led the strike, the International Union of Mine, Mill and Smelter Workers, had been redbaited and expelled from the CIO, as the latter had been from the AFL in 1938.

The film was an independent production financed by this union. Initially slated for the pivotal role of Esperanza was the blacklisted actress wife of Herbert Biberman, Gale Sondergaard, but it soon became clear that this would perpetuate the opposite of their intentions, the opportunity of Mexican-Americans to portray themselves on film. The role went to the acclaimed Mexican film newcomer Rosaura Revueltas. She would later recall, "When I read the script I said, 'Well, I'll do this picture if this is the last thing I'll ever do.' It was since then I haven't been able to work again in Mexico." For the role of Ramon, actor Rodolfo Acosta had been contracted but withdrew under pressure from the major studios. Ultimately, the role went to Juan Chacon, the recently elected president of Mine-Mill Local 890. Blacklisted character actor Will Geer was cast as the manipulative sheriff, while other roles were filled with actual strikers and their wives.

The film opens with the narrator, Esperanza Quintero (Rosaura Revueltas), a Chicana who is expecting her third child. Her husband, Ramon Quintero (Juan Chacon), a zinc miner, supports a strike when a miner is injured. The sheriff (Will Geer) and owner Hartwell (Melvin Williams) are convinced that Ramon is the ringleader and have him arrested and beaten. At the very same moment, Esperanza gives birth to a daughter. Both husband and wife call each other's name as if connected by some transcendental bond. When Ramon is finally released, a Taft-Hartley injunction prevents the men from picketing. At a meeting, the wives propose that they take over the picketing, much to the chagrin of Ramon and others. Esperanza makes a decision to join the picketing and is subsequently arrested along with other women. Ramon and the other men find themselves transposed in the chores and tasks of their wives and begin to develop a consciousness about their sexism and chauvinism.

When Esperanza is released, a confrontation occurs between her and her husband, who refuses to accept her in a new role. The sheriff and his men attempt to evict them and begin to remove their furniture. However, the men, women, and children of the union and town surround the evictors, who back down. Hartwell, too, accepts the victory of the strike. At last, Ramon recognizes the crucial role played by the women and his wife: "Esperanza . . . thank you . . . for your dignity. You were right. Together we can push everything up with us as we go." Esperanza (whose name means hope in English) comments omnipresently, "Then I knew we had won something they could never take away—something I could leave to our children and they, the salt of the earth, would inherit it."

The shooting of the film proved to be an arduous undertaking. A hostile press and a red-baiting and intimidated Hollywood film industry used their formidable power and influence to harass, malign, and obstruct the filming. Denied the technical resources, Biberman and Jarrico had to edit, score, and dub the film clandestinely. As things got worse, the last sequence of the eviction had to be shot at Will Geer's ranch in Topanga Canyon with Chicanos volunteering as extras. Politicians also vented their hysteria on the film. On February 24, 1953, Congressman Donald Jackson (D-Ca.) in the House stated:

> I bring to the attention of the Congress, and through it to the American people, some facts regarding a picture now being made under Communist auspices in Silver City, New Mexico. . . . This picture is being made . . . not far from . . . Los Alamos [by] men and women who [are] part of the pro-Soviet Secret apparatus in this country. . . . This picture is deliberately designed to inflame racial hatreds and to depict the United States as the enemy of all colored peoples. . . . I shall do everything in my power to prevent the showing of this Communist-made film in the theaters of America. . . .[6]

Even the reclusive and reactionary billionaire Howard Hughes got into the self-righteous posturing and proposed that "the Congress and the State Department . . . act immediately to prevent the export of this film to Mexico or anywhere else."[7]

As an end product of all the provocation, Rosaura Revueltas was arrested on February 25, 1953, by immigration investigators and held without bail. At the hearing, she would write later:

> I heard the government attorney describe me as a "dangerous woman" who ought to be expelled from the country. At times he referred to me as "that girl." Since I had no evidence to present of my "subversive" character, I can only conclude that I was "dangerous" because I had been playing a role that gave stature and dignity to the character of a Mexican-American woman. . . .[8]

She returned voluntarily to Mexico where she was also effectively blacklisted by the Mexican film industry. She would write:

> There were bitter memories I could not leave behind. But I also carried home with me the spirit that had made this picture possible, the determination that would see it completed, and the inner assurance that a handful of ignorant and frightened men could never prevent it being shown to the peoples of the world.[9]

Some needed footage of Rosaura and her voice-over were made secretly in Mexico to complete the film. All this effort was a testament to the dedication of the Hollywood filmmakers who completed the film amid all the provocation.

The film managed to get only scant bookings in the United States. However, even some major critics were impressed, although most qualified their statements that the film was "slanted." Others, however, like Pauline Kael, were representative of the times and wrote that the film was as "clear a piece of Communist propaganda as we have had in many years." *Variety* (March 17, 1954) commented:

> It is, however, a propaganda picture which belongs in union halls rather than motion picture theatres where audiences come for entertainment and not lectures couched in dramatics. . . . Because it treats a somewhat isolated situation from a distinctly biased point of view, "Salt" will do only harm to the U.S. outside

the U.S. . . . Yet as a piece of film artistry, "Salt" achieves moments of true pictorial excellence. Rosaura Revueltas, a Mexican actress playing the wife of a strike leader, gives a taut, impressive performance that has real dimension. Juan Chacon, a union leader in real life, turns in a credible acting job. . . .

The *New York Times* (March 15, 1954) stated:

It is somewhat surprising to find that "Salt of the Earth" is, in substance, simply a strong pro-labor film with a particularly sympathetic interest in the Mexican-Americans with whom it deals. . . . Miss Revueltas, one of the few professional players, is lean and dynamic in the key role of the wife who compels her miner husband to accept the fact of equality, and Juan Chacon, a non-professional, plays the husband forcefully. . . . The hard-focus, realistic quality of the picture's photography and style compels its characterization as a calculated social document. It is clearly intended as a special interest film.*

In 1954, the film won Czechoslovakia's Film Festival Grand Prize. In 1956, it garnered the Académie du Cinéma de Paris award as the best exhibited in France the previous year. Rosaura Revueltas was honored as Best Film Actress. The film won numerous other awards in Europe, the socialist countries, and Third World countries. With the passage of time, the film acquired the status of a cult classic.

In the history of the Chicano/Hispanic image in American film, *Salt of the Earth* was a milestone. It was the first American film seen through the eyes of a Chicana woman. Previously, an occasional film had had a woman's perspective, more often from that of a career woman with social mobility (e.g., Katharine Hepburn and Barbara Stanwyck). However, to have a woman of color as the main protagonist and omnipresent narrator was not only novel, but revolutionary.

The film explores the destructiveness that emanates from the divisiveness of sexism and racism. Through the relationship

---

*Copyright © 1954 by The New York Times Company. Reprinted by permission.

of Esperanza and Ramon, we witness the inability of both to understand the degree and source of their oppression. As the labor struggle progresses, so do their consciousnesses to a realization of the "indivisibility of equality." Esperanza tells Ramon, "Why are you afraid to have me at your side? Do you still think you can have dignity only if I have none? . . . The Anglo bosses . . . you hate them for it. 'Stay in your place, you dirty Mexican,' that's what they tell you. But why must you say to me, 'Stay in your place.' Do you feel better having someone lower than you? . . ."

Racial antagonism among the workers themselves impedes initially the unity of the union to the benefit of the power structure. Frank Barnes and Jenkins are ignorant of Mexican culture, and Ramon is distrustful of Anglos. Ramon is referred to variously as "Ray" or "Pancho," and he blames "those Anglo dames" for his wife's growing activity in the strike. It is when the strikers resolve the divisiveness of sexism and racial antagonism that they can create the unity that will prove victorious.

Mexican culture is omnipresent throughout the film. Spanish is depicted as the cultural anchor and source of strength ebbed in history. Three songs parallel the three main components of the film: "Las Mañanitas" symbolizes the resiliency of family and culture; "La Adelita" represents the emerging emancipation of women; and "No Nos Moveran" symbolizes the strength of the unity of labor.

The film admirably intertwines themes of sexism, racism, labor, culture, community, and the power of collective action versus the mystique of rugged individualism.

Trial (1955, MGM)

Perhaps the key film of the decade that depicted Chicanos as ideological disciples was the rambling, cold-war–induced courtroom drama *Trial*.

The film chronicles the prosecution of a Mexican youth, Angel Chavez (Rafael Campos), for the murder and attempted rape of a white girl, apparently somewhere in the U.S. Southwest. A law professor with little courtroom experience, David

Blake (Glenn Ford), and a seasoned trial attorney, Barney Castle (Arthur Kennedy), are enlisted as his defense team. A politically ambitious prosecutor, John J. Armstrong (John Hodiak), attempts to charge Chavez with manslaughter, but Castle rejects this. A racist mob attempts to storm the prison. The jailer, Sanders (Robert Middleton), is in sympathy with the mob and comments that "the boy will have a legal hanging."

Subsequently, the case becomes a cause celebre. Castle is revealed to be single-mindedly Communist by Abbe Nyle (Dorothy McGuire), herself a fellow traveler. Blake appears to attempt to railroad the youth to make him a Communist martyr. Finally, Chavez comes to a trial presided over by a Black judge (Juano Hernandez) and is found guilty. When Blake attempts to appeal the verdict, he is fired by Castle. Ultimately, Chavez is sent to an industrial school after the prosecutor relents, and Blake reveals the sinister designs of Castle.

The film is severely handicapped by simplistic polemics and cold-war myopia. It depicts Chicanos and their community as unable to think and organize without the patient plodding of ideological missionaries. Moreover, the film portrays Chicanos and all principled progressive elements as fatally flawed with gullibility and ulterior motives. Also, in evidence is the attitude that Chicanos are innately crime oriented. For example, when attorney Castle first meets Angel in the jail cell and is told by him that he is innocent, Castle proceeds to slap Angel around and shouts at him to admit his guilt.

Despite all the simplistic and melodramatic excesses, the film received some glowing reviews, obviously perpetuating the distortions. The *Hollywood Reporter* (August 2, 1955) wrote:

> Every American should see it. Indeed, no American can afford not to see it. And every European should see it too, for "Trial" will at long last, prove to them that Americans, in their approach to the tides of history, are not stupid, not childish, and not naive.... There is a sweet groping innocence about Rafael Campos that makes him a perfect casting as the prisoner....

Variety (August 3, 1955) stated:

Beyond the human interest and immediacy of saving the sympathetic Mexican boy from the gallows is the broader story—a
theme never before developed on the screen—of how the Communist Party seizes upon an authentic instance of local bigotry and
pumps it up into a national cause celebre for the raising of funds
and the making of a class war martyr. . . . As the Mexican symbols
of local "race prejudice," Kathy Jurado, the mother, and Rafael
Campos, her son, both give intelligent performances, a habit with
Miss Jurado, a new displace on the part of the young man. . . .

Motion Picture Daily (August 2, 1955) commented:

Don M. Mankiewicz's Harper's prize novel and screenplay, is a
shocker and frightening at times in its depiction of the emotions
which rule the thinking and behavior of some Americans. . . .

Viva Zapata! (1952, 20th Century)

One of the most famous U.S. films made about the Mexican
Revolution is Elia Kazan's *Viva Zapata!* Judged in hindsight,
the film's merit results from the considerable skill of Marlon
Brando and Anthony Quinn, rather than from its grossly distorted and falsified version of Mexican history.

Director Elia Kazan would later recollect in his autobiography:

I'd started making notes on a film about Emiliano Zapata in 1944.
It's the first film I made from an idea that attracted me—a revolu-
tionist fights a bloody war, gains power, then walks away—one I
started and saw through to the end.[10]

It is obvious from these statements that Hollywood and Kazan
had never read Mexican history. Emiliano Zapata (1879–1919)
was a literate and small landowner from the southwestern Mexican state of Morelos, who in alliance with Pancho Villa
(1877–1923) represented the truest aspirations of the peasantry
and poor for social justice during the Mexican Revolution
(1910–20). With the overthrow of corrupt dictator Porfirio Díaz

93

in May 1911, Francisco I. Madero was elected president. Threatened by political and social reform, the counter-revolution, led by General Victoriano Huerta, assassinated Madero and overthrew the government. Zapata and Villa defeated Huerta and marched into Mexico City only to be confronted by another opportunistic counter-revolutionary group led by General Carranza and a clique that included Generals Obregon and Calles. Unable to defeat Zapata's guerrillas, Carranza had him assassinated on April 10, 1919. Subsequently, after Carranza's defeat, Villa was assassinated in an ambush on July 20, 1923, on the orders of Obregon and Calles.

Needless to say, history is not what novelist-turned-screenwriter John Steinbeck and Kazan portrayed. Several factors contributed to the substantial distortion of historical facts, one of them being the second round of the HUAC hearings and Kazan's testimony as a friendly witness. Producer Darryl Zanuck had first attempted to film in Mexico, but the Mexican film technicians' union correctly demanded script changes. Noted Mexican cinematographer Gabriel Figueroa confronted Kazan and posed the question, "Suppose a Mexican company came up to Illinois to make a picture about Abraham Lincoln's life with a Mexican actor playing the lead, what would you think about that?"[11] Kazan remained unconvinced and attributed the problems to a Communist conspiracy: "We knew that the Communists in Mexico would try to capitalize on the people's reverence for Zapata by working his figure into their propaganda—much as Communists here quote Lincoln to their purpose. . . ."[12] Consequently, the film was shot in south Texas.

Not surprisingly, the Right attacked his ambiguous stance. Some critics accused him of glorifying a Communist rebel, to which Kazan took issue. Nevertheless, the fictional character of Fernando, according to Kazan, represented "the Communist mentality." The character "typified the men who use just grievances of the people for their own ends, who shift and twist their course, betray any friend or principle or promise to get power and keep it."

However, besides the self-serving polemics of Kazan, there are other numerous misrepresentations. Early in the film Zapata is portrayed as a groping illiterate, which is pure Hollywood fantasy. One scene has two Zapatistas as proverbial ideological disciples:

Fernando: In the United States, the government governs, but with the consent of the people.
Pablo: That's right.
Fernando: They have a President, too, but he governs with the consent of the people. Here, we have a President, but no consent. . . .

The historical fact is that Mexicans had known democracy before Díaz and were hardly in need of a lesson on democracy (especially since slavery had been abolished since 1824). Another scene has Zapata and Villa sleeping under a tree in traditional Hollywood fashion while a guard comments, "They're deciding the fate of Mexico." At one point, Villa asks Zapata if he can read, to which Zapata nods in affirmation, apparently having become literate overnight. Villa then states, "Then you're the President. There isn't anyone else. Do I look like a President? There isn't anyone else." Kazan's proposal that Zapata walked away from power is myth. Zapata and Villa left Mexico City (leaving a provisional president) for a major campaign against Carranza's forces and not for the reason of giving up political power or evading responsibility. The film also takes historical liberties with Zapata's brother Eufemio (Anthony Quinn), portraying him as a reckless amoral semibarbarian who appears to do more drinking and womanizing than actual fighting. Kazan also denigrated the worth and merit of leaders and leadership, saying that all will inevitably "desert" and "change" and cautioning viewers not to look for leaders.

Marlon Brando infused his portrayal of Emiliano Zapata with respect and nobility as well as with human flaws. Anthony Quinn played Eufemio Zapata effectively and captured some of the inarticulate passion of revolution. For his performance, he became the first Chicano/Mexicano to win an Academy Award for Best Supporting Actor. Among the number of Hispanic players who were featured in addition to Quinn were Margo, as a Soldadera, and Movita, in a bit part as the farmer's runaway wife who lives with Eufemio. The film received generally enthusiastic reviews, especially noting Brando and Quinn's performances. However, Hollywood continued to document history with cultural myopia and historical amnesia. *Variety* (February 5, 1952) stated that the "[p]icture misses in that the ideas and ideals with which it deals come over too symbolically, and it lacks the humanness and heart that could have cinched popular appeal. . . ." *Time* (February 11, 1952) noted:

> "Viva Zapata!" makes the Tiger out to be a pretty tame cat. According to history, Zapata was not only a great folk hero and agrarian emancipator, but also a cruel, cunning Guerrero Indian whose notorious Death Legion made human torches of the enemy and staked living men to anthills. . . . The cast includes such acceptable Latin types as Anthony Quinn and Margo, and such less acceptable Latin types as Jean Peters. In the title role, Marlon Brando, wearing a spit-curl hairdo, drooping mustachios and cartooned sombrero, slouches and mumbles his way through the excitement in a deadpan Brando voice. . . .*

The *Los Angeles Times* (February 13, 1952) wrote:

> Brando . . . comes through with punchful moments that will unquestionably evoke popular plaudits. . . . Top-flight . . . [is] Anthony Quinn in his semi-amusing delineation of brother of the title character. . . . Portrayals that need special recognition apart from those mentioned are given by . . . Margo as Soldadera. . . .

The *Motion Picture Guide,* for example, states, "Although Brando presents an idealized version of the great leader, he was in reality more barbaric, and did not hesitate to execute his enemies en masse. . . ."[13] Thomas wrote, "Certainly it is an idealized concept of Emiliano Zapata, whom historians claim was far more self-seeking and bloodier than as depicted by Zanuck, Steinbeck and Kazan. . . ."[14] It is apparent that Hollywood was malnourished in regards to Mexican history.

---

*Copyright © 1952 by Time Inc. Reprinted by permission.

The Players

The 1950s saw Hollywood's introduction of five well-established Mexican actresses and one Spanish one: Maria Elena Marquez, Mirosalava, Rosenda Revueltas, Rita Macedo, Katy Juarado, and Sarita Montiel. During the decade, on-location filming all over the world, wide-screen Cinemascope, and the introduction of beautiful foreign actresses were Hollywood's attempts to enhance movie attendance to combat the rising threat of television.

Maria Elena Marquez made her American film debut in William Wellman's underrated and striking tale of fur trappers, *Across the Wide Missouri* (1951, MGM), opposite Clark Gable and Ricardo Montalban but was thereafter disappointed by offers to typecast her as an Indian maiden. She went back to Mexico, returning for one American film at the end of the decade. Mirosalava, Czech-born but Mexican-bred, debuted in her teens in American film in Robert Rossen's impressive *The Brave Bulls* (1951). However, like Marquez, she would not succumb to the stereotypical roles subsequently offered and returned to Mexico for some notable films like Buñuel's *Ensayo de un Crimen* (1955). She returned to make one more U.S. film before committing suicide in 1956. Rosenda Revueltas was an established Mexican star when she was brought in to star in Herbert Biberman's *Salt of the Earth* (1954), scripted by Oscar-winning screenwriter Michael Wilson (*A Place in the Sun*, 1951), and soon the film became a cause celebre. Both Biberman and Wilson ran afoul of the notorious and self-righteous HUAC for refusing to testify on their political beliefs and those of others. They, along with the film's crew, were harassed by government authorities, and the film colony was generally cowed into moral acquiescence. Revueltas was deported as an undesirable alien and never allowed to return. The film's distribution was limited until the 1960s, when the film was exhibited to universal acclaim. Rita Macedo was brought to star with Arturo De Cordova in *Stronghold* (1952, Lippert), an adventure drama set in the French Occupation of Mexico. Dissatisfied by the film effort, she returned to a flourishing career in Mexico in such films as Buñuel's *Nazarin* (1968). Katy Jurado was brought in to star in Budd Boetticher's realistic bullfighting film *The Bullfighter and the Lady* (1951) and the next year scored even more impressively in the Western classic *High Noon* (1952), scripted by another victim of the infamous HUAC Committee, Carl Foreman. That bright promise, however, was never fully fulfilled in the poisonous climate of "foreign" hysteria, jingoism, and racial intolerance, and she was soon relegated to supporting roles in mostly undistinguished films. The sixth import was the Spanish-born Sarita Montiel, who debuted in *That Man from Tangier* (1953) but was more impressive in Robert Aldrich's popular *Vera Cruz* (1954, United Artists), set during the French Occupation of Mexico. Hollywood, however, could not lure her to stay, and after two more films, she left to make films in Spain and Mexico.

Three other Hispanic actresses came to the fore during the decade: Argentinean-born Linda Cristal, Puerto Rico's Rita Moreno, and Susan Kohner, daughter of Lupita Tovar. Both Cristal and Moreno were inevitably typecast as Latin sexpots, Cristal in *Cry Tough* (1959) and Moreno in *Latin Lovers* (1953), and while neither obtained top-ranked stardom, they had by the 1960s won recognition as fine actresses. Moreno would become the first Hispanic actress to win an Academy Award, as Best Supporting Actress in *West Side Story* (1961, United Artists). Kohner met with modest success at the end of the 1950s and the beginning of the 1960s, retiring after marriage. She had become the first Hispanic to be nominated for an Academy Award, for her performance as Lana Turner's daughter in the remake of *Imitation of Life* (1959, Universal).

Male Hispanic stars were less prominent and in evidence during the quiet conformist 1950s, when idols on the screen were the blond and blue-eyed Tab Hunter, Aldo Ray, Troy Donahue, Marilyn Monroe, Jayne Mansfield, Kim Novak, and Sheree North, among others. Hollywood imported two established stars: veteran Mexican-born comedian Mario Moreno "Cantinflas" and Argentinean heartthrob Fernando Lamas. Cantinflas, already hailed as the world's foremost comedian by no less an authority than Charles Chaplin, made an impressive Passepartout in Michael Todd's star-studded *Around the World in Eighty Days* (1956, United Artists). Thereafter, however, it was difficult to translate his particular play-on-words type of comedy, and he made only one more American film. Lamas would have a short vogue with the resurgence of the Latin lover in a series of Technicolored films paired with one of the reigning film beauties, such as Lana Turner in *The Merry Widow* (1952, MGM).

A trio of younger Hispanic actors also made promising starts, but their potential was never fully realized: Los Angeles–born Lalo Rios, Dominican Republic-born Rafael Campos, and Mexican-born Rodolfo Acosta. Rios was discovered by soon-to-be blacklisted and expatriate director Joseph Losey and cast in *The Lawless* (1950), dealing with Mexican migrant workers. Thereafter he scored another triumph in a "sleeper," *The Ring* (1952), in which he played a Chicano boxer struggling out of the East Los Angeles barrio. Subsequent film roles never came his way, and he was relegated to small parts in inconsequential films, Orson Welles' *Touch of Evil* (1957) being an exception. Campos debuted as one of the young hoods in Richard Brooks' *The Blackboard Jungle* (1955) and scored even more forcefully as a Mexican youth accused of murder in Mark Robson's courtroom drama *The Trial* (1955). Thereafter, though, he suffered Rios' fate. Acosta, an established Mexican character actor, made his American debut in the low-budget *Pancho Villa Returns* (1950) and afterward was typecast in scores of mostly routine films as a Mexican bad man or Indian, many of these Westerns. Another prominent Mexican character actor in the 1950s was Pedro Gonzalez. Gonzalez made his U.S. film debut in *Wings of the Hawk* (1953) and thereafter essayed basically the same amiable comic relief character in two dozen films.

Notes

1. Rodolfo Acuña, *Occupied America* (New York: Harper & Row, 1988).
2. Robyn Karney, ed., *The Movie Stars Story* (New York: Crescent Books, 1984).
3. Gary D. Keller, ed., *Chicano Cinema* (New York: Bilingual Peviee Press, 1985).
4. Michael Wilson, *Screenplay—Salt of the Earth* (New York: The Feminist Press, 1975).
5. Ibid.
6. Ibid.
7. Ibid.
8. Ibid.

9. Ibid.
10. Elia Kazan, *A Life* (New York: Alfred A. Knopf, 1988).
11. *Saturday Review*, April 5, 1952.
12. *Saturday Review*, April 5, 1972.
13. Jay Robert Nash, *The Motion Picture Guide 1927–1983* (Chicago: Cine-books, 1987).
14. Tony Thomas, *The Films of Marlon Brando* (Secaucus, N.J.: Citadel Press, 1973).

CHAPTER SIX
The 1960s—the Invisible Minority

I took you out of the beanfields and gave you respectability!
—One-Eyed Jacks (1961)

When the legend becomes fact, print the legend.
—The Man Who Shot Liberty Valence (1962)

The great battleground for the defense and expansion of freedom today is the whole of the southern half of the globe: Asia, Latin America and the Middle East. The land of the rising people. Their revolution is the greatest in human history. They seek an end to injustice and exploitation. More than an end, they seek a beginning.
—Pres. John F. Kennedy (1962)

I care about my people, my village, my Mexico. . . . This is their land and no one is going to drive them away. . . . If I can take guns I will go with them. . . .
—Angel in The Wild Bunch (1969)

The 1960s were the apex of the cold war. The era was characterized by unprecedented political strife: revolution, assassination, racial riots, and military invasions to maintain hegemony. On the North American continent, the first socialist revolution had brought socialism to Cuba, and in the United States, a Chicano movement developed by the end of the decade, finally putting to disrepute the myth that Hispanics were the "invisible minority."

The decade began with promise and expectation as a young President John F. Kennedy took office. He stated that "those who possess wealth and power in poor nations must accept their

101

own responsibility. They must lead the fight for those basic reforms which alone can preserve the fabric of their society. Those who make peaceful revolution impossible make violent revolution inevitable."

However, those with "wealth and power" did not desist, but sought to maintain and prolong their control. Nationalist liberation movements flourished, challenging moribund empires, such as the British and Portuguese in Africa and Asia, and new hegemonies such as the United States in Latin America. The United States invaded Cuba in 1961 and the Dominican Republic in 1965, and Soviet forces invaded Czechoslovakia in 1968. The Alliance for Progress gave way to a policy of containment with Green Berets, military training, and advisers. In 1962, the Cuban Missile Crisis brought the world to the brink of nuclear annihilation. Racial integration met with increasing violent resistance, and Mexican farm workers began to organize around an incipient union led by Cesar Chavez. In November, President Kennedy was assassinated, bringing an abrupt end to Camelot and paving the way for President Johnson's Great Society and "War on Poverty." Increasing U.S. involvement in Vietnam diverted funds from going to the social agenda, alienating the poor, minorities, and intellectuals. In 1968, Martin Luther King and Robert Kennedy were assassinated, hundreds of ghettos broke into riots, and the antiwar movement became a mass movement. The FBI escalated a wave of illegal activities, from harassment to wiretaps and shootouts with the Black Panthers, which became commonplace by the end of the decade. A "law and order" presidential candidate, Richard M. Nixon, made a spectacular political comeback by gaining the presidency.

In 1967, Reies Lopez Tijerina of New Mexico led the Alianza de los Pueblos Libres (Alliance of Free City-States) to struggle for violated land grants. According to U.S. figures, Chicanos comprised 10 percent of the population in the Southwest, but accounted for 19.4 percent of Southwest casualties in the Vietnam War. In the meantime, relatives of Chicano soldiers in Vietnam were accused of "stealing jobs" and were being deported. In December 1969, the National Chicano Moratorium Committee held its first demonstration. By the end of the decade, the

Chicano and Hispanic, in political terms, were no longer the "invisible minority."

The Films

The Hollywood film industry continued to decline in the 1960s in both quantity and quality. Several factors contributed to this outcome. First, previously moribund film industries in Europe and the Far East (India and Japan, especially) reestablished themselves and became more competitive. Second, the personal manner of running the Hollywood studios by autocratic moguls came to a complete end, when many functions were taken over by talent agency personnel. The studios themselves had been taken over by multinationals such as Gulf-Western, who were more interested in making short-term profits than in making quality films. Third, the rise of television and professional sports, (e.g., basketball and baseball) limited the number of film goers. Fourth, Hollywood continued to only acknowledge reluctantly the predominance of its youthful audience, until the breakthrough event of *Easy Rider* in 1969. Finally, the decade witnessed a remarkable turnover in the stars and personnel in American films, in a scale only comparable to the silent-to-sound period. The majority of the stellar names of Hollywood's Golden Age died or retired by the end of the 1950s or early 1960s (e.g., Bogart, Power, Flynn, Gable, Cooper, and Ladd).

The Hispanic in the United States was the second largest minority by the beginning of the decade, but an invisible minority in political and economic power. This lack of political power, coupled with the policy of containment in Latin America, shaped the image of the Chicano and Hispanic in American film. The image of the Hispanic in the 1960s, with minor exceptions, was of two kinds, that of the subservient, ideological disciple type, unable to think for himself, and that of the amoral bandit and the cantinera woman. The majority of these films were Westerns in which the fear of lawlessness was a common theme. Two other discernable genres were those films with the Mexican Revolution as a background and the historical films. The fate of the Hispanic implied in these films was either to be benignly docile, in accordance with the Monroe Doctrine or to be stigmatized as bandits and annihilated like the revolutionaries in Latin America. In real life, the decade saw the flourishing of numerous guerrilla movements in Latin America, and it was typical for the decrepit and corrupt military dictatorships that the guerrillas challenged to brand them as "bandits."

The ideological disciple films had begun in the previous decade, with the advent of the cold war. Invariably, these films depicted Mexicans as pathetic, childlike figures, humble but cowardly, incapable of defending or fighting for their interests or rights without some condescending and fearless, messiahlike Anglo hero. The most representative of these films during the decade were *The Magnificent Seven* (1960, United Artists), *Guns of the Magnificent Seven* (1969, United Artists), and *The Magnificent Seven Ride* (1972, United Artists). The former film was based on Akiro Kurosawa's *Seven Samurai* (1954). In the original, a Japanese village is pillaged frequently by a band of marauding bandits. The villagers pool their meager resources and hire seven Japanese samurai warriors to protect them. In the Americanization of the story, the warriors became seven Anglo gunfighters, the marauding bandits became Mexicans, as did the hapless villagers. Neither the Manifest Destiny and Monroe Doctrine philosophy nor the racism and stereotyping could have been more explicit. These elements can also be found in other films of the 1960s.

The resurgence of the Mexican bandit was given impetus by the phenomenon of the "spaghetti Western," which emerged in Italy in the mid-1960s but was popularized by Sergio Leone's *Fistful of Dollars* (1966, United Artists) and its sequels, *For a Few Dollars More* (1967, United Artists) and *The Good, the Bad and the Ugly* (1970, United Artists). They catapulted a relatively unknown Clint Eastwood, as the enigmatic "Man with No Name," into major film stardom. The series was based on another Kurosawa classic, *Yojimbo* (1961), in which Toshiro Mifune had played the sardonic and enigmatic samurai. Scores of spaghetti Westerns followed, most of them filmed in Italy and Spain, and some even in Germany, where a series of them starred expatriate American film stars like Stewart Granger and Lex Barker. Most of the others starred former "names" like Guy Madison, Eddy "Kookie" Byrnes, Gilbert Roland, Steve Reeves, and Gordon Scott, among others. One common denominator in all these films was that all the villains were invariably Mexican *bandidos,* and all Mexican women were *cantineras.*

These new bandidos were a new breed, "good-bad *bandidos.*" The "good" referred to their technical skills, ingenuity, and persistence, and to a fast draw. In these amoral films, the Anglo hero descended to the level of the stereotypical Mexican bandit. The latter, unlike the equally amoral Anglo counterpart, was an innately and extraordinarily violent, greasy-looking, treacherous, insatiably oversexed drunkard, intellectually and technically inferior to the Anglo hero. Thus, scores of these bandits were killed with a high level of frequency in these films. A partial list of spaghetti Westerns includes *Ace High* (1969, United Artists); *Death Rides a Horse* (1969, United Artists), with Lee Van Cleef; *God Forgives, I Don't* (1969, American International), with Terence Hill; *Day of Anger* (1969, National General), with Lee Van Cleef; *Adios, Gringo* (1968, Translux) and *Flaming Frontier* (1968, Warner Brothers), with Stewart Granger; *A Stranger in Town* (1968, MGM) and *Any Guy Can Play* (1968, Raf), with Gilbert Roland and Eddy Byrnes; *The Ugly Ones* (1968, United Artists), *Seven Guns for the MacGregors* (1968, Columbia), and *The Brute and the Beast* (1960, AI), with Franco Nero; *Payment in Blood* (1968), with Guy Madison and Eddy Byrnes; *A Minute to Pray, a Second to Die* (1968, MGM), with Tony Anthony; *The Big Gundown* (1968, Paramount), with Lee Van Cleef; and *A Bullet for the General* (1968, Avco), with Gina Maria Volante. The amoral spaghetti Western would come to a climax with Sergio Leone's superior *Once Upon a Time in the West* (1969, Paramount), filmed in the U.S. Southwest, in which the hero turns out to be a Mexican gunfighter called the "Man with Harmonica" (Charles Bronson).

The more traditional Mexican bandit continued into the 1960s with *The Magnificent Seven. The Outrage* (1964, MGM) was based on yet another Kurosawa classic, *Rashomon* (1951), about a bandit's rape of a rancher's wife. In translation into English, the bandit became a Mexican one, Juan Carrasco (Paul Newman), and the rancher and the wife become, predictably, Anglos. Not since Wallace Beery's *Viva Villa* had there been such a caricature of a Mexican *bandido,* dripping with such a thick accent, grease, violence, and over-sexuality. In the British-made *The Singer Not the Song* (1961, Warner Brothers), Dirk Bogarde unconvincingly played Anncleto, an atheistic Mexican bandit, who runs a small town. He is enraged at the arrival of a Roman Catholic priest (John Mills) and begins killing peasants alphabetically. In *Rio Conchos* (1965, 20th Century), Tony Franciosa played yet another stereotypical Mexican bandit, Rodriguez, who pays for his treachery before the last reel. In *The Appaloosa,* the horse of a buffalo hunter (Marlon Brando) is stolen by a sadistic Mexican bandit, Chuy Medina (John Saxon), which results in a deadly confrontation. In *Blue* (1969, Paramount), Ricardo Montalban played a Mexican bandit, Ortego, whose adopted Anglo son (Terrance Stamp) turns against him. In *MacKenna's Gold,* a sheriff (Gregory Peck) defends his new-found treasure against an unsavory *bandido,* Colorado (Omar Sharif). *Bandidos* prevent peace-loving Confederates (John Wayne, Rock Hudson) from joining the Juáristas in *The Unde-feated* (1969). In *Butch Cassidy and the Sundance Kid* (1969, Woth), the two outlaws decimate the Bolivian army, singlehand-edly, and good-humoredly.

The third type of film common in the decade was that with the Mexican Revolution as a backdrop. Influenced by the amorality of the spaghetti Westerns, the films portrayed both the reactionary federales government forces and the liberal revolutionary forces as decadent. The federales were depicted as pompous, class-conscious, and corrupt and the revolutionaries as promiscuous, drunken, dirty, and violent. These films typically had Anglo soldiers of fortune or ideological mentors supplying technical and political expertise. In *The Professionals* (1966, Paramount), several soldiers of fortune, formerly fighters (Burt Lancaster, Lee Marvin, Robert Ryan) in the Revolution, are paid to abduct the present wife (Claudia Cardinelli) of an important rancher (Ralph Bellamy) by a revolutionary, Jesus Reza (Jack Palance). They easily perform the feat without a single casualty, only to discover at the end that the alleged wife had voluntarily left the corrupt husband. In *100 Rifles* (1969, 20th Century), one superstud, Black sheriff (Jim Brown), on the trail of a Yaqui Indian (Burt Reynolds) who robbed U.S. banks to buy guns for his people, is captured relatively easily by the sheriff, who proceeds to seduce the Indian's promiscuous girlfriend, Sarita (Raquel Welch), at will. The image of Pancho Villa (Yul Brynner) in *Villa Rides* (1968, Paramount) is an improvement over that in *Viva Villa*. The military skill, daring, and ingenuity is displayed, although the overly eager trigger-happiness of General Fierro (Charles Bronson) borders on caricature.

The most serious, impressive, and famous of these Mexican Revolution background films is Sam Peckinpah's controversial *The Wild Bunch* (1969, Warner Brothers), chronicling the demise of an aging, anachronistic gang of the Old West, seeking a tragic redemption in the Mexican Revolution.

A fourth type of film in the decade was the revisionist historical film. The John Wayne–directed *The Alamo* (1961, United Artists) reprised the accumulated romanticized myths with some cold-war allegories. A subsequent film, *Viva Max* (1969, Commonwealth United), had a modern day, buffoonlike Mexican general (Peter Ustinov), who recaptures the Alamo and, in the process, recycled stereotypes of the 1930s. In the programmer *Frontier Uprising* (1961, United Artists), a stalwart Anglo frontier scout (Jim Davis) battles hordes of Mexicans and Indians, trying to carry out Manifest Destiny in California. The mammoth and star-studded *How the West Was Won* (1963, MGM) dedicated only a fleeting second to the dispossession of the Southwest from Mexico and had one single Mexican character, a bandit (Rodolfo Acosta) involved in the exciting train robber finale.

Joaquin Murietta was depicted in a trio of low-budget films. He was portrayed as a revenge-filled man who becomes almost demented, by Carlos Thompson, in *The Last Rebel* (1961, Hispano) and by Jeffrey Hunter, in the Spanish-filmed *Murietta* (1965, Warner Brothers). In the third, *The Firebrand* (1962, American Pictures–Fox), Murietta (Valentin De Vargas) eludes successfully his pursuers and returns to Sonora, Mexico. More recent history was depicted in *Hell to Eternity* (1960, Allied Artists), that of Mexican-American marine hero, Guy Gabaldon (Jeffrey Hunter), in which he is portrayed as a cultural eunuch. Finally, derision, ridicule, and caricature were the trademarks, circa 1930s, in *Che!* (1969, 20th Century), the purported story of Latin American revolutionary Ernesto "Che" Guevara.

The fifth type of film attempted a more honest and realistic presentation of the Mexican and Hispanic. The Marlon Brando–directed *One-Eyed Jacks* (1961, Paramount) provided insightful portrayals of strong and independent Mexican women for Pina Pellicer, as Brando's girlfriend, and Katy Jurado, as Karl Malden's abused wife. In *Dime with a Halo* (1963, MGM), Barbara Luna played a hard-working woman, looking after her younger brother in the Tijuana shantytown. These images were not the derogatory norm in the portrayal of Chicana, Mexican, and Hispanic women. If the dominant stereotype of the Hispanic male was the bandit, his female counterpart was the *cantinera* or prostitute. In the spaghetti Westerns, swarms of seedy, over-sexed, hard-drinking, and promiscuous Hispanic women populated the saloons and bedrooms. Their portrayals in U.S.-made films were no different. Thus, in *The Alamo's* (1960, United Artists) Flaca (Linda Cristal), we are expected to believe the implausible fiction that a beautiful Mexican woman is easily seduced by an alien mercenary (Davy Crockett), on the very eve he is conspiring to steal land from her country. In *The Appaloosa* (1966, Universal), Trini (Anjanette Comer) suddenly develops an overwhelming hatred for her Mexican bandit, Chuy Medina (John Saxon), when she meets a great White scout, Matt Fletcher (Marlon Brando). In *The Professionals* (1966, Paramount), the *soldadera* Chiquita (Maria Gomez) spends all of her time cavorting around, flimsily dressed and seemingly satisfying the sexual needs of an entire regiment. In *100 Rifles,* Sarita (Raquel Welch), although spoken for by Yaqui Joe (Burt Reynolds), is seduced at the whim of the American superstud sheriff (Jim Brown). Loyalty, honor, and self-respect were not virtues attributable to Mexican women.

In 1969, two breakthrough films were released. In *The Royal Hunt of the Gun* (1969, Renk), Hollywood provided a sympathetic view of Inca king Atahualpa (Christopher Plummer), at the hands of the avaricious Pizzaro (Robert Shaw). In 1967, the first recognized Chicano film was released, *I Am Joaquin,* a documentary chronicling two hundred years of history, based on

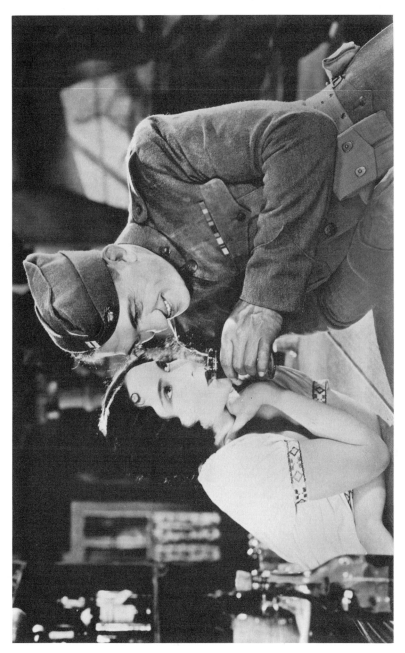

Dolores Del Rio (1905–83), in her star-making role in Raoul Walsh's *What Price Glory* (1926) with Victor McLagen. *What Price Glory* © 1927 Twentieth Century Fox Film Corporation. All rights reserved.

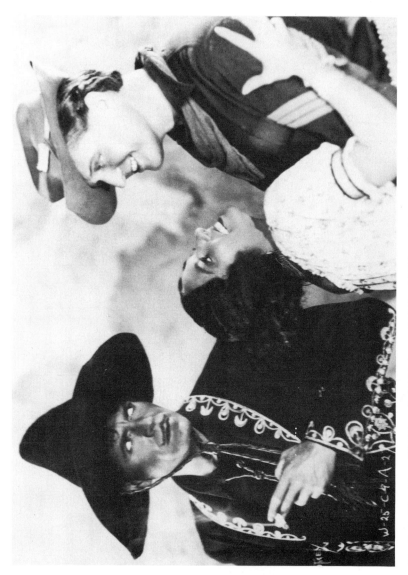

The first of the Cisco Kid films, *In Old Arizona* (1929), with Warner Baxter in his Oscar-winning performance as the Kid, Dorothy Burgess, and Edmund Lowe. *In Old Arizona* © 1929 Twentieth Century Fox Film Corporation. All rights reserved.

Ramon Novarro (1899–1968) meets Myrna Loy in *The Barbarian* (1933), one of his best sound films.

Gilbert Roland (1905–94), one of the most durable of Mexican-born stars. Typecast as a "latin lover" in the twenties and thirties, the Cisco Kid in the forties, and thereafter evolving into an all-purpose actor of depth. © 1932 Turner Entertainment Co. All Rights Reserved.

Maria Montez's (1920–51) most frequent co-star was Jon Hall (four films). Here they romance in *Arabian Nights* (1943).

Arturo De Cordova (1908–73), the established Mexican film star, was brought to Hollywood in 1943 and went on to star in nine films, including the excellent *A Medal for Benny* (1944). Copyright © by Universal City Studios. Inc. Courtesy of MCA Publishing Rights. a division of MCA Inc.

Ricardo Montalban (b. 1920) as a Chicano boxer in John Sturges's *Right Cross*.

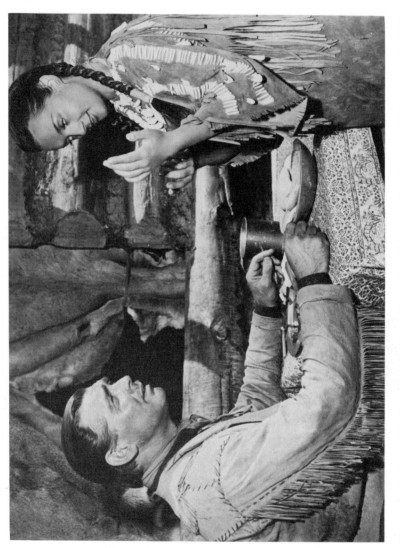

The award-winning Mexican actress Maria Elena Marquez made her Hollywood debut opposite Clark Gable in *Across the Wide Missouri*.

Rosaura Revueltas in *Salt of the Earth* (1954). Courtesy of producer Paul Jarrico.

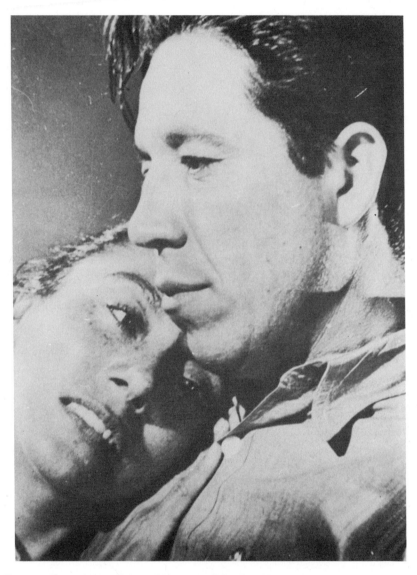

Rosaura Revueltas and Juan Chacon in *Salt of the Earth* (1954). Courtesy of producer Paul Jarrico.

Juan Chacon in *Salt of the Earth* (1954). Courtesy of producer Paul Jarrico.

Pedro Armendariz (1912–63) as Francis I in *Diane* (1955), which co-starred Lana Turner. © 1955 Turner Entertainment Co. All Rights Reserved.

Mario Moreno Cantinflas (1911–93), Mexico's greatest comedian, made two U.S. films, *Around the World in 80 Days* (© 1956 Michael Todd Co., Inc.), with David Niven, Marlene Dietrich, and Frank Sinatra, and *Pepe* (1960). Courtesy of Warner Bros.

Pina Pellicer (1935–64), who made a brilliant debut opposite Marlon Brando in *One-Eyed Jacks* (1961), and starred in the Mexican film classic *Macario* (1960).
Courtesy of Pilar Pellicer.

Sam Peckinpah's complex presentation of the two Mexicos during the Mexican Revolution, *The Wild Bunch* (© 1969 Warner Bros.–Seven Arts, Inc.), with Ernest Borgnine, William Holden, and Warren Oates. Courtesy of Warner Bros

Pina Pellicier and John Gavin in *Pedro Paramo* (1965).

Chicano playwright, actor, and director Luis Valdez (b. 1940), here portraying a Cesar Chavez–like union organizer opposite Richard Pryor in *Which Way Is Up?* (1977). Copyright © by Universal Studios, Inc. Courtesy of MCA Publishing Rights, a division of MCA Inc.

Enrique Muñoz and Adriana Rojo in Jesús Salvador Treviño's *Raices de Sangre* (1979), the first Chicano-Mexico co-production effort. Photo by George Rodriguez. Courtesy of Jesus Salvador Treviño.

Guillermo Gil, Adriana Rojo, and Malena Doria in a scene from *Raíces de Sangre*, written and directed by Jesús Salvador Treviño. Photo by George Rodriguez. Courtesy of Jesús Salvador Treviño.

Daniel Valdez and Edward James Olmos in Luis Valdez's *Zoot Suit* (1981).

Barbarosa (1982) showcased three generations of Chicano/Mexican film stars: Isela Vega from the sixties, Gilbert Roland from the twenties, and Alma Martinez from the eighties. Copyright © by Universal City Studios, Inc. Courtesy of MCA Publishing Rights, a division of MCA, Inc.

Elipidia Carillo (b. 1961) and Jack Nicholson in *The Border* (1982). Copyright © by Universal City Studios, Inc. Courtesy of MCA Publishing Rights, a division of MCA, Inc.

Alma Martinez. Used by permission.

Silvano Gallardo. Used by permission.

Chicano comedian, writer, director Cheech Marin (b. 1946) and Kamila Topez in *Born in East L.A.* (1987). Copyright © by Universal City Studios, Inc. Courtesy of MCA Publishing Rights, a division of MCA. Inc.

Cheech Marin. Copyright © by Universal City Studios, Inc. Courtesy of MCA Publishing Rights, a division of MCA, Inc.

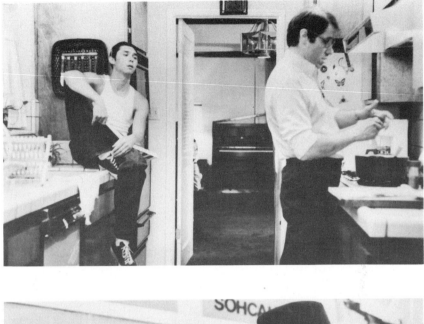

Edward James Olmos and Lou Diamond Phillips in *Stand and Deliver* (© 1988 Warner Bros., Inc.). Courtesy of Warner Bros.

Chicano actor and director Edward James Olmos (b. 1947).

the epic poem by Rodolfo "Corky" Gonzalez and produced by Luis and Daniel Valdez of Teatro Campesino.

The following are representative films of the decade.

The Alamo (1960, United Artists/Batjec)

The Alamo was filmed at the height of the cold war and, as such, is an allegory of East-West relations. It recycled all the Alamo myths and revised history with rabid jingoism.

The film was starred in, directed by (in his directorial debut) and produced (to the tune of $15,000,000) by John Wayne, the all-time box-office attraction in American cinema. According to the film's press kit, Wayne explained his perception of the film, " . . . however, this is not a story that belongs only to Texas; it was filmed to convey to Americans and people everywhere a sense of the debt they owe to all men who have died fighting for freedom." This concept of freedom was dubious since an independent Texas was to introduce the institution of slavery. Indeed, one of the most pathetic characters is Jethro (Jester Hairston), an aged Black slave of Jim Bowie (Richard Widmark), who is finally given his freedom in the midst of the siege (when he could hardly expect to get out), and who, once given his "freedom," decides to stay to fight to establish slavery in Texas. Later, Jethro gives his life protecting his master.

The Mexican characters are equally pathetically portrayed. When Davy Crockett (John Wayne) and his men arrive in San Antonio, they find droves of happy-go-lucky cantineras, who immediately fraternize with the very people who will dispossess them of their land. They dance to "La Adelita," which is unfactual, as the song did not exist until the Mexican Revolution (1910–20). As for the Mexican men, they are nothing but emotionless mannequins with thick serapes on their shoulders, presumably worn so they can sleep at a moment's notice. Late February and early March (when the Alamo battle took place) is very warm and humid in Texas, and to wear serapes in such weather is not only physically unhealthy, but preposterous. The real-life character of Juan Seguin (1806–90), one of the key leaders of the Texas revolt and an actual participant in the battle (which he later lived to regret), is shown condescendingly as an

137

octogenarian, in one brief scene where he is treated with due contempt by Travis (Laurence Harvey). No further mention is made of him or of his involvement.

Numerous other historical revisions abound. In the middle of the siege, the besieged run out of food and so some half-dozen of the filibusters sneak out, quietly and efficiently kill three times their number of Mexican soldiers, and gallop off with a herd of longhorn cattle, back to the Alamo: pure Hollywood fiction. Later, just before an attack, the filibusters comment on how pretty the Mexican army looks. After the attack has been repulsed and the battleground is strewn with piles of corpses, one filibuster says, "You know, I was proud of them even as I was killing them." General Santa Ana is never developed as a character and is shown as an expressionless observer. No effort whatsoever was made to show the Mexican side of the conflict. All Mexican characters are a throwback to the worst of the Hollywood stereotypes, circa 1930s. Only one Mexican character, Lieutenant Reyes (Carlos Arruza), is shown with any semblance of common decency. According to the film's press kit, this character was "the courier sent by Santa Ana to the Alamo, first, to demand surrender, then to offer safe evacuation for the non-combatants. He represents the gallantry, dignity and bravery of Mexican soldiery." The commodity of dignity is something sorely missing in reference to Mexican characters. At the end of the battle, Mrs. Dickinson (Joan O'Brien), her infant daughter atop a donkey, and a Black boy depart the strewn battlefield in a silhouette reminiscent of the infant Jesus, Mary, and Joseph, to the sentimental strains of Dimitri Tiomkin's music score.

The film was nominated for numerous Academy Awards, including Best Picture, but failed to recoup its expensive cost at the box office. John Wayne lost heavily, having invested much of his personal fortune, and was left, at the age of fifty-two, on the verge of bankruptcy. It would take him several years to recover. A political conservative and hawk most of his life, he diametrically shifted his ideological position in 1979, by supporting the Panama Canal treaties and actively campaigning with General Omar Torrijos in Panama to help pass a referendum in support.

The film was shot on location in Bracketville, Texas, where director Jesus Treviño would later film a more historically accurate motion picture, *Seguin* (1981).

Che! (1969, 20th Century)

The film *Che!* was the prototypical movie made by Hollywood about Latin America and its revolutionary upheaval after the Cuban Revolution in 1959. Hollywood's perception of Hispanics, as previously mentioned, during the era was reduced to two types: ideological disciples who conformed to the gospels of the Monroe Doctrine, and/or the rebels/dissidents who necessitated that they must be destroyed, denigrated, and/or simply ridiculed.

Producer Sy Bartlett stated to the *Hollywood Reporter* (September 5, 1969), "This story was done with the greatest attempt at objectivity, and we have been criticized for not taking a point of view which is precisely what we set out to do." The film's director, Richard Fleischer, had another point of view when interviewed by *Newsweek* (December 9, 1968), "We're dealing with one of the phenomena of our time. As of this moment he's a tremendous symbol for young people all over the world. But I'm not so sure that five years from now anyone will remember him, because there's no residue, no substance to the man. When you analyze it, Che is a big loser." History would prove Fleischer to be naively mistaken in reference to Guevara's continued appeal in Latin America.

According to historical fact, Ernesto "Che" Guevara (1928–67) was born to a middle-class family in Argentina. Asthmatic since childhood, he earned his nickname, "Che," from the common Argentinean expression that means: "hey, you!" Before and after graduating from medical school, he traveled throughout Latin America, becoming aware of the poverty and injustice firsthand. He was present in Guatemala in 1954, when the CIA-sponsored invasion overthrew the democratically elected and reform-minded President Arbenz. He obtained political asylum in Mexico, where he met Fidel Castro and other Cubans seeking to overthrow the dictator Fulgencio Batista. In the subsequent revolution, he emerged as military theoretician, diplomat, and economic minister. He disappeared suddenly in 1965. It would be revealed that he had fought alongside the remnants of Patrice Lumumba (who had been murdered by pro-West forces), partisans in the Congo and, later, he was leading a guerrilla movement in Bolivia. Wounded in battle, he was taken prisoner, and then executed by U.S.-trained counter-insurgency special forces on October 9, 1967.

The finished film does not begin to document the historical context of Guevara, the Cuban Revolution, or Latin America or the complex political, cultural, and economic realities. These omissions were obvious to veteran producer Darryl Zanuck, who commented, "I wish the late Errol Flynn were alive, as he (Guevara) personally participated in the last phase of the overthrow of Batista, and had commissioned or authorized Errol to contact me about making a film on the birth of Castro's Cuba."[1] The film underwent several screenplay changes. Formerly blacklisted screenwriter Michael Wilson, one of the Hollywood Ten and Writer of *Salt of the Earth* (1954), was engaged to work on another draft. Eventually, however, screenplay credit was assigned to Michael Wilson and Sy Bartlett and story to Sy Bartlett and David Karp. Additionally, the film carries a disclaimer stating "none of the various texts written on Che Guevara, nor his published diary penned by the revolutionary during the Bolivian episode, was utilized in the final treatment from which this screenplay was adapted." Deleted from the film was everything before the Cuban Revolution. Also eliminated was anything about the corruption, poverty, and repressive nature of the Batista and Barrientos (in Bolivia) regimes, the Bay of Pigs, the Cuban Missile Crisis, the Congo campaign, and historical characters (Regis Debray, Inti Peredo, Tania). Detached from a historical context, the film promulgates ambiguity and simplistic political myopia. At the end, the film promotes the idea that Che is a deluded buffoon and the object of derision.

Mexico banned the film outright, which angered producer Sy Bartlett, who stated to anyone who would listen, "I'd be glad to take him on, a young man who audaciously questions some of the world's most professional observers and people who were on the scene. I'd like to know who this expert is who challenges the authenticity and the objectivity of 'Che!'. . . ." The dubious "professional observers" were never made public. Reviews of the film were surprisingly conscientious of the film's appalling flaws. The *Motion Picture Herald* (June 11, 1969) stated:

> As such, the film will not attract the college audience to whom Che is something of a New Left hero. The portrayal of motivation is much too superficial and the political complexities treated in too cursory a manner for any of the artists involved to rationalize the product as a serious analysis. . . . Jack Palance's excessively mannered performance as Castro adds to the one-sided portrayal of the relationship. . . .

Variety (May 29, 1969) wrote:

> Che talks in vague terms about his theories of revolution, but his comments on the U.S. are confined to a few references to "Yankee imperialism," always quickly stated in the middle of a sentence about something else. The specific reasons for bitterness of many Latin American intellectuals and guerrillas toward the U.S. are hardly mentioned. . . . It had been taught that at least "Che!" would attempt to explain just what was the charisma inherent in this leader which has caused such a cult and mystique to develop after his death to the point he is worshipped as saint by many youth elements. . . . But the effort in "Che!" appears to be entirely one of demystification, a denial of Guevara's appeal. . . .

Time (June 13, 1969) noted:

> The men who made "Che!" chose folly. As scenarists Michael Wilson and Sy Bartlett saw it, the Cuban Revolution was just a Caribbean comic strip drawn in that country's green and peasant land. . . . Striving to placate all factions, the film actually represents none. One moment Che is a cultural hero; the next he is a messianic psychopath.

Leone's Trilogy: A Fistful of Dollars (1966), For a Few Dollars More (1967), and The Good, the Bad, and the Ugly (1968)

Italian director-screenwriter Sergio Leone's trilogy of Italian Westerns, *A Fistful of Dollars, For a Few Dollars More,* and

The Good, the Bad and the Ugly revitalized the moribund Western genre with what became known as the "spaghetti Westerns." Unfortunately, in the process, it brought back the most racist stereotypes from the pre-1920s period.

Leone had served a long apprenticeship as an assistant director with some notable American directors filming in Italy during the 1950s: Robert Wise *(Helen of Troy,* 1955), William Wyler *(Ben Hur,* 1959), Raoul Walsh *(Esther and the King,* 1961), Fred Zinnemann *(A Nun's Story,* 1959), and Melvyn LeRoy *(Moment to Moment,* 1965). He made his directorial debut with *The Colossus of Rhodes* (1961).

It may be recalled that Martin Rott's *The Outrage* (1964) had been derived from Kurosawa's *Rashomon* (1951), and John Sturge's *The Magnificent Seven* (1969), from Kurosawa's *The Seven Samurai* (1956). Leone's *For a Fistful of Dollars* was similarly based on yet another Kurosawa film, *Yojimbo* (1962). One element that all three derivations shared, besides their Japanese source, was that all villains and/or bandits were exclusively Mexican, whereas in Kurosawa's versions, all characters were Japanese. *A Fistful of Dollars* chronicled the story of the violent and amoral Anglo gunfighter, the "Man with No Name" (Clint Eastwood), who is hired as a mercenary by two bands attempting to control a town. He plays both sides against each other, taking money from both and contributing to the destruction of both camps. At the end, he leaves the town, the population reduced to the now-prosperous coffin maker, a bankrupt bartender, and a pathetic bell ringer.

The film is a flawed effort, marred by a clear lack of authenticity. The predominantly Italian cast is totally unconvincing as Mexicans. The majority of the Mexican characters are bandits: unkempt, brutal, violent, greasy, treacherous. The film perpetuates the belief that the only good Mexicans are dead Mexicans, as they, once more, are unable to control themselves or other Mexicans. Although Leone attempted to present a rustic Old West look, the architecture and geography betray him. The dubbing is also deficient and distracting.

The film, nevertheless, revitalized the overused Western genre for several reasons. For one, Leone infused his films with an operatic visual style, impressive spacial compositions of extreme close-ups and background, and Ennio Morricone's eerie musical score, consisting of grunts, groans, and stereolike gunfire. Second, by the time of the film's appearance (it was filmed in 1964, but released in the United States in 1967), the Western genre had suffered from overexposure on film and television. Finally, the stars and directors who had contributed to make the Western a uniquely American genre had departed or were about to depart the scene: actors Gary Cooper, Alan Ladd, Randolph Scott, and Joel McCrea, among others, and directors John Ford, Howard Hawks, and Anthony Mann. While Leone contributed, he also borrowed western lore. The *Washington Post* commented that Leone "has drawn heavily upon his experience from both William Wyler and Fred Zinnemann. Accordingly, his picture offers both evidence of adequate documentation on the lore of the Old West and creditable performances by the actors impersonating the typical heroes and villains of lore. . . ."

For Clint Eastwood, an ex-Universal contract player (1955–58) of feature roles and costar of the television Western, *Rawhide* (1959–65), the role of the "Man with No Name" propelled him to international prominence. The film became a worldwide hit. Eastwood had been paid $15,000 for *A Fistful of Dollars,* and for his second Leone film, his fee climbed to $50,000. The initial reviews indicated that the Western genre was undergoing a revolutionary change. The *Los Angeles Herald-Examiner* noted, "If 'A Fistful of Dollars' doesn't blaze a new trail in Western, shoot-'em-up style motion pictures, it'll be a miracle of this preposterous age, and you will be wise not to bet against it. . . . " It was an accurate prediction. Although the spaghetti Westerns predated Leone's efforts, it was Leone's films that brought them to international renown and spawned their onslaught for almost another decade. According to Frayling, "Well over 300 spaghetti westerns were released in Italy between 1963 and 1969 alone; the peak year for production was 1966–1967 (when 66 were made). Fewer than 20 percent of these spaghettis have been distributed internationally. . . . "[2] Later, locales would include Spain and even West Germany.

Leone's second spaghetti Western, *For a Few Dollars More* (made in 1965, but released in the United States in 1967), was budgeted at $550,000, as opposed to the $80,000 of its predecessor. The film brought back the "Man with No Name" (Eastwood). He establishes an unpredictable alliance with an aging gunfighter, Colonel Douglas Mortimer (Lee Van Cleef), in pursuit of psychopathic Mexican bandit Indio (Gran Mario Volante). Indio has a large reward on his head and is planning to rob a supposedly impregnable bank in El Paso. What motivates Mortimer is not the bounty, but revenge. Indio had previously raped and murdered his sister. After a final gunfight, which Indio loses, the "Man with No Name" departs, with a cart filled with corpses of Mexican bandits.

Gran Mario Volante, who had portrayed John Wells, another Mexican bandit in *A Fistful of Dollars,* returned to play Indio. Indio is the Hollywood embodiment of a caricature Mexican *bandido*. He is duly violent, treacherous, and brutal. He is willing to kill his entire gang for the sake of the bank's loot. He is nevertheless unable to discover that the "Man with No Name" garnered the trust of his gang by having simply freed one of his men from prison. Indio spends an inordinate amount of time under the influence of marijuana and laughing sadistically. He takes special delight when the "Man with No Name" 's ulterior motives are discovered and he is beaten to a pulp.

The "Man with No Name" in this film is transformed into a superhero, like James Bond. His ability to decimate a whole gang singlehandedly and cart them off, all in a day's work, is reflective of this transformation. Even his inherent cruelty is cause for glorification. On one occasion, he grabs a little Mexican boy by the throat and barks at him, "Listen to me, you sawed-off little runt, how many were there?" In another scene, after the "Man with No Name" has killed half a dozen Mexicans, one of them grapples about, apparently only wounded. The "Man with No Name" observes him coolly and then shoots him dead.

A Fistful of Dollars proved to be a commercial hit. As a consequence, Eastwood's salary for the third Leone Western, *The Good, the Bad and the Ugly* (1967), climbed to $250,000, plus a percentage of the profits. The veteran Lee Van Cleef, who had been living on residuals and unemployment insurance when selected for his role, went on to become a star in scores of spaghetti Westerns. Reviewers were considerably cool. The *New*

144

York Daily News commented, "More than two dozen people get killed in one way or another, so the cost is large." The *New York Times* reviewer stated, "That this film is constructed to endorse this exercise of murderers, to emphasize killer bravado and generate glee in frantic manifestations of death is, to my mind, a sharp indictment of it as so-called entertainment in this day." Despite the critics' hostility to the gratuitous violence, no comment was made of the racist stereotype of Mexicans.

Leone's third spaghetti Western, *The Good, the Bad and the Ugly*, set during the Civil War, was the longest (161 minutes), and most expensive (more than one million dollars). It revolves around the "Man with No Name"'s (Eastwood's) efforts in an uneasy partnership with a crude and brutal Mexican bandit, Tuco (Eli Wallach), to find a fortune of loot buried in the unmarked grave of a man named Bill Carson. In the process, they raise some money through the "Man" turning in the bandit for bounty. The "Man" then helps him escape. They find an abandoned carriage and a dying Bill Carson, who tells them where the loot is buried. However, each is only able to hear part of the information, and thus they are dependent on each other. They are captured by a Union sergeant, Sotenza (Lee Van Cleef), who is looking for the fortune himself. Sotenza is unable to extract the information from the pair, even after torture, and the three establish a precarious alliance. Trapped in a battle, the "Man with No Name" uncharacteristically comments that he has never "seen so many men wasted so badly." It all ultimately results in a three-way gunfight in a large cemetery.

The film is complex and finely detailed in period, but marred by the ludicrous, caricature Mexican bandit Tuco. It is a grotesque and repugnant character greatly overplayed by Eli Wallach, who had played another similar caricature in *The Magnificent Seven* (1960). The *New York Times* (January 25, 1968) commented on the excesses, "Wallach makes his eyes dance, he emits horrible gastrointestinal noises to communicate emotion and laughs incessantly. . . . " *Time Magazine* (February 9, 1968) wrote, "Bad is the word for the wooden acting, and Leone's addition to the cramped values and stretched probabilities of the comic strip. And ugly is his insatiable appetite for

145

beatings, disembowelings and mutilations, complete with close-ups of mashed-in faces and death-rattle sound effects." The *Los Angeles Times* stated: "In many ways, the success is not hard to understand. The stylized Western is taken further from reality, and Leone has a sense of style, garish and derivative but showing that he has paid close heed to the better American models. . . . "

While the bandit Tuco is the only major Mexican character, there is a pervasive anti-Mexican ambience. In one scene, Tuco's brother Pablo, a friar, states, "Where we were born, one is only a bandit or a priest." But then, one thing shared in common by most of the scores of spaghetti Westerns was the image of the Mexican man as a greaser and bandit and the Mexican woman as a cantinera or an unvirtuous señorita. Leone's last Western, *Duck, You Sucker* (1972), set during the Mexican Revolution, had another repugnant caricature of a Mexican bandit (on that occasion, played by Rod Steiger). Sergio Leone, admittedly a very gifted director, attempted to make up for his fixation of Mexicans as bandits in his career's masterpiece, *Once Upon a Time in the West* (1969), in which the hero is finally a Mexican gunfighter. Like D. W. Griffith's reputation, because of his portrayal of Blacks in *The Birth of a Nation,* Leone's reputation is marred by a prejudiced view of Mexicans in his spaghetti Westerns.

The Magnificent Seven (1960, United Artists)

Made at the height of the cold war, this film represents the apex of films portraying Mexicans as helpless and cowardly ideological disciples.

The Magnificent Seven was a remake of famed Japanese director Akiro Kurosawa's classic *Seven Samurai* (1954), which won Hollywood's Academy Award as Best Foreign Film. The film chronicled the tale of seven down-and-out samurai warriors in feudal Japan, who came to the defense of a village against a warlord and his band of marauders. Yul Brynner had initiated the process of the remake and made arrangements with Anthony Quinn to costar. The film was to be produced by Brynner's Alciona Productions. Subsequently, Brynner sold the rights to Mirisch Productions, and Quinn sued for breach of contract. Quinn and Brynner settled out of court. Set to direct was the very successful John Sturges, who had made such films as the socially conscious *Right Cross* (1950) and *Bad Day at Black Rock* (1955), and the well-known *Gunfight at the O.K. Corral* (1957). He later stated, "My thought was that the original film held the basis for a story and characters that would make a very good western. We developed that story to the best of our ability without regard as to whether or how it differed."

Sturges and his cast went to Mexico to shoot the film. The director submitted his script to the Mexican government as required and was informed by Jorge Ferretis, the official censor, that the script was anti-Mexican, correctly demanding changes. Sturges unreasonably resisted, "The idea of Americans coming into Mexico to do a job involving physical prowess and courage for the Mexican government presented an instant censorship problem. We had difficulty selling the idea that the villagers were farmers, men of peace—not an aspect limited to Mexicans!"[3] He further stated, "The censor was just picking on anything that might be objected to by some member of the lunatic fringe. I think his only concern was that there must be nothing that someone in Mexico might conceivably consider anti-Mexican. . . . "[4] A petulant Sturges concluded, "If it weren't for the censor, Mexico would be a wonderful country for making movies. But as it is now, it is okay so long as you are making an American movie about a boy and his dog."

At the heart of the matter is the gross amount of racism and ideological vanity that the film perpetuates. In the original Kurosawa film, all the characters (samurai, farmers, marauders) had been Japanese. In its American translation, the samurai became Anglo gunfighters, the farmers became indolent and cowardly Mexican peasants, and the marauders became violent and slimy Mexican bandits. The Mexican villagers, apparently located somewhere in northern Mexico, are some of the worst stereotypes since the dawn of American cinema. After the bandits' fast intrusion, they quiver in confusion and chaos. One peasant says, "We must do something." "But what?" asks another. "I don't know," cries another. Then, according to the precepts of Social Darwinism, they opt to travel to the United States to seek protection from seven misfit gunfighters. Apparently,

Sturges and his writers were unaware that Mexicans have historically fought against injustice and invasion, be it either in the Mexican-American War or during the French Occupation. Moreover, the villagers in the film never attempt to turn to the government authorities for assistance, but like loyal ideological disciples, they flock to the north. The film implies that Latinos cannot think or act for themselves. The allegorical message proposed is that such character deficiencies can only be resolved by the Manifest Destiny of the Monroe Doctrine to impose a protectorate hegemony on Latin America.

The most ludicrous performance of all was given by Eli Wallach as the archetypical Mexican bandit Calvero. Grossly overacting his character, he turned it into a throwback to the silent cinema greaser characters: greasy, unkempt, buffoonlike, violent, and barbarian. Unfortunately, he would reprise such a travesty in *The Good, the Bad and the Ugly* (1968). Then–German heartthrob Horst Buchholz is totally miscast as Chico, the young Mexican peasant-turned-farmer, as is Russian character actor Vladimir Sokoloff as the village elder. Some of the minor characters were Mexican players, among them, Jorge Martinez de Hoyos, Valentin De Vargas, and Enrique Lucero. Famed Mexican director-actor Emilio Fernandez was hired to choreograph the dances and cast extras. The most impressive of the Mexican cast was the lovely Rosenda Monteros, who played the village girl, Petra. She had made her U.S. film debut in *A Woman's Devotion* (1956) and later appeared in another U.S. film, *She* (1965), and one Mexican feature, *Un Extraño en la Casa* (1966). Charnez notes: "The rest of the Mexican actors, for the most part, do not have speaking roles. Those parts are taken by Hollywood actors, who fake the accent badly. . . . "[5]

The film was commercially successful mainly because of the box-office pull of Yul Brynner and his fast-rising, charismatic costars (Steve McQueen, James Coburn, Charles Bronson, Robert Vaughn). The film spawned several sequels, which became more mediocre and low budget as they progressed: *Return of the Seven* (1966), *Guns of the Magnificent Seven* (1969), and *The Magnificent Seven Ride* (1972).

One-Eyed Jacks (1961, Paramount)

Marlon Brando's directorial debut film, *One-Eyed Jacks,* an offbeat and somber Western, provides two of the best-developed Chicano/Mexican film roles in Hollywood's checkered history.

The making of the film was plagued by schedule delays (December 1958 to October 1959), the departure of the originally assigned director, Stanley Kubrick (who was then replaced by Marlon Brando), a rise in budget from $1,800,000 to close to $6,000,000, and excessive length. Brando shot more than one million feet of film, adding up to four hours and forty-two minutes. Producer Frank P. Rosenberg and his editors, with the apparent exclusion of Brando, then spent several months editing the film down to two hours and twenty-one minutes. The film, produced by Brando's own production company, Pennebaker Productions, was finally released in March, 1961.

The film chronicled the tale of two American outlaws, Rio (Brando) and Bad Longsworth (Karl Malden), who rob a bank in Mexico in 1880 and are trapped when one of their horses is killed. Longsworth is designated to leave and return with another horse, but when he finds a mount, he rides off to the United States with the loot. Rio is captured and imprisoned for five years before he breaks out with the help of a friend, Modesto (Larry Duran). Bent on revenge, Rio, Modesto, and two others (Ben Johnson, Sam Gilman) head for Monterey, California, where Longsworth has become sheriff and has taken a Mexican wife, Maria (Katy Jurado). She has a teenage daughter, Louisa (Pina Pellicer). Rio does not reveal to the guilt-ridden Longsworth that he was imprisoned as a result of the latter's betrayal. Rio nevertheless loathes Longsworth's hyprocisy and seduces Louisa as a form of contempt. In the morning, Rio suffers pangs of conscience:

Rio: I shamed you. I wished to God I hadn't.
Louisa: You only shamed yourself.

From the beginning, the character of Louisa is developed fully with human depth. Returning home, she is confronted by the slimy deputy, Lon (Slim Pickens):

149

Lon:	I reckon I know where you been.
Louisa:	I was just walking.
Lon:	Let's go for a little walk, you and me. One more ain't gonna make no difference.

Rio, guilt-ridden because of what he has done, kills a man mistreating a bar girl and is subsequently arrested, is publicly whipped, and has his gun hand broken by a rifle butt. After several weeks, he finally recovers the use of his hand as his desire for revenge grows. Two of his friends, Amory (Ben Johnson) and Johnson (Sam Gilman), become impatient and leave. When Modesto refuses to join them, he is killed. Louisa visits Rio to inform him she is pregnant, and he confesses his love for her. Blamed for Johnson and Amory's failed attempt to rob the bank, Rio is again arrested. Making a daring escape, he engages Longsworth in a gunfight in which he kills him. Before he leaves, he promises Louisa that he will return.

The scenes between Maria, the mother, and Louisa, her daughter, convey a gentle intimacy. Both scenes are done completely in Spanish and reflect credible and deep-seated feeling about Louisa's loss of virginity and, later, her pregnancy. Both women are acutely aware of the loss of respect by the stepfather and the town, and of the consequence of becoming an unwed Chicana/Mexican mother in an anti-Mexican California. Yet both recognize the weakness and power of love. The mother is forgiving and understanding, while her husband breaks out into a self-righteous rage and abuse: "I took you out of the beanfields and gave you respectability." Neither Louisa nor Maria is the conventional and traditional Hollywood Latina; they are independent-minded and possess their own senses of values and the strength to standup for their convictions.

Modesto is another full-fledged Mexican character. Although most of the assortment of characters are filled with duplicity and treachery, he proves to be Rio's most loyal friend. It is a loyalty that he pays for with his death.

Amory:	We're going to take the bank right now.
Modesto:	You mean, just the two of you?

Amory:	Kinda' of figure maybe three. You in or you're out?
Modesto:	Not me, it's no good. If we go in we make a lot of trouble for Rio. . . .
Amory:	I'm real disappointed in you, greaseball, ain't you, Harve?
Modesto:	Malditos!
Amory:	You've had a good life, *cholo* (gang member).

The film accentuates the Mexican influence in Anglo California, on its architecture and other facets of culture such as the town fiesta. It also recognizes the early influx of Chinese immigrants. Among the Hispanic cast are Mexican Rodolfo Acosta as the leader of the rurales and Puerto Rican actress Miriam Colon as a redheaded beauty.

Critical reaction was mixed, many of the critics inevitably raising the issues of the film's delays and expenditures beyond budget and pointedly blaming Brando. However, with time, the film has acquired a cult following. The *New York Times* wrote:

> At his acting peak, Marlon Brando also elected to direct himself. The result is an extraordinary sort of Western drama, proceeding in two contrasting styles, one hard and realistic, the other lush and romantic. . . . The realism is curiously surrounded by elements of creamed-cliche romance—Brando's tender idyll with a charmingly delicate Mexican girl, played by Pina Pellicer—and a kind of pictorial extravagance. . . . [6]

Tony Thomas wrote:

> Brando's *One-Eyed Jacks*—a title that refers to the duplicity of man—is not a film to dismiss or forget. It lingers in the mind because of its visual beauty and the intensity of some of its scenes. . . . [7]

Others have taken a more dim view: "Jurado is only a prop and Pellicer, reportedly a Rosenberg discovery, is unconvincing and unattractive as the naive girl. . . . [8] Suffice it to say that Pina Pellicer in her film debut won international acclaim and the Best Actress Award at the San Sebastian Film Festival.

The Professionals (1966, Columbia)

Richard Brooks' *The Professionals,* set during the Mexican Revolution after the counter-revolution had begun to triumph in 1917, is a film with old-fashioned heroic Western characters. It also perpetuates the Manifest Destiny of Anglo mercenaries in Mexico, who were able single-handedly to alter Mexican history.

The film chronicled the story of a powerful rancher, J. W. Grant (Ralph Bellamy) hiring a group of professional gunmen, Dolworth (Burt Lancaster), Farden (Lee Marvin), Ehrengard (Robert Ryan), and Sharp (Woody Strode) to rescue his wife, Maria (Claudia Cardinel). She has been kidnapped by one Captain Jesus Reza (Jack Palance), a Mexican revolutionary. The men hired had at one time fought on the side of Pancho Villa and Reza and had entered Mexico City with the revolutionary army. Now, the counter-revolutionary forces of Carranza (recognized by the United States) have the Villistas on the defensive in the north. The group fights its way into Reza's camp and rescues Maria, who they discover is in love with Reza. In their retreating battle, Chiquita (Maria Gomez), Dolworth's former girlfriend, is killed and Reza is wounded. Reza attempts to appeal to Dolworth's former idealism.

Dolworth: Perhaps since time began there has been one revolution. . . . When the dead are buried and the politicians return the revolution it adds up to one thing, a lost cause.

Reza: You want perfection or nothing, you are too romantic, compadre. The revolution is like a great love affair. In the beginning she is a goddess, a holy cause. But all love affairs have a terrible enemy, time. We see her as she is, not a goddess or holy cause. But like a whore, she was never pure, holy, perfect. And we run way, another lover, another cause. Quick sordid affairs, lost but no love, passion but no compassion. . . . And then we realize that without love, without a cause we are nothing. We leave because we are disillusioned, we return because we need a cause, we die because we are committed. . . .

In actuality, Maria has married Grant to raise money for the revolution. The group realizes that Maria and Reza are really the captives and get them free. Grant confronts Farden and tells him, "Bastard!" "Yes, sir!" responds Farden. "In my case, an accident of nature. But you're a self-made man!"

Technically, *The Professionals* is a well-crafted film, but it is plagued by acts and feats that are blatantly unrealistic. The film perpetuates the myth of four Anglo mercenaries single-handedly decimating an entire army of Villistas revolutionaries. Historically, this feat is something that the counter-revolutionary army of Carranza and/or General Pershing's Expeditionary Army together or alone were unable to accomplish, and yet we are led to believe that four Anglo mercenaries are able to carry it out without one single casualty. Besides purporting to show Mexican incompetence in war and arms, the film perpetuates the racist stereotype of Mexican women as promiscuous sexual objects. The character of Maria, for example, has prostituted herself to Grant to raise money for the revolution. When rescued by Dolworth, she tells him of Grant, "My husband stole millions from this land, our land. If we can keep the revolution alive for even one more day then I'll steal and cheat and whore!" She then proceeds to entice him, baring her breasts so that he can release her. Dolworth's former girlfriend, Chiquita, is another typical stereotype.

Dolworth:	How's your love life?
Chiquita:	Terrific!
Dolworth:	Don't you ever say no?
Chiquita:	Never!
Dolworth:	Anybody?
Chiquita:	Everybody!

Reviews were favorable. Few of them commented critically on the film's sense of unrealistic portrayal of the exploits of the four Anglo mercenaries. The military experience in Vietnam had yet to shatter the myths of American invincibility. *Films in Review* wrote:

[Brooks] has a U.S. millionaire (made to seem a stinker by Ralph Bellamy) hire four soldiers-of-fortune . . . to go into Mexico and

153

rescue his wife. . . . How they accomplish this won't seem credible even to a twelve year old. . . .

Newsletter stated: "It's a film in the tradition of Vera Cruz, say, rather than Shane. . . . " Predictably, *The Professionals* went on to become one of the top-grossing films of 1966.

Villa Rides! (1968, Paramount)

Mexican revolutionary Pancho Villa (1877–1923) was brought back Hollywood-style after a ten year absence *(Villa!* [1958]) in Paramount's *Villa Rides!,* the most recent and last Hollywood film about him.

The film's original screenplay was written in 1959 by Sam Peckinpah, who had planned to direct a film about Villa himself. After *Major Dundee* (1965) had been cut and altered without his consent and he had been fired from *The Cincinnati Kid* (1965), Peckinpah had been forced to sell his script about Villa. Yul Brynner, who had been cast to play the role, demanded that the screenplay be rewritten and questioned Peckinpah's accuracy regarding Mexico. Peckinpah, in turn, replied, "I've spent a great many years in Mexico, I married a Mexican girl, and I know Mexican history."[9] The screenwriter brought in to do the rewrite was Robert Towne, years before he would earn recognition as the writer of *Chinatown* (1974) and *Shampoo* (1975). He would later denounce the film, and Peckinpah went public with his disgust about the historical liberties taken. Perhaps, because of a sense that the Mexican government censors would rightly object to the typical Hollywood distortions, the film was shot entirely in Spain. In any case, the film would later be banned in Mexico.

Historically, the film had one asset: *Motion Picture Herald* (March 27, 1988) stated:

Villa invented or rediscovered military tactics that left his enemies in awe. He was a political-sociological thinker who organized his army as a weapon for peace and his peaceful countrymen as an army in reserve. One of his tradition-breaking departures was his use of aircraft in guerrilla-type warfare. . . .

154

Villa Riders! was the first Hollywood film to chronicle his inno-vation of air power in war. The film revolved primarily around this and his friendship with an Anglo flyer, Lee Arnold (Robert Mitchum), in the lean years of 1912 to 1913. Predictably, how-ever, the film turned out to be a superficial and trivial enactment of an important part of Mexican history. Adding to the lack of believability was the incongruous non-Mexican/Hispanic cast: the Russian-born Yul Brynner as Villa, the Lithuanian Charles Bronson as General Fierro, the Italian Maria Grazia Buccello as Fina, the Czech Herbert Lom as General Huerta, and the British Alexander Knox as President Francisco I. Madero. The only effective actor in the film was Mitchum, underestimated as the laconic American flyer.

The definitive filmic portrayal of Pancho Villa is that of Pe-dro Armendariz in Ismael Rodriguez's trilogy of Mexican films: *Asi Era Pancho Villa* (1957), Pancho Villa y la Valentina (1958), and *Cuando Vivo Villa Es la Muerte* (1958). Critical reaction to *Villa Rides!* was expectedly hostile. The *Los Angeles Times* (July 31, 1968) commented:

> Perhaps if Sam Peckinpah had had the chance to direct the script he wrote for "Villa Rides" it might have been worthy of the legend-ary Pancho Villa. The result is that deadliest kind of picture, the one that's neither good nor bad but merely routine. . . . Mitchum, easily the more talented of the two, seems to walk his way through a role that wasn't much to begin with. (It's one of those "composites" of various actual men and as such has the uninten-tionally offensive effect of making it seem that Villa couldn't have gotten by without the help of this resourceful American. . . . Bryn-ner, on the other hand, hasn't much to give. . . . His Pancho Villa cannot stand comparison with Brando's subtle Zapata. . . .

The Wild Bunch (1969, Warner Brothers)

One of the most important and controversial films of the decade was Sam Peckinpah's *The Wild Bunch*.

Especially irksome to some self-righteous critics were the slow-motion scenes of violence. Typical of the reviews of the film was that of highbrow critic Judith Crist, writing in *Look* magazine (January 9, 1968):

> To the horror of the puritans and Neanderthals among us, we're in a no-holds-barred era as far as the content of film is concerned. . . .

It would seem that such reviews were faintly hypocritical in light of the fact that real scenes of violence from the Vietnam War were on display on prime time television every day. The assassination of Lee Harvey Oswald and the police riot at the 1968 Chicago Democratic Convention had been carried "live." In the 1960s, filmmakers inevitably ran into conflict when they attempted to challenge the pristine image of the American character: sexual, political, or otherwise.

Unfortunately, the controversy over the violent scenes in *The Wild Bunch* detracted from the fact that the film attempted one of the more complex and serious interpretations of the Mexican Revolution. It is important to mention that several versions of the film exist. Producer Phil Feldman and the studio took the film from director Sam Peckinpah and edited the film down to 143 minutes. A vastly reconstructed version in 1986 restored the film to the original 190 minutes.

The movie was filmed on location in Parras, Coahuila, Mexico, and utilized a large number of Mexican players, including Emilio Fernandez, semiretired from directing; the rarely seen Elsa Cardenas, who had been so impressive in *Giant* (1956, Warner Brothers); and newcomer actor-director Alfonso Arau.

The film is set in Texas in 1913, as the Old West is in its final death throes and death of another kind is coming with the onset of World War I. An old outlaw gang (the Wild Bunch—William Holden, Jaime Sanchez, Ernest Borgnine, Warren Oates, Ben Johnson, Bo Hopkins) attempts to rob a bank, but they are set up to be ambushed by a posse of bounty hunters (Strother Martin, L. Q. Jons) led by an ex-member of the gang (Robert Ryan) and financed by a vengeful railroad owner (Albert Dekker). The remnants of the bunch escape as a temperance union begins marching down the street. They go to Mexico with what they believe is loot. As they near the Rio Grande, Angel (Sanchez) exclaims, "Ay Mexico lindo!" To this, Tector (Johnson) retorts, "I don't see no lindo, I just see more of Texas."

At their hideout, they are met by an old timer (Edmond O'Brien), but they are shocked to find that the alleged loot is nothing more than metal washers. The leadership of Pike Bishop (Holden) is questioned by the bigoted Gorch brothers (Johnson, Oates), who bait and threaten Angel. Pike and Dutch (Borgnine) side with Angel. Pike warns them, "You're not getting rid of anybody. We're gonna stick together just like it used to be. When you side with a man you stay with him and if you can't do that you're like some animal. You're finished: We're finished! All of us!" Pondering their future, Pike tells them, "We got to start thinking beyond our guns. Those days are closing fast." Tellingly, on their way to Angel's village for a rest, Pike falls off his horse, and Tector smirks, "How the hell you're gonna side with anybody when you can't even get on your horse?"

In his village, Angel discovers that a renegade general, Mapache, in the pay of the usurper Huerta, has killed all the young men and that his girlfriend (Sonia Amelio) has willingly gone with him. The bunch decides to seek employment with Mapache. Angel dissents, "I'm not going to seek guns for that devil to rob and kill my people. . . . I care about my people, my village, my Mexico . . . this is their land and no one is going to drive them away. . . . If I can take guns I will go with them." To this, Pike replies, "One case, you give up your half of the gold." Angel agrees. At Mapache's camp, in a sudden anger, Angel kills Teresa while she is in Mapache's arms. Convinced by the bunch that it is not an assassination attempt on his life, Mapache hires them to rob a U.S. Army shipment of guns.

The bunch carries out the action, although pursued by the U.S. army and the bounty hunters. In the process, Angel saves Dutch when trapped in the train. A case of guns is given to the Villista villagers, and the rest is taken to Mapache. Mapache learns about the deception, and when Angel and Dutch take the last case, Angel is captured and tortured. "And Angel?" asks Mapache. Dutch replies, "He's a thief, you take care of him."

Pike lashes out at Dutch's treachery, "He gave his word!" Dutch replies, "That's not what counts! It's who you give it to!"

Pursued once more by the bounty hunters, the bunch seeks a respite at the Mapache camp, accepting the general's invitation to the celebration even as Angel is being dragged around tied to a car. They seek solace with prostitutes, and Pike, totally disillusioned even with his tarnished code of loyalty and himself, decides to end it all in pursuit of one noble act, that of rescuing Angel. The bunch confront Mapache requesting Angel, who has his throat cut, and the final battle begins.

After the battle, the bounty hunters plunder the remains, but Deke (Ryan) abandons them. The bounty hunters are subsequently killed by the Villista villagers. Some of the villagers arrive with Sykes (O'Brien), who tells Deke, "Me and the boys here got a job to do. Wanna come along? It ain't like it used to be, but it'll do."

Peckinpah rendered the two Mexicos of the Revolution through the allegorical characters of Angel, the flawed but resolute Villista and Mapache, the decadent and corrupt counter-revolutionary. Indeed, Angel, as his name implies, is a redeeming messenger of fate for the wayward bunch. Pettit in his extensive work on Peckinpah noted:

> His commitment to my people, my village, Mexico, separates him from the Bunch, who are committed only to each other until Angel's execution takes them to their own deaths—if not for Angel's values, at least for his spirit. It is Angel who wins our sympathy early in the action by flinging the Bunch's racism in their faces, and it is Angel who shows the Bunch an alternative to Mapachismo by taking them to his native village. It is Angel who gives his fellow Villistas a case of ammunition, throwing Mapache into the fit of rage that leads to the film's violent climax. It is Angel who is the catalyst for both the physical destruction and the moral resurrection of the Wild Bunch. By awakening his fellow outlaws to the moral dimensions of the revolution, Angel serves as the spiritual center, the conscience, the moral burden, and, ultimately, the redeemer of the Bunch. . . .[10]

In the restored version, Mapache is shown to be a multidimensional character. In the battle scene at the train tracks, Mapache's army takes a beating at the hands of Pancho Villa's *dorados*. Mapache suppresses his desire to retreat when he notices the unmistakable signs of hero worship in a little boy. In the aftermath of the battle with the Villistas, Mapache exhibits touching concern as the wounds of his men are tended to. One of his adjutants tells him, "With the new guns, this wouldn't have happened." Later, when he has acquired the guns, he tells the little boy. "Con esos rifles y esa metralladora les voy a abujerar esos desgraciados Villistas." Mapache is vicious and cruel, but only with those that threaten his people.

Peckinpah often pays homage to the Villistas, sometimes at the expense of the bunch. When the Villistas surround the bunch unnoticed to pick up their rifles, a frustrated but admiring Lyle cries, "They made damn fools of us, Mr. Bishop!" Later, Pike remarks, "They ever get armed with good leaders this whole country will go up in smoke."

Some Anglo characters are shown to have deficient skills and traits. General Pershing's troopers defending the arms shipment train prove to be incompetent and bungling, unable to discern the daring act of the bunch taking the arms. The bounty hunters' excessive anxiety causes the civilian deaths at the bank robbery. Later, while in pursuit of the bunch, the bounty hunters nervously initiate fire until Deke screams at them, "Don't shoot; it's the army, you idiots!" In the end, their absent-minded greed leads to their quick demise at the hands of the Villistas.

From the beginning, Peckinpah portrays the Wild Bunch as killers and thieves, but human and thrivingly vital and tarnished. Unlike *Butch Cassidy and the Sundance Kid* (1969, 20th Century), they are not pristine romanticized good-bad men. Within this context, the controversial carnage at the end of the film is a metaphor for the death throes of one era and the childbirth of another.

The Players

In the 1960s, Hispanic players were less visible than in previous decades. For all practical purposes they constituted an "invisible minority."

One reason was that the vast majority of films requiring Hispanic roles were in the spaghetti Westerns, which were produced in Italy, Spain, and Germany and thereby utilized non-Hispanic players for the most part. Second, in U.S. films, most Hispanic roles were in Westerns, which were greatly reduced in number because of the overexposure of the genre on television (e.g., *Wagon Train, Bonanza, Cheyenne,* etc.). Another reason was that in non-Westerns Hispanic characters were exclusively played by non-Hispanic actors, such as the World War II Chicano hero Guy Cavaldron played by Jeffrey Hunter in *Hell to Eternity* (1960), Zorro played by Guy Williams in the *Sign of Zorro* (1961, Disney) and the Chicano gunfighter Elfego Baca, played by Robert Loggia in the television series.

A fourth reason contributing to the situation was the death or retirement of well-known Hispanic players. Pedro Armendariz, who alternated between Mexican, American, and European films, died in 1963. Ramon Navarro, the first Hispanic star, made his last film appearance in *Heller in Pink Tights* (1960, Paramount), went into semiretirement, and was killed in 1968. Dolores Del Rio was semiretired but came back for two last Hollywood films, *Flaming Star* (1960) and John Ford's *Cheyenne Autumn* (1965, Warner Brothers). Gilbert Roland, Ricardo Montalban, and Katy Jurado worked infrequently and mostly on television. Rosenda Revueltas was effectively barred from entry and blacklisted. Maria Elena Marquez, Rita Macedo, and Sarita Montiel were never employed by Hollywood in the 1960s. Rita Hayworth worked only sporadically until the end of the decade. The only visible Hispanic star for the most part was Anthony Quinn.

Finally, while a familiar Hollywood cliche excuse was that there were "no qualified Hispanic actors and actresses," the studios made little, if any, attempt to find them or to develop them. Periodically, during the decade, Hollywood utilized established Mexican stars in insignificant small roles that were not conducive to a star's return. Thus, they squandered the talents of the internationally acclaimed and Luis Buñuel–favorite Silvia Pinal in *The Guns of San Sebastian* (1968, MGM) and Pilar Pellicer in *The Day of the Evil Gun* (1968, MGM). Others, such as David

Reynoso, Aurora Clavel, Alfonso Arau, and Emilio Fernandez, suffered similar fates.

One exception was the young and talented Pina Pellicer, who made her impressive film debut in Marlon Brando's *One-Eyed Jacks* (1961, United Artists) and seemed slated for a brilliant career. Sadly, after four subsequent Mexican films, she committed suicide in 1964. Jaime Sanchez was another promising newcomer who made impressive impact in *The Pawnbroker* (1965, Warner Brothers) as a troubled Puerto Rican youth and as Angel in Sam Peckinpah's *The Wild Bunch* (1969, Warner Brothers). Unfortunately, the fact that his career languished thereafter can only be attributed to Hollywood's latent racism and continued stereotyping. A third promising newcomer was the sensitive Mexican actress Ana Martin, who was brought in to star in *The Return of the Gunfighter* (1968, MGM) opposite the veteran Robert Taylor, but never again employed by Hollywood. By the end of the decade, however, an obscure bit player, Raquel Tejada, had been transformed into Raquel Welch and became the reigning sex symbol of American cinema. It could only happen in Hollywood.

Notes

1. Jack Leonard, "Will the Real Che Guevara Please Stand Up and Die for Our Popcorn?" *New York Times Magazine,* December 8, 1968, p. 57.
2. Christopher Frayling, *Spaghetti Westerns* (London: Routledge & Paul, 1981).
3. Ibid.
4. Ibid.
5. Casey St. Charnez, *The Films of Steve McQueen* (Secaucus, N.J.: Citadel Press, 1984).
6. Howard Thompson, ed., *The New York Times Guide to Movies on T.V.* (Chicago: Quadrangle Books, 1970).
7. Tony Thomas, *The Films of Marlon Brando* (Secaucus, N.J.: Citadel Press, 1973).
8. Jay Robert Nash, *The Motion Picture Guide 1927–1983* (Chicago: Cinebooks, 1986).
9. *Take One* interview, 1969.
10. Arthur Pettit, *Images of the Mexican Revolution in Fiction and Film* (Bloomington: Indiana University Press, 1981).

CHAPTER SEVEN

The 1970s—Round Up the Usual Suspects

If a man gives you freedom, it is not freedom. Freedom is something only you must take.

> —Jose Dolores (Evaristo Marquez)
> in *Burn* (1970, United Artists)

"You say you're defending freedom and democracy.
. . . Your methods are war, fascism, and torture.
. . . Surely you agree with me, Mr. Santore?"

> —Hugo (Jacquez Weber)
> in *State of Siege* (1973, Cinema 5)

The 1970s were characterized by continued hostility in East-West relations. In Latin America, insurgencies against corrupt and predatory military cliques withstood the United States' onslaught of dollars and counter-insurgency efforts. In the United States, dubious acts of political morality compelled a president to leave office. Chicanos and Hispanics continued to press for social change.

The United States' withdrawal from Vietnam finally came about in March 1973. The promise of peace with the signing of the Strategic Arms Limitation Treaty looked bright, but it was dampened by the movement of Soviet troops into Afghanistan in 1978 and the formidable insurgencies in El Salvador and Nicaragua. In July 1979, Sandinista guerrillas in Nicaragua toppled the forty-four–year-old repressive Somoza dynasty, which had been supported unwaveringly by the United States. Elsewhere, the OPEC (Organization of Petroleum Exporting Countries) raised oil prices, which resulted in an energy crisis revealing the vulnerability of industrialized nations. The placement of nuclear weapons in Europe by the United States further increased East-West tensions. In 1979, the client state of the Shah of Iran was unceremoniously overthrown.

Latin America continued to experience the economic and political metamorphosis of a continent attempting to disengage itself from United States hegemony. In 1973, the constitutionally elected President Salvador Allende of Chile was overthrown by a U.S.-sponsored military coup. The continued U.S. support of the bankrupt policy of the status quo characterized by oppressive military regimes (e.g., Stroessner in Paraguay, Duvalier in Haiti, and Pinochet in Chile), billion dollar foreign debts, economic underdevelopment, and political dependency continued. Millions of undocumented Mexican workers seeking employment in the United States were accused of "stealing jobs," which further exacerbated anti-foreign feelings.

President Richard M. Nixon resigned his office in disgrace in August 1974, and the moral fiber of the nation was severely tested by the Watergate hearings. The emphasis on "human rights" by President Jimmy Carter was a refreshing new shift in foreign policy. Domestically, however, the efforts of ethnic minorities for equality was undermined by the Bakke case (1976).

The 1970s witnessed the fragmentation of the Chicano movement, the end of the Vietnam War, the abandonment of federal support for affirmative action, and acceptance of the inevitability of poverty. The postwar recession and sectarianism sapped energies and shifted focus. Acuña notes:

> In the 1970s, Mexicans again became bandits, blamed for stealing jobs. They were made outlaws in order to criminalize them, to justify paying them less and hounding them like the bandits of old, while at the same time demonstrating the pseudo-need to appropriate more funds to the INS. Many poor and middle-class Chicanos "believed" that the undocumented worker had invaded their land and taken their jobs. In the face of this hysteria, Chicano leaders witnessed their finest hour. . . . [1]

The Republican party courted Cubans and middle-class Chicanos. Some of the demands of the Chicano movement came to fruition: Chicano and Latin American Studies departments and bilingual education, among others.

The Films

In the 1970s, the Hollywood film industry witnessed the continued decline of box-office receipts and the exodus of paying customers for television. The industry managed a desperate comeback of sorts with some new and very independent directors and landmark films. The dominant image of Chicanos/Hispanics in the decade mirrored their image portrayed in the news media and their perception by government: illegal aliens, bandits, gang members, *cantineras,* and violence-prone revolutionaries.

A disastrous box-office glut affected Hollywood between 1969 and 1971. The numerous expensive films that flopped and other studio losses had not been as great since the period, from 1931 to 1932, at the height of the Depression. Numerous management changes took place under conglomerate guidance that barely managed to keep the studios in business. Fueled by inflation, film budgets rose to an average of seven million dollars and by the middle of the next decade, to twelve million dollars.

Producers-directors became common, as did maverick independent producers. True film "stars" became a scarce commodity. Karney noted:

> A star, in the past, was the incarnation of a particular stereotype. When the stereotypes were good of their kind there was much fun to be had in meeting them in as many situations as the ingenuity of the screenwriter could muster. . . . The old stars scarcely even acted. But the new stars act away as if their lives depended on it. . . . The lessons of Stella Adler and the Actor's Studio had been taken to heart and interiorized. The '70s were a decade of studious professionalism. . . . [2]

Despite the "studious professionalism," most of the film fare of the decade was either escapist in nature or true to old tested-and-tried Hollywood formulas that provided movie goers solace from the disenchantment of Vietnam, Watergate, inflation, and the energy crisis. Films included *Love Story* (1970, 20th Century), *The Exorcist* (1973, Warner Brothers), George Lucas' *American Graffiti* (1972, Universal), and *Close Encounters of the Third Kind* (1977, Columbia). Sequels, remakes, and film gadgetry became a staple of the decade, becoming increasingly repetitive, redundant, and inane. Periodically, offbeat and insightful films were made by maverick directors: Francis Ford Coppola's *The Godfather* (1972, Paramount) and *Godfather II* (1974, Paramount) explored the darker side of the free enterprise economic system; Sydney Lumet's *Network* (1976, MGM) dealt with the pervasive influence of television; Martin Scorsese's *The Taxi Driver* (1976, Columbia) chronicled the alienation and violence of the mean streets; Roman Polanski's *Chinatown* (1974, Paramount) and Alan J. Pakula's *All the President's Men* (1976, Warner Brothers) questioned the political morality of the nation.

The Black exploitation films reached their height during the decade and lost their initial impetus of truly addressing the Black community's cultural and political needs. They stagnated into the typical and routine of Hollywood mainstream films of simple-minded revenge, violence, and sex.

The Chicanos/Hispanics inevitably turned up in the roundup of the usual suspects: illegal aliens, bandits, gang members, catineras, and violence-prone revolutionaries.

The decade saw the welcome decline and demise of the spaghetti Western and its caricature *bandidos* and *cantineras*. To the very end, the genre retained its singularly stylish but unrepentive image of the Mexican as barbarian. In *Adios Sabata* (1971, United Artists), Sabata (Yul Brynner), an American soldier of fortune, is joined with a Mexican bandit, Scudo (Pedro Sanchez), and his henchmen to steal a gold shipment from Maximilian's occupation forces for Juarez's nationalist ones. The sequel, *Return of Sabata* (1972, United Artists), with Lee Van Cleef, was permeated with Mexican *cantineras* and *bandidos*. In *The Mercenary* (1970, United Artists), an American hired gun, Douglas (Franco Nero), teams up with a Mexican desperado, Eufemio (Tony Musante), to rob banks and free revolutionaries. In *A Bullet for Sandoval* (1970, United Artists), a feared Mexican bandit (Ernest Borgnine) is killed in a knife fight duel in a bullring at the hands of a Confederate deserter (George Hilton) after he has gone on a rampage over northern Mexico. In *A Town Called Hell* (1971, Benmar), a priest and ex-revolutionary (Robert Shaw) seeks refuge in a town run by an evil Mexican bandit (Telly Savalas) and an assorted number of henchmen. Typical characters and geography were covered in other spaghetti oaters: *Today We Kill . . . Tomorrow We Die!* (1971, Cine), *Catlow* (1971, MGM), *Blindman* (1972, Fox), and *Compañeros* (1970, Tritone). One of the genre's most ambitious entries was Sergio Leone's *Duck, You Sucker* (1972, United Artists), set during the Mexican Revolution. It involved a fugitive Irish revolutionary, Sean Mallory (James Coburn), joining a gang of revolutionaries headed by Juan Miranda (Rod Steiger). Unfortunately, the caricatured Mexican characters, especially the one played by Steiger, undermined any believability.

Mexican portrayals in domestic Westerns weren't any more believable or less stereotypical. In *Barquero* (1970, United Artists), Maria Gomez played yet another *cantinera*, Nola. In *Cannon for Cordoba* (1970, United Artists), General Pershing enlists the aid of an intelligence officer (George Peppard) to end the marauding of a band of bandits headed by Cordobe (Raf Vallone). In *Machismo—40 Graves for 40 Guns* (1970, BI), another Mexican bandit gang runs amuck headed by Hidalgo (Robert Padilla). Other Mexican desperados appeared in *Macho Callahan* (1970, AE) played by Pedro Armendariz, Jr.; in *Scandalous John* (1971, Disney), by Alfonso Arau; and in *El Condor* (1970, NG), by Patrick O'Neal. In *The Magnificent Seven Ride* (1972, United Artists), the third and last sequel to *The Magnificent Seven* (1960), Chris (Lee Van Cleef) leads his motley crew to rescue some widowed White women from another band of murderous Mexican bandits. In *The Revengers* (1972, NG), an embittered Civil War veteran (William Holden) leads six convicts to track down a renegade White man who had murdered his family and sought refuge in a Mexican town, populated exclusively by bandits, robbers, and murderers. In *Two Mules for Sister Sara* (1970, Universal), the Juaristas appear incapable of defeating the French Occupation forces without the technical efforts and fearless daring of a lone Anglo mercenary (Clint Eastwood). Eastwood is equally benevolent to Chicanos (Stella Garcia, John Saxon) who have been dispossessed of their land in *Joe Kidd* (1972, Universal). Howard Hawks' *Rio Lobo* (1970, NG) featured something unusual in the decade. A Mexican Confederate officer, Cardona (Jorge Rivero), is instrumental in helping a colonel (John Wayne) in tracking down a fugitive who is guilty of stealing a shipment of gold. In *The Wrath of God* (1972, MGM), a defrocked priest (Robert Mitchum) is hired by a revolutionary to assassinate the local cacique (Frank Langella). In *Valdez Is Coming* (1971, United Artists), a Mexican-American sheriff (Burt Lancaster) wreaks havoc on a wealthy rancher (Jon Cypher) who has caused the death of an innocent Black man.

Hispanics in films with contemporary settings had no less demeaning images. In *Trackdown* (1976, United Artists), a cowboy big brother (John Mitchum) searches for a country girl caught up in the low-life of Los Angeles, where the hero confronts scores of Chicano gang members. In another similarly witless film, *Assault on Precinct 13* (1976, TR), a multicultural gang lays siege to a police station. No real motivation is offered other than the seemingly innate violence of these gang members. Another film, *Walk Proud* (1979, Universal), purported to chronicle the gang rites of passage of Emilio (Robby Benson with brown contact lenses and brown makeup) who is in love with a rich Anglo girl (Sarah Holcomb). The interracial couple only finds happiness when Emilio discovers that his father is an Anglo and thus he is only half Chicano. In the more believable *Boulevard Nights* (1979, Warner Brothers), one hard-working brother, Raymond (Richard Yniguez), attempts to remove his younger brother Chuco (Danny de la Paz) from the gang life. Although the latter film might have been well intentioned, its ultimate failure to capture the life of cholos/pachucos lay in the inability of the non-Hispanic filmmakers to perceive the world from the inside looking out: a threatening world of racism, discrimination, poverty, and injustice.

In *Which Way Is Up?* (1977, Universal), Richard Pryor played a California grove worker who finds himself involved politically and sympathetically in the plight of Mexican farm workers (Daniel Valdez and the Teatro Campesino). A less sympathetic image was presented in *Up in Smoke* (1978, Paramount), wherein Pedro de Pacas (Cheech Marin) and Man

167

Stoner (Tommy Chong) played a pair of traveling down-and-out marijuana-induced rockers. While the film (the first for Cheech and Chong) went on to rake up sizeable profits, it little profited the Chicano image. Other Hispanics appeared in small roles in *Dog Day Afternoon* (1975, Warner Brothers), with Chu Chu Malava playing a Puerto Rican boyfriend; in *Blue Collar* (1978, Universal), with Jimmy Martinez as a union organizer; in *The Big Fix* (1978, Universal), with Ofelia Medina as a barrio suspect investigated by a sixties' radical–turned detective (Richard Dreyfuss); in *The Goodbye Girl* (1977, MGM), with Pancho Gonzalez and Jose Machado as muggers; in *Grease* (1978, Paramount), with Lorenzo Lamas as a fifties' rocker; in *Midway* (1976, Universal), with Erik Estrada, who is nicknamed Chili Bean by his comrades-in-arms; in *Red Sky at Morning* (1970, Universal), with Desi Arnaz, Jr., as a Chicano youth in New Mexico; in *Mr. Majestik* (1974, United Artists), with Linda Cristal as a union activist Chicana; and in *The Last Movie* (1971, Universal), with Stella Garcia as a Peruvian *cantinera*.

A handful of the decade's films dealt in depth with the historical realities of Latin America: colonialism and neocolonialism. Gillo Pontecorvo's *Burn* (1970, United Artists) uncompromisingly depicted the revolutionary uprising on a Caribbean island during the colonial period. A film, Costa-Gavras' *State of Siege* (1973, Columbia), chronicled the true story of a kidnapping of an AID counter-insurgence expert (Yves Montand) by the Tupamaros guerrillas in Uruguay. The two films are among the most perceptive and powerful ever made about colonialism and neocolonialism and its political, economic, and psychological consequences for Latin America. A third, but lesser film, Sam Peckinpah's dark *Bring Me the Head of Alfredo Garcia* (1974, United Artists) captured some of the moral ramifications of the appropriation of the Mexican Revolution by the counter-revolution.

In conclusion, the dominant image of the Chicano/Hispanic in American cinema was that of a reel suspect, imitating the alleged real suspect as perceived by government and the communications media.

The following are representative films of the decade.

Boulevard Nights (1979, Warner Brothers)

Among the spate of youth gang–oriented films at the end of the late 1970s and early 1980s, *Boulevard Nights* is the best one. Yet some felt that it was controversial and a disservice to the Chicano community.

The late 1970s saw the emergence of a brief Hollywood trend of ethnic gang films. Walter Hill's *The Warriors* (1979, Paramount), about a New York gang, became notorious when its exhibition in some theaters resulted in three gang murders. *Walk Proud* (1979, Universal) had Bobby Benson (with brown contact lenses) totally unconvincing as a gang leader of mixed parentage in love with a rich White girl. A series of other gang films made on lower budgets cashed in on the trend by glorifying and perpetuating the stereotype of Chicanos/Hispanics as one-dimensional violence-prone gang members. Several years later, Luis Valdez's *Zoot Suit* (1981, Universal) chronicled the 1942 Sleepy Lagoon incident with more mature depth and skill. *Boulevard Nights* is a notch below *Zoot Suit* and several above the rest of the gang films.

Producer Bill Benenson stated, "I think we made a genuine effort with 'Boulevard Nights' to tackle a serious social problem (gangs). Still, there were people with legitimate complaints and expressing genuine feelings."[3] Executive producer Tony Bill said, "The film relates to a real-life struggle that's going on, the struggle of young people who are basically rootless and joining up with an easily identifiable peer group."[4] The film was shot almost entirely in the sprawling barrio of East Los Angeles, utilizing an almost all-Chicano film cast headlined by Richard Yniguez.

The film documented the story of the efforts of an older brother, Raymond Avila (Richard Yniguez), to convince his younger brother, Chuco (Danny De la Paz), to leave the gang life and his preoccupation with cruising Whittier Boulevard. Raymond is an ex-serviceman who works in an auto shop and is about to marry Shady Landeros (Marta Du Bois). He gets his brother a job at the shop but soon proves himself unable to be responsible. After getting high and having a confrontation, Raymond is ultimately fired. The experience has the effect of further drawing Chuco into his gang. After a gang member is beaten by a rival gang, warfare results. At Raymond and Shady's wedding celebration, a rival gang member accidentally kills Mrs. Avila (Betty Carvalho) while aiming at Chuco. Overcome with anger, both Raymond and Chuco determine on retribution despite Shady's efforts to the contrary. Chuco, on his own, tracks down his mother's killer but is mortally shot as his brother attempts his rescue. Raymond and Shady are left alone to contemplate their past and possible future.

The film's Chicano cast and East Los Angeles location added much to the film's convincing reality. The inclusion of such real-life car clubs as the Imperials and such well-known spots as Whittier Boulevard contributed ambience and context sadly lacking in other gang films. The Chicano family's strong ties of unity and loyalty are in evidence. The character of Shady is a strong one, loyal and caring but with a sense of independent critical thinking, all too aware of the excesses of gangs and the residue of the gang life style. It is she who prods Raymond out of his prolonged fascination with car clubs and cruising. She attempts to get him a job in a factory in Montebello (a nearby suburb of Los Angeles), to which Raymond angrily retorts, "You mean you ain't nothing until you work in an office and wear a suit and all that shit?" Raymond aspires to have his own auto shop and realizes the importance of responsibility, respect, and consideration. However, it is here that the film is most flawed. Education is never mentioned as being a viable option for reasonably persevering people such as Raymond and Shady. The film fails to acknowledge the historical fact that the Chicano movement evolved out of the East Los Angeles high school walkouts of 1970 and the numerous efforts of many community organizations to promote education as a priority issue. No alternatives are documented to demonstrate that Chicanos can be more than simply gang members and auto mechanics or that there are many groups and individuals attempting to repair the social fabric damaged by gangs.

The gang violence in the film is not glorified but is shown as a believable possibility within the context of the characters' actions. The main criticism levelled at the film by the Chicano community was not necessarily directed at the film's well-intentioned will but at the fact that Hollywood rarely made films about Chicanos/Hispanics. When it infrequently did, it focused on the negatives rather than on the positives such as chronicling the contributions of Chicano/Hispanic doctors, attorneys, engineers, or teachers. Seen within this context, such film efforts exhibited a certain opportunism on the part of Hollywood. Professor Armando Morales, of the UCLA Department of Psychiatry, stated for example:

> 5% of any population segment, Hispanic, Black or Anglo, is criminal. The remaining 95% is law-abiding. Media have the obligation to show that 95%! . . . In order to have an impact on the racist perceptions regarding Hispanics, film and TV must show positive role models—attorneys, judges, doctors, teachers, etc. We need a true reflection of our position in society.[5]

It was on this basis that the film was picketed in many Chicano communities.

Critical response to the film was mixed. The *New York Times* (March 23, 1979) decried that it:

> trivializes the Mexican-American experience by equating it with the melodrama of many other minor movies about gang wars. The film, written by Desmond Nakano and directed by Michael Pressman, is so busy trying to meet the needs of a conventional narrative that it appears to have no point of view about its characters. . . . With the possible exception of Mr. De la Paz, whose haunted looks suggest someone deeply troubled, the actors are not very good.*

Variety (March 23, 1979) wrote:

> To label "Boulevard Nights" simply another gang picture because its milieu is the streets of East Los Angeles would be doing the . . . production a disservice. Unfortunately, the film fails to carve out a separate identity of its own, rehashing a familiar story about

---

*Reprinted by permission.

inter-family conflicts. . . . While the acting throughout "Boulevard Nights" is first-rate, especially from Yniguez, de Bois and screen new-comer De la Paz, there is simply not enough to distinguish the pic from a number of previous ethnic-set mellers.

The *Los Angeles Herald-Examiner* (March 23, 1979) commented:

> The movie is so fearful of its subject—gang warfare in East L.A.—that it gives "responsibility" a bad name. . . . Chuco, in De la Paz's prehensile performance, almost matches DeNiro's Johnny boy—and, perhaps, James Dean—as often as he echoes them.

The *Los Angeles Times* (March 23, 1979) wrote:

> Modest, earnest, honest, authentic, dramatic and effective drama photographed in and largely populated by the East Los Angeles barrio, may evoke protests—and has—but seems unlikely to provoke overt violence.

Chicano journalist Frank Del Olmo noted that:

> [the] cause of gang violence, barely touched on in "Boulevard Nights," is another shortcoming in an otherwise well-intentioned effort. But perhaps the saddest exclusion is the film's failure to mention that there are people working, often very hard and at great sacrifice, to help the real-life Chucos of East Los Angeles and other barrios. . . .[6]

Burn (1970, United Artists)

Burn is one of the most powerful, incisive, and uncompromising films ever made in its indictment of slavery and colonialism. Half-heartedly promoted by United Artists, it was lambasted by politically motivated U.S. critics. Since then, the film has deservedly become a cult film.

The film was made as a result of Marlon Brando's political activism and his desire to make a film relevant to socioeconomic conditions. He had been deeply involved in the support of civil rights activities in 1960s and had been greatly distressed by the assassinations of Robert Kennedy and Martin Luther King. He sought a film vehicle to express his disillusion and outrage. On one occasion, he stated to Toronto entertainment reporter Sid Adilman:

> I was overcome by the Martin Luther King assassination. I have been concerned lately with man's predacious nature. More and more I feel it is difficult to achieve a rapprochement with oneself and with the fact of man's tendency to behave aggressively.[7]

About his motives for the film, Brando stated:

> You can say important things to a lot of people. About discrimination and hatred and prejudice. I want to make pictures that explore the themes current in the work today.[8]

The film chronicled the efforts of one Sir William Walker, (Marlon Brando) in 1845, who as an agent of the British government attempts to initiate a revolution in the Portuguese Caribbean island colony of Quemada. He develops and trains for leadership a Black dockworker, Jose Dolores (Evaristo Marquez), to lead the rural revolt and a mulatto, Teddy Sanchez (Renato Salvatori), to lead in the towns and cities. When Dolores makes a final triumphant entrance into the capital, he discovers that Sanchez has been selected as the new leader by the sugar-growing class. Illiterate and uneducated in the ways of government and diplomacy, Dolores finally agrees to disband his army and disappears into obscurity.

Ten years later, a new revolution erupts. Walker is recalled by the corruption-ridden Sanchez regime to quell the revolt led by his former friend Dolores. Peasants are forcefully removed from strategic areas of guerrilla activity, and villages and forests are burned. Attempting to stop some of the excesses, Sanchez fires Walker, but Sanchez is promptly arrested and shot for treason. British troops arrive to assist government troops. Ultimately, the guerrillas are defeated, and Dolores is captured.

Dolores tells an inquiring soldier, "If a man gives you freedom, it is not freedom. Freedom is something only you must take." Dolores turns down Walker's and the general's offer of exile, choosing to be executed and to become a martyr to his countrymen against colonialism. As he is led to the scaffold, Dolores tells Walker, "You say civilization belongs to the Whites. But what's civilization? And for how long?"

The film was directed by Gillo Pontecorro, who had made *The Battle of Algiers* (1969). The film was cowritten by Pontecorro and Franco Solinas who had begun writing spaghetti Westerns and would later also write *State of Siege* (1973). The haunting musical score was composed by Ennio Morricone of the Sergio Leone spaghetti Westerns fame. Most of the film was shot on location in Colombia. What gives the film some of its raw and uncompromising power is Pontecorro's use of nonprofessional actors, among them Evaristo Marquez as Jose Dolores.

The film met with critical hostility and outright animosity in some quarters. Released at the tail end of the polemical 1960s, it was dismissed by many as one more dogmatic statement against the status quo. But the film cannot be easily so dismissed, for it is a deeply analytical and penetrating overview of colonialism and neocolonialism and the destructive impact on the social fabric of a people. What Pontecorro and Solinas did was synthesize the historical experience of colonialism and neocolonialism, especially in Latin America. The Walker character is obviously modeled after the historical filibuster William Walker, who forcefully attempted to establish Nicaragua as a U.S. slave state, and the meddlesome, intrigue-ridden U.S. ambassador Henry Lane Wilson, who conspired with General Huerta in 1912 against the democratically elected President Madero. Jose Dolores is a composite of numerous nationalist and revolutionary leaders: Augusto Sandino of Nicaragua, Emiliano Zapata of Mexico, Patrice Lumumba of the Congo, and Ernesto "Che" Guevara of Argentina. Their lives and deaths have become synonymous with struggles against colonialism and neocolonialism. It is a film filled with passion but based on historical fact.

Critical response, especially in the United States was mixed. *Variety* (October 21, 1970) wrote:

Indeed, the presence of Marlon Brando is the major fault although other casting is almost as ineffective. . . . Gillo Pontecorro . . . here has mishandled what is, at least, a generally professional cast. Even Evaristo Marquez, touted during production as a previously untrained and untried find, is impressive only physically. . . . Pontecorro, who seems to like filming revolutionary movements in countries other than his own, has come up with a fictionalized version of one of Gualtiero J. Copetti's documentaries.

The *Los Angeles Herald-Examiner* (December 18, 1970) commented:

"Burn" is a film to gaze and brood over. It is a film about idealism fractured by doubts, truth smeared by heroics. It is a film about freedom and inquisition, politics, economics, power and faith. . . . Brando has soured the plumminess of the voice he used in "Mutiny on the Bounty." It matches well the pain of indifference, the knowledge of lack of understanding which dwells within Walker. He rivets our attention with the ache of his poise. . . . Evaristo Marquez has great presence . . . yet he can only really symbolize the man struggling to make himself worthy of the myth which he knows will wing wide from his gallows.

The *Los Angeles Times* (December 16, 1970) wrote:

A remarkable movie that not only boasts one of Brando's finest performances but also marks Pontecorro's growth as an artist. . . . Brando draws upon his formidable combination of intellect and virility to create a man who has the kind of lofty sagacity that gives him his potential for tragedy.

Duck, You Sucker (1972, United Artists)

Sergio Leone's *Duck, You Sucker,* set during the Mexican Revolution, propagated all the stereotypes and historical revisions first employed by *Viva Villa!* (1934). The passage of almost forty years attested to Hollywood's inertia to change.

The film is set in Mexico in 1914, chronicling the activities of a Mexican bandit, Juan Miranda (Rod Steiger), his aged father, and six crude and repulsive sons. Juan encounters Sean Mallory (James Coburn), a fugitive Irish revolutionary who suffers with recurring memories of the struggle in his homeland. Sean possesses uncanny skills for explosives, and Juan convinces him to join him in robbing a supposedly unpenetrable bank vault. At the city where the bank is located, they meet a group of revolutionary conspirators planning to take over the city. They join their efforts in attacking the bank. The bank turns out to be full of prisoners, and Juan becomes a revolutionary hero. Juan, Sean, and their followers subsequently blow up a bridge and decimate one of Huerta's battalions. The treachery of one revolutionary, Dr. Villega (Romolo Valli), results in the murder of a dozen urban revolutionaries and the capture of Juan. Juan and Sean uncover the traitor and then lead a train loaded with dynamite into the enemy camp. Sean is killed in the ensuing battle.

The film perpetuates only two types of Mexicans: the old landed aristocracy, who are snobby, arrogant, greedy, and decadent, and the peasantry, who are cruel, violence-prone, promiscuous, and destructive. The role of Juan Miranda is the Hollywood prototype of the Mexican bandit and ranks up with the most racist and pathetic stereotypes, such as those of Pancho Villa in *Viva Villa!* (1934), Calvera in *The Magnificent Seven* (1960), Juan Carrasco in *The Outrage* (1964), and Tuco in *The Good, the Bad and the Ugly* (1967). Predictably, Miranda is cruel, violent, and destructive. When Sean first meets him, Mallory states in incredulous surprise, "So, you can read!" Despite his sympathy for Pancho Villa's revolutionary cause, Miranda states, "My country is me and my family." Even after he has been thrust the mantle of leadership, he says, "I don't want to be a hero. All I want is the money." Once more a foreigner, in this case, an Irishman, possesses the unique technical skills to catapult the Mexican revolutionary forces to success. Rod Steiger's performance as Miranda is abysmal, replete with an accent as guttural in sound as a man drowning. Filmed in Italy, the geography is totally unconvincing.

Critical response was cool. The *Los Angeles Times* (June 29, 1972) wrote:

It stars Rod Steiger as a Sancho Panza–like Mexican bandit with James Coburn as his Don Quixotê, a disillusioned Irish terrorist turned silver prospector, who get caught up in the revolution. . . . Because Leone deliberately exaggerates everything with such consistency and imagination he creates a pathetic fallacy that is at once poignant and amusing.

Time (March 31, 1972) stated:

The best thing about Sergio Leone's movies is their charming and infectious childishness. So gaudy that they seem to have been splashed across the screen with finger paints, so wildly illogical and improbably giant toyboy and the plots from comic books. . . . The result of all this is diverting but far from consistent, even in its craziness. There are frequent longueurs and too many conversations about the meaning of revolution that are stupid even by Leone's standards.

Joe Kidd (1972, Universal)

The Western *Joe Kidd* perpetuated the stereotype of Chicanos as ideological disciples incapable of determining their own destiny.

Directed by John Sturges, who had made the grossly stereotyped *The Magnificent Seven* (1960), *Joe Kidd* is set in Sinola, New Mexico, in 1900. Luis Chama (John Saxon) is a Mexican-American leader who protests the dispossession of his people's land by rich Anglo cattlemen. The Spanish land grants are disregarded, and the Chicano families are driven out. A gunfighter, Joe Kidd (Clint Eastwood), rescues the prejudiced judge (John Carter) from being kidnapped by Chama and his followers. An Anglo posse is formed, led by a racist rancher, Frank Harlan (Robert Duvall), but Kidd refuses to side with him until his small ranch is raided. At this juncture, Kidd joins the posse and captures one of the leaders, Helen Sanchez (Stella Garcia), and several followers. The posse threatens to kill five of them if Chama does not surrender. Kidd and Helen fall for each other (rather unconvincingly in light of the circumstances). Kidd begins to feel Harlan is too extreme. Imprisoned by Harlan, he escapes and frees Helen and the others. Helen and Kidd make their way to Chama, who is uncaring about the murder of the hostages and appears to be more concerned with his glory. Kidd captures Chama, takes him back to Sheriff Mitchell (Gregory Walcott), and rides off with Helen.

The story is obviously patterned after the real-life struggle of Chicanos/Mexicanos to have their Spanish land grants recognized by U.S. courts. The Luis Chama character is patterned (in a distorted manner) after Reies Lopez Tijerina, who had organized Alianza de los Pueblos Libres (Alliance of Free City-States) in 1963, in New Mexico, to recover land taken from Chicanos/Mexicanos. A raid on a courthouse resulted in a massive manhunt for his followers. The real-life Tijerina became a Chicano hero, but continued government harassment resulted in several years in prison. In the film, the Luis Chama character perpetuates the supposition that Chicanos/Mexicanos cannot develop leaders loyal to the cause of justice and thereby Anglo ideological messiahs are necessary to expose these misleaders. The film also repeats the proverbial Hollywood convention of the Latina (in this case an activist one) abandoning her Latino lover for the Anglo hero. Here, one is expected to believe that Helen Sanchez turns her back on her man and her people's cause for Kidd, who is a member of a racist posse that has imprisoned her.

While Puerto Rican John Saxon imbued Luis Chama with ethnicity and fire of passion, it is Stella Garcia, in the flawed written role of Helen, who gives the film's outstanding performance. The *Los Angeles Times* (July 19, 1972) wrote:

Set in New Mexico, it forthrightly depicts injustices to Mexican-Americans, which strikes a note of contemporary awareness without seeming to strain for relevance. . . . Stella Garcia stands out as Chama's spirited aide.

The *Los Angeles Herald-Examiner* (July 20, 1972) commented:

Ultimately Kidd comes to sympathize with the cause of the Mexicans in a property squabble. Well that's not quite true. Essentially

178

Kidd doesn't really give a damn one way or the other, but gets more perverse satisfaction backing the underdog and coming out tops. . . . Stella Garcia and Lynn Marta are the ladies who as usual in such movies get little more attention than a quick fumble or a swift leer when they get in the way.

Raices de Sangre/Roots of Blood (1974)

Jesus Salvador Treviño *Raices de Sangre* was the first film to explore the common economic destinies of Chicanos and Mexicanos. It stands also as the only Mexican-financed film ever written and directed by a Chicano.

The film tells the story of a Harvard-educated Chicano lawyer, Carlos Rivera (Richard Yniguez), who returns to his hometown of Socorro, Texas, located along the border of Mexico, and works one summer for the Barrio Unido Community Center. Rivera is reluctantly involved in the center's efforts to organize the workers on both sides of the border in one *maquinadora* (U.S.-owned plant on the Mexican side of the border) and in a factory owned by a multinational corporation. Lupe (Roxano Bonillo-Guianini), an activist, and Rivera's boyhood friend Juan (Pepe Serna) are instrumental in making Rivera understand the socioeconomic conditions that demand political activism.

In Mexico, Roman Carvajal (Ernesto Gomez Cruz) is fired from the garment *maquinadora* for bucking the company union. Hilda Gutierrez (Malena Doria) and Rosamaria Mejia (Adriana Rojo) organize the women workers in conjunction with Juan and the Barrio Unido's efforts. At a rally in Socorro, the police attack those peacefully assembled (a re-creation of the 1970 East Los Angeles Chicano Moratorium, a nonviolent anti–Vietnam War demonstration that resulted in several deaths, including that of journalist Ruben Salazar). Juan is wounded and later dies as a result. Mexican and Chicano workers hold a candlelight march along the border fence to commemorate Juan. From the Mexican side, Carvajal cries, "Que viva la raza!" From the U.S. side, Rivera responds with, "Que viva la raza unida!"

The film was financed by Conacine, a Mexican government corporation responsible for energizing the national film industry in the 1970s. Director Jesus S. Treviño stated:

I made "Raices de Sangre" to examine the question of who the Chicano is and who the Mexican is. . . . As I got more into the subject matter, I began to realize that a film like "Raices de Sangre" could not only explain the Chicano reality to the Mexicans but could also explain the Mexican reality to Chicanos.[9]

The film explored the diversity within the movement for change: the uncertainty of some, the ignorance of others, and the fear of still others. It documented the machinations of multinationals at the expense of underpaid and overworked workers and the impact of the border upon culture and language and the commonality of history. Treviño said:

I'm hoping that English-speaking people in this country will be able to see the film and learn something from it. When American tourists go to Mexico and see all the poverty, which is especially out of proportion in border towns like Tijuana, they wonder, why all these poor people? They don't realize that many economic factors that originate here in the U.S. cause it. In fact, the decisions made in American boardrooms have a direct effect on the life of the Mexican, which is often that he cannot feed his children.[10]

The film was shot in Mexicali, Mexico, and the scenes of the U.S.-owned garment factory in an abandoned Mattel Toy factory, which itself had moved to the cheaper labor area of Taiwan after real-life workers had organized in order to demand higher pay. The film was released with Spanish and English subtitles. It was released in Mexico in 1976 to excellent commercial and critical reception. Subsequently, it was released in the United States in 1979.

The *Los Angeles Times* (June 3, 1970) commented:

"Raices de Sangre" is an ambitious film that dramatizes the plight of Chicanos and Mexicans who are subjected to economic exploitation on both sides of the U.S.-Mexican border.

Variety (June 4, 1979) wrote:

A solidly made call to political involvement and activism which effectively points up the problems of Mexicans on the border in very human terms. . . . Writer-director Jesus Treviño stages that action simply and forcefully. . . . Richard Yniguez is significantly more effective here than he was earlier this year in "Boulevard Nights". . . . Remainder of the cast is uniformly earnest and strong. Neo-realist and Third World cinema often seems somewhat remote from American concerns, but "Raices de Sangre," through its evenhanded considered polemics and sheer proximity, brings another culture's problems a lot closer to home.

State of Siege (1973, Columbia/Cinema 5)

Costa-Gavras' *State of Siege* was deemed controversial in some quarters. This logically emanated from the deeply political, historically based, and uncompromised presentation of contemporary Latin America.

Greek-born director Constantin Costa-Gavras was already established as a progressive filmmaker by the time *State of Siege* was made. He had acquired international recognition with the political thriller *Z* (1969), a powerful indictment of the repressive Greek military junta, and *The Confession* (1970), which chronicled the political excesses in Czechoslovakia.

Costa-Gavras has stated:

The cinema has never, or rarely, or insufficiently, tackled the reasons that are behind hunger or war. That's what the political film is trying to do today—define these causes and reasons. In my view, the cinema is a way of showing, exposing the political processes in our everyday life. . . . [11]

With regard to why he made the film, he said, "We wanted to make a film that would influence the viewing public never again to see an American embassy as a simple embassy, but as an espionage center, a control center, a political pressure group."[12] The film was shot in Chile while President Allende was still in power (he would subsequently be overthrown and assassinated in a U.S.-sponsored military coup in 1973). Costa-Gavras explained the reason for the film's location site:

For two essential reasons. First of all, because it was absolutely necessary to shoot the film in Latin America, and Chile is the only country where there is freedom, almost complete freedom without any problems of censorship or pre-censorship. And then, because this country's cinematic set-up permitted us to shoot a film of this importance."[13]

The film was a coproduction of the United States, France, Italy, and Germany.

Screenwriter Franco Solinas, who had cowritten *The Battle of Algiers* (1966) and *Burn* (1970), stated:

I write scenarios which generally deal with political themes because in my opinion politics is a fundamental matter. I'm not interested in psychological stories; I have no use for literature in the traditional sense. . . . Politics gets to the bottom of problems, then it is the most important and necessary subject of our time. Politics gets to the bottom of problems, doing it through real events and not by playing on the emotions. . . . [14]

The film was a reenactment of the historical Daniel Mitrone, who had worked for the U.S. Agency for International Development (AID), which among other goals had as a priority the training and assisting of Latin American military and police forces. Information released after Mitrone's death revealed his involvement in Uruguay's right-wing regime as an anti-insurgency expert and adviser on torture and political assassination (in league with death squads).

The film begins in the 1970s in a South American capital (Montevideo, Uruguay) with the search-in-process for Philip Michael Santore (Yves Montand), who has been kidnapped by the Tupamaros (named after Tupac Amaro, one of the last Inca kings to resist the Spanish conquest). Santore's dead body is found in a car, and after a funeral sequence, the film flashbacks to chronicle how this political act has brought the right-wing regime to a crisis.

Mitrone was abducted several days earlier and, in a secret location, is interrogated. Gradually, the guerrillas present proof that Mitrone had worked closely through the AID to overthrow the democratically elected President Bosch in the Dominican Republic in 1965 and the Goulert government in Brazil. In the meantime, a flurry of negotiations takes place. One of Santore's close friends, the zealous Captain Lopez (Renato Salvatori), conducts extensive operations to find the guerrillas. One elderly journalist (O. E. Hasse) is a sort of "everyman," through whose efforts the various layers of government deception and crisis are observed. In the Congress, as the functions of Santore are gradually made public, discussion is focused on "this deluge, this mob of do-good Americans." The Tupamaros offer the release of Santore in exchange for 150 political prisoners.

Eventually, the guerrillas confront Santore about complicity with the apparatus of government to abduct, torture, and murder political dissidents. Santore admits some things. One guerrilla leader, Hugo (Jacques Weber), tells him, "You say you're defending freedom and democracy. . . . Your methods are war, fascism, and torture. . . . Surely you agree with me, Mr. Santore?" Finally, exasperated and frustrated, Santore lashes out, "You are subversives, Communists. You want to destroy the foundations of society, the fundamental values of our Christian civilization, the very existence of the free world. You are an enemy who must be fought in every possible way." Hugo tells him, "I don't think we have anything more to say to each other." Santore responds, "I don't either."

The government manages to arrest Hugo and some of the other Tupamaro leaders, and this makes them less reluctant to negotiate. Realizing this impasse, the guerrillas vote on whether to permit Santore to live. Their inability to follow through with their threat will exhibit weakness for their cause and organization. Days after Santore's body is found, another AID man arrives attached to the embassy. He is watched closely by people, possibly Tupamaros, who know what he represents.

State of Siege is a long way from *Viva Villa!* The former documents the historical context of contemporary Latin American reality, while the latter distorts and deforms history. The Tupamaro guerrilla leader Hugo and journalist Carlos Ducas are light years far removed from the one-dimensional Latin lovers, Wallace Beery's illiterate barbarian and baffoon Pancho Villa, or the submissive Don Arturo Bodega. The main objective to the film raised was the alleged glorification of political assassination and the Tupamaro guerrillas. But then, Hollywood had always glorified Manifest Destiny and the wholesale dispossession of land from Indians and Mexicans and the Social Darwinistic hegemony over Latin America. The dubious exploits of Davy Crockett, Jim Bowie, and Kit Carson and "gunboat diplomacy" had been dutifully glorified for almost a century in literature and film. Obviously, characters such as Hugo and Carlos Ducas posed a greater threat than Latin lovers, caricature bandits, or submissive ideological disciples to the sensitivities of Social Darwinists for they are characters that represent cultural and political independence, possessing a desire for self-determination. Female characters, although relatively less important than the male characters, are equally three-dimensional and are shown with the capacity for leadership, strength, and conviction. In conclusion, the film proved unnerving to some because it showed the harsh economic and political reality of Latin America, an image that had always been distorted or romanticized to fit the dream factory of Hollywood.

Critical response was generally positive. The *Los Angeles Times* (May 16, 1973) wrote:

> "State of Siege" is a strong, disturbing and notably competent film . . . a tract, but a cold and skillful tract with expert performances by a large cast. . . . Notable supporting roles include Renato Salvatori as a police captain, Jean-Luc Bideau and Jacques Weber as rebel leaders. . . .

The *Los Angeles Herald-Examiner* (May 19, 1973) commented:

> The film is documentary in tone, harsh but unflamboyant in both its visual and verbal statements. . . . The actors are kept deliberately low-key so that even such a star as Yves Montand is barely recognizable, displaying no qualities which might remind us that he has ever been featured anywhere else before. Denied gloss and gimmick, playing characters with no private lives and only political emotions, the actors triumphantly manage to create fully realized individuals. . . .

The *New York Daily News* stated: "A powder keg film, enormously forceful, vitally important." The conservative *Wall Street*

Journal wrote, "Masterful film. It treats its audience with respect. It has a complex and brilliant narrative structure. It is great art." *Cosmopolitan* referred to it as "a powder keg of dynamite. The most important political film of this decade."

Two Mules for Sister Sara (1970, Universal)

Two Mules for Sister Sara, along with *The Professionals,* perpetuated and celebrated the mythical prowess of Anglo filibusters in Mexico and their ability to single-handedly alter the course of history.

The initial screenplay was written by the always evocative Budd Boetticher, who at one point was slated to direct. However, after several script changes (the last credited to Albert Malz, one of the Hollywood Ten), the independent-minded Boetticher was replaced by Don Siegel. Siegel would subsequently direct Clint Eastwood in four other films. The additional talents of the noted Mexican cinematographer Gabriel Figueroa and the Leone-Eastwood spaghetti Western music composer Ennio Morricone were recruited. Elizabeth Taylor had originally been considered for Sister Sara, but extravagant salary demands were rejected. Shirley MacLaine took over the role. Clint Eastwood would state, "The film is really a two-character story, and the woman has the best part—something I'm sure Shirley noticed. It's a kind of 'African Queen' gone West."[15] The film was shot on location in Cocoyoc, Mexico.

Hogan (Clint Eastwood) is a soldier of fortune hired by the Juarista forces to fight against the French Occupation forces (1861–66). He runs across Sister Sara (Shirley MacLaine), who is about to be raped, and rescues her. He accompanies her to the Juarista camp. On the way he attempts to dynamite a French train with ammunition, but is wounded by a Yaqui Indian. Sara removes the bullet and bandages and subsequently helps him blow up the train. Upon their arrival at the camp, she reveals that she has detailed information on the layout of a French fort. Colonel Beltran (Manolo Frabegas) confers with Hogan about strategy. A plan is devised by the group. With the gate opened, the Mexican guerrillas and, with Hogan's prolific use of dynamite, the French are defeated. Sara reveals to the suspecting Hogan that she is a former prostitute. They make love, acquire some of the loot, and ride off.

Two Mules for Sister Sara is a personable and well-crafted film but a deceptive one. Hogan carries with him an unabashed sense of superiority. When Sara asks him if he has any sympathy for Juarista's cause he replies, "Not theirs or anybody else's." When he arrives to meet a contact at a village on the fourteenth, he complains with typical Hollywood assumption of Mexican idleness that his contact will not be there until the next day. Later, at the Juarista camp, he complains disparagingly to Colonel Beltran about his military capabilities, "Less than a hundred rifles, a few machetes and not much more. Even drunk, the French are going to blow your heads off!" Before attacking the fort, Beltran rebukes him on his arrogant carelessness, "I have my mind on my men, all you have in your mind is money." The film additionally promotes the belief that, but for Hogan's superior skills, the Juáristas are incapable of defeating the French. Historical facts disprove this as the Mexican people defeated the highly regarded French army without Anglo military advisers.

Reviews were mixed, but the film was a commercial success. The *Los Angeles Herald-Examiner* (July 15, 1970) wrote:

> A solidly entertaining film that provides Clint Eastwood with his best, most substantial role to date. . . . Greed is his primary motivating force. But always, in the end, he does the right thing—if for the wrong reasons. . . . Miss MacLaine is a good counterpart. . . . The cinematography of Gabriel Figueroa stunningly captures the barrenness and the heat of the desert. . . .

The *Los Angeles Times* (July 15, 1970) commented:

> With his admirably hard, clean style—the movie for the most part is well-staged against stunning rugged locales—Siegel is also adept at getting the widest range and variation out of Eastwood. . . .

The Players

The decade saw a significant decline in the number of Chicano/Hispanic players in Hollywood films. Several political, economic, and social factors account for this.

First, Hollywood continued with a myopic perception that prevented it from acknowledging the Chicano/Hispanic population as a viable film market, as it had acknowledged the Black community. In the latter, the Black exploitation films had developed, and although the films never achieved expectations and potential, they provided a tangible opportunity for Blacks to enter the film industry in various capacities. Second, the decline of the civil rights movement as a cohesive force and the federal government's abandonment of a commitment to affirmative action and equality provided the film industry with a convenient device to provide only token changes or simply to perpetuate its historical continuity. Third, the economic recession and inflation gave vent to the pervasive jingoism that had always been present just below the surface of this society. The simplistic accusation that Mexicans were "stealing" jobs and the vulnerability of the industrialized West in its dependency on foreign oil resulted in antiforeign feeling, of which the Mexican was the most visible victim. Thus, Mexicans once more become convenient villains and objects of derision. Fourth, Hispanic roles which were usually in Westerns, virtually disappeared as a result of the decline of the genre in American cinema and the advent of the foreign-made spaghetti Westerns.

The decade provided only one bonafide Chicano film star in Cheech Marin. Marin, part of the Cheech and Chong comedy duo, had acquired a significant cult following in clubs and albums by the time the team had made its successful film debut in *Up in Smoke* (1978, Paramount). Their other film efforts would prove to be equally commercially successful. The popular Mexican action star Jorge Rivero was imported to costar in one film, Howard Hawk's *Rio Lobo* (1970). Richard Ynguinez, a talented Chicano actor, appeared to have a promising career after *Boulevard Nights* (1979), but thereafter, predictably languished in inconsequential films and television. Teatre Campesino alumnus actor-singer-writer Daniel Valdez made his film debut in *Which Way Is Up?* (1977) but would have to wait for another film to fully blossom on film, in *Zoot Suit* (1981). Journeymen Chicano actors Pepe Serna and Henry Darrow, among others, worked regularly on film and television, never quite receiving the merited opportunities.

Hollywood's continued obsession with Latinas as sexual and exotic dark ladies resulted in the importation of established Mexican film stars Isela Vega and Ofelia Medina and Nicaraguan model Barbara Carrerra. The attractive and extremely popular Isela Vega starred to good advantage in three U.S. films: *Bring Me the Head of Alfredo Garcia* (1974), *Drum* (1976), and *Barbarosa* (1982). Unfortunately, her age (late thirties, an anathema in Hollywood especially in relation to women) and her desire to retire prevented her from consolidating her English-language film career. Ofelia Medina, a rising film and television actress, made an impressive U.S. film debut in the stylish *The Big Fix* (1978), but thereafter, no other roles developed. The third, Barbara Carrerra, made her film debut as a Chicana señorita in the offbeat *The Master Gunfighter* (1975) and thereafter was typecast as a dark lady of seduction in a career that, although not spectacular, has been durable and significant. Chicana actress Stella Garcia made impressive impact in a pair of films, Dennis Hopper's *The Last Movie* (1971) and then opposite Clint Eastwood as a strong-willed Chicana in *Joe Kidd* (1972), but quickly thereafter faded into obscurity.

Notes

1. Rodolfo Acuña, *Occupied America* (New York: Harper & Row, 1988).
2. Robyn Karney, ed., *The Movie Stars Story* (London: Crescent Books, 1984).
3. *Los Angeles Times,* April 12, 1981.
4. *Los Angeles Times,* March 23, 1979.
5. *Los Angeles Times,* April 12, 1981.
6. *Los Angeles Times,* March 17, 1979.
7. Tony Thomas, *The Films of Marlon Brando* (Secaucus, N.J.: Citadel Press, 1973).
8. Ibid.
9. *Los Angeles Times,* June 3, 1979.
10. Ibid.
11. Franco Solinas, *Screenplay-State of Siege* (New York: Ballantine Books, 1973).
12. *Los Angeles Times,* April 22, 1973.
13. Ibid.
14. Ibid.
15. *Los Angeles Times,* June 22, 1969.

CHAPTER EIGHT
The 1980s—the Decade of the Hispanic?

The decade that began with the gunboat theatrics of the Reagan administration ended with a historical thaw of United States–Soviet Union relations. Domestically, the changing demographics influenced some policy makers to deem it the decade of the Hispanic.

The decade began precipitously with the U.S.-orchestrated boycott of the Moscow Olympics in response to the continued Soviet troop presence in Afghanistan. The incoming Reagan administration waged an eight-year covert war against Nicaragua and a more overt one in El Salvador and reverted to the morally bankrupt policy of gunboat diplomacy with Reagan's invasion of Grenada. The lack of popular support for such abrasive policies induced obsessed cold warriors to establish a clandestine dual government apparatus that resulted in the Iran-Contra scandal and a constitutional crisis. In the Middle East, the Palestinian question continued to be unresolved. Europe moved closer to a unified economy, and Japan became the third most important industrial nation. In the latter part of the decade, the emergence of a new Soviet leader, Mikhail Gorbachev, and his politics caused unprecedented and historical political and economic changes across the world.

In the United States, the increased migration of Central American refugees fleeing their countries' repressive regimes and Mexican workers departing from an economy unable to absorb them further intensified nativism and jingoism. Acuña notes that "ex-CIA director William Colby had stated in 1978 that Mexican migration represented a greater threat to the United States than the Soviet Union."[1] Moreover, the Reagan administration's insensitivity to continued racism in the nation set the stage for a climate of increased racial incidents, a growth of right-wing extremist groups, such as the Ku Klux Klan, and a proliferation of greedy and self-righteous demagogue evangelists who appealed to the always latent xenophobia. In California, in 1986, an "English Is the Official Language" proposition was passed. Mexicans and Latin Americans continued to be accused of "stealing jobs," while paying taxes and benefiting minimally from social services.

In political and economic terms, the 1980s were not the decade of the Hispanic. However, they were the beginning of positive long-term changes. During the 1970s, the population of Hispanics grew from nine million to some fourteen million, an increase of some 61 percent, in comparison to 9 percent for non-Hispanics. The continuation of such a demographic trend indicates that Hispanics, by the year 2000, will become this nation's largest minority, and some 60 percent of these will be Chicanos or Mexican-Americans. Such a historical event symbolizes that in the foreseeable future the indigenous mestizos of the Southwest will be in a position to regain their cultural, political, and economic ascent. Other factors may prove instrumental to shaping the future political agenda of Chicanos especially. According to Acuña:

> In 1980 in California, the median age of Mexican-Americans was under 22; by the year 2000, the median age would be about 26. The majority of white North Americans were over 30 years in 1980, and, by the turn of the century, the majority would be over 35. The graying of "America" in all probability will result in a greater reluctance on the part of society to pay for education, a policy change that would greatly affect Chicanos.[2]

It remains to be seen whether the future demographic advantage of the Chicano/Hispanic will be transcended into an equally historic attainment of equality and justice at long last.

The Films

The 1980s finally saw the acknowledgement by Hollywood of the rapidly growing and viable Chicano/Hispanic market. In addition to becoming more prominent because of this realization, Latin Americans became an omnipresent image in the mass communications media, as a result of the Reagan administration's interventionist policy in Latin America, in Grenada, Nicaragua, and El Salvador. This sudden and benevolent interest in Latinos was sparked by the spectre of revolution. This in turn motivated the Hollywood film industry liberals and conservatives to sprinkle their casts with more Hispanic players and to finance films that finally began addressing Chicano/Hispanic history, culture, and issues. The latter was an event that was unprecedented in Hollywood.

The film industry underwent a major transition during the decade. The advent of video cassettes brought a technological and economic revolution to films. The invention, which was introduced early in the decade, quickly blossomed, and by the end of the decade, accounted for some 80 percent of film receipts. Cable television was another development that contributed to film revenues. Ultimately, both video and cable television undermined regular television, as the latter had previously done to motion pictures. Revenues from foreign markets markedly increased because of a renewed popularity of U.S. films and the faltering of movie industries abroad, especially in Mexico and Latin America. While the film maxim that "movies are better than ever" was not necessarily valid, American films of the decade were full of technological marvels and special effects with which foreign films could not compete.

By middecade, six studios accounted for almost 90 percent of domestic receipts. Two new important studios emerged, Orion Pictures and Tri-Star Pictures, both administered by displaced studio personnel. By 1986, they accounted for some 24 percent of features produced. The old studios were now permanently under the ownership of vast conglomerates. Finler noted: "The problems experienced by Fox and MGM/UA and changes in ownership of both, meant that the share of the six majors fell to an all-time low of only 64% in 1986. . . . "[3]

Film fare in the 1980s leaned heavily toward an endless array of repetitive sequels: *Rocky III, Return of the Jedi, Rambo III, Jaws II,* and so forth. Technological wizardry was another staple in which Hollywood overindulged. A few mainstream

191

films had enduring worth: *Ordinary People* (1980, Paramount), *Raging Bull,* (1980, United Artists), *Reds* (1981, Paramount), *Gandhi* (1982, Columbia), *Sophie's Choice* (1982, Universal), *Terms of Endearment* (1983, Paramount), *Amadeus* (1984), *Wall Street* (1987, Woth), *Fatal Attraction* (1987, Paramount), and *Running on Empty* (1989, Warner Brothers). The star system, the last vestige of the old Hollywood, continued to disintegrate as film newcomers appeared and then floundered rapidly. Most of the old guard stars and directors who had come upon the scene in the 1930s and 1940s passed away from the scene: George Raft, Duncan Renaldo, Mae West, Raoul Walsh, in 1980; Melvyn Douglas, Allan Dwan, Gloria Grahame, Ann Harding, William Holden, Robert Montgomery, Natalie Wood, William Wyler, in 1981; Ingrid Bergman, Henry Fonda, Henry King, Fernando Lamas, Eleanor Powell, King Vidor, in 1982; Luis Buñuel, George Cukor, Dolores Del Rio, David Niven, Pat O'Brien, Gloria Swanson, in 1983; Richard Burton, Jackie Coogan, Janet Gaynor, Carl Foreman, James Mason, Walter Pidgeon, William Powell, in 1984; Anne Baxter, Henry Hathaway, Margo, Orson Welles, in 1985; James Cagney, Emilio Fernandez, Cary Grant, Ray Milland, Vicente Minelli, Donna Reed, in 1986; Fred Astaire, Madeleine Carroll, Rita Hayworth, John Huston, Danny Kaye, Mervyn LeRoy, Robert Preston, Randolph Scott, Raquel Torres, in 1987; John Houseman, Trevor Howard, in 1988. The passing of these unique talents left the Hollywood film industry more artistically impoverished.

A diverse Chicano/Hispanic image was presented in four recognizable types of films: (1) mainstream features; (2) narcotraficante films, (3) xenophobia/revenge films, and (4) an emerging body of work classified as Chicano/Hispanic films.

Mainstream films of the decade often had Hispanic cast members, but, predictably, in incidental roles as characters who were at times less than role models. In *9 to 5* (1980, 20th Century), Roxana Bodilla was a secretary; in *Fort Apache, the Bronx* (1981, 20th Century), Rachel Ticotin was a Puerto Rican nurse who was a junky; in *Back Roads* (1981, Warner Brothers), Miriam Colon was a Chicana madam; in *Whose Life Is It Anyway* (1981, MGM), Alba Omsas was a benevolent nurse; in *S.O.B.* (1981, Paramount), Bert Rosario played an ignorant Mexican gardener unable to recognize his employer's attempt at suicide; in *Death Wish II* (1982, Filmways), Silvana Gallardo played a domestic raped and murdered; in *One from the Heart* (1982, Columbia), Raul Julia was a sleazy Latino gigolo; in *The Last American Virgin* (1982, Cannon), Louisa Moviz was a sex-starved older Hispanic woman catering to white teenagers; in *Bad Boys* (1983, Universal), Esai Morales was a vicious Puerto Rican hoodlum; in *Stick* (1985, Universal), playwright-turned-actor José Perez was an inept cop who gets himself killed; in *Down and Out in Beverly Hills* (1986, Touchstone), Elizabeth Peña was a promiscuous Mexican domestic; in *Colors* (1982, Orion), Trinidad Silva was a violence-prone *cholo;* in *Tequila Sunrise* (1988, Warner Brothers), Raul Julia was a Mexican cop involved in drug smuggling, and in *Moon Over Parador* (1988, Universal), Julia was a proverbial corrupt and brutal Latin American general; in *Lust in the Dust* (1985, New World), Lanie Kazan played a Mexican cantinera. Hollywood belatedly began to chronicle the Vietnam War in films, in which each featured a bit part for a Chicano soldier: in *Platoon* (1986, Orion), this soldier was played by Francisco Quinn (Anthony's son); and in *Full Metal Jacket* (1987, Warner Brothers), played by Sal Lopez. Other mainstream films that had Chicano/Hispanic roles were *Zorro, the Gay Blade* (1980, 20th Century), with George Hamilton as the title character; *Stir Crazy* (1980, Columbia), with Karmin Murcelo; *Seems Like Old Times* (1980, Columbia), with Dolores Aquirre; *Barbarosa* (1982, Universal), with Isela Vega, Gilbert Roland, and Alma Martinez; *Heartbreaker* (1983, Monorex), with Fernando Allende; *Paris, Texas* (1984, 20th Century), with Socorro Valdez; *Let's Get Harry* (1986, Tri-Star), with Elipidio Carrillo; *The Penitent* (1988, Cineworld), with Raul Julia; and *An Officer and a Gentleman* (1982, Paramount), with Tony Plana.

A second type of film, the xenophobia/get even films were directly influenced by the historically revisionist *Rambo* (Sylvester Stallone) and *Missing in Action* (Chuck Norris), inane adventure fantasies in which both characters win the lost Vietnam War. Motivated by simplistic self-righteousness and cold-war fanaticism, these lone avengers convert themselves into missionaries of Social Darwinism and Manifest Destiny. These films returned to the worst of the racist stereotypes, specifically about

Chicanos and Latin Americans. In *The Kidnapping of the President* (1980, Crow International), Latin American guerrillas fighting right-wing military dictatorship take the U.S. president hostage. In *Lone Wolf McQuade* (1983, Orion), Chuck Norris plays a lone Texas Ranger who single-handedly thwarts a gang of gunrunners stealing U.S. Army arms and selling them to Central American guerrillas. In *Last Plane Out* (1983, New World), Nicaraguan dictator Anastacio Somoza is portrayed as a "good ol' boy" and befriended by another "good ol' boy" (Jan Michael Vincent). In *Red Dawn* (1984, MGM), the United States is invaded by ruthless and violence-prone Nicaraguan, Cuban, and Soviet paratroopers, and the scenario is similar in *Invasion U.S.A.* (Cannon), in which Chuck Norris is once more another messianic one-man army. In *Heartbreak Ridge* (1986, Warner Brothers), a broken-down cold warrior (Clint Eastwood) leads a group of inner-city recruits into a glorious invasion of Grenada.

The third type of film image that proliferated about Chicanos/Hispanics was that of the narco trafficker. The fact that this nation had become the number one consumer of illegal drugs was obligatorily ignored, and, according to one interview given by Chuck Norris, he claimed that it was really the Russian KGB that was involved in the smuggling of drugs into the United States. Additionally, the media's increasing coverage of the drug scourge resulted in the search for convenient villains, instead of the methods of prevention. Chicanos and Hispanics became the convenient suspects and malefactors, who were perceived as evil foreigners attempting to undermine the moral fiber of the nation. The Latino stereotype as a narcotraficante was on display in *High Risk* (1981, AC), *Vice Squad* (1982, Avco), *Scarface* (1983, Universal), *Romancing the Stone* (1984, 20th Century), *Code of Silence* (1985, Orion), *Cocaine Wars* (1985, Concord), *Firewalker* (1986, Canon), *Above the Law* (1988, Warner Brothers), and *Crocodile Dundee II* (1988, Paramount), among others. The old Mexican *bandido* stereotype was resurrected for *The Three Amigos* (1986, Orion), in which three Anglo film stars (Chevy Chase, Steve Martin, Martin Short) go to Mexico to protect helpless Mexican peasants from a gang of despicable Mexican bandidos (Alfonso Arau, Tony Plana).

Finally, the emergence of films addressing the social concerns, history, and cultural milieu of Chicanos/Hispanics during the 1980s came to fruition after fifty years of gradual evolution. The Hollywood Spanish-language films of the 1930s had established a precedent for the economic considerations of the Chicano/Hispanic market, while the premature Chicano cinema of the early 1950s had been a conscious attempt to dispel the myths of the "melting pot" and the flaws of the American Dream. The first Chicano movement film, *I Am Joaquin* (1967) and other documentaries, such as Jesus Treviño's *Yo Soy Chicano* (1973), were important in defining the cultural and historical consciousness of Chicanos and Mexicanos. Treviño would later direct the first Chicano-Mexican coproduction, *Raices de Sangre* (1979).

In the meantime, two other Hispanic cinemas had begun to develop: the Puerto Rican and Cuban-exile cinemas. The former had begun in 1912, in the silent era, and had continued with the first Puerto Rican sound film, *Romance Tropical* (1934). Thereafter, some independent filmmakers addressed critically the relationship of Puerto Rico with the United States. The divergent Cuban-exile cinema had begun with *PM* (1969), a short film about the night life in old Havana, and culminated with *El Super* (1979), concerning a nostalgic Cuban superintendent who relocates in Miami from Queens, New York. Noriega advocates that:

Hispanic cinema must embrace—not negate—our differences, if we are to discover the cultural glue that holds us together. As Chicanos, for example, we have a double consciousness: one of ourselves and another of the dominant culture. But the idea of a Hispanic cinema holds out the possibility of a third consciousness; one, in fact, that makes "us" the majority in this hemisphere. . . . [4]

The breakthrough came when Luis Valdez wrote and directed *Zoot Suit* (1982, Universal), which chronicled the events of the Sleepy Lagoon and Zoot Suit riots in Los Angeles in 1943, which resulted in an international incident. The events were seen through the eyes of Henry Reina (Daniel Valdez) and a Faust-like pachuco (Edward James Olmos). Jesus Treviño's *Seguin* (1981, PBS) covered the Texas uprising against Mexico that

195

dispelled the benevolent myths of historical revision. *The Ballad of Gregorio Cortez* (1983, Embassy) depicted the turbulent life of Gregorio Cortez (Edward James Olmos), a Mexican farmer already immortalized in a corrido in the latter part of the nineteenth century in south Texas. Gregory Nava's *El Norte* (1984, Cinecom International/Island Aive) documented the trek of a Guatemalan brother and sister (Zaide Silvia Gutierrez, David Villapando) through Mexico and ultimately to the Los Angeles barrio. *Crossover Dreams* (1985, CF) presented, in an almost autobiographical manner, the desire of one Rudy Veloz (Panamanian Ruben Blades) to make a musical crossover into the elusive and mainstream American Dream. *Latino* (1986, Orion) examined the moral choices of Eddie Guerrero (Robert Beltran), a Chicano soldier training contras in Honduras to fight against people similar to his own. Luis Valdez's *La Bamba* (1987, Columbia) chronicled the short life of legendary Chicano rocker Ritchie Valens (Valenzuela). The Cheech Marin–directed and written *Born in East L.A.* (1987, Universal) depicted the plight faced by many Chicanos, that of being deported by the INS. *Stand and Deliver* (1988, Warner Brothers) documented the true story of Bolivian-born teacher Jaime Escalante (Edward James Olmos) working with East Los Angeles Chicano high school students. Finally, *Break of Dawn* (1988, Cinewest) depicted the true story of Pedro Gonzalez (Oscar Chavez), the first Spanish-speaking radio broadcaster in the 1930s. All the aforementioned films met with enthusiastic critical success, and most of them with commercial success as well.

Several other films addressed past and recent Latin American history effectively and intelligently. *The Mission* (1986, Warner Brothers) was a powerful indictment of the colonization of the Indians by the Spanish and Portuguese with the collusion of the Vatican. Chilean director Miguel Littin's *Alsino and the Condor* (1983, Libra/Cinema 5) humanized the victims of the U.S.-sponsored contra war in a way that the media never could. *Walker* (1987, Universal) chronicled the misdeed of the American filibuster William Walker (Ed Harris), who attempted to make Nicaragua a slave state. Costa-Gavras' *Missing* (1982, Universal) depicted the true story of Ed Horman (Jack Lemmon), whose son, Charles Horman (John Shea), was murdered by the U.S.-supported Pinochet military dictatorship. The Argentinian-made *The Official Story* (1985, Almi Pictures) chronicled the plight of families of the "disappeared" under the reign of the military dictatorship, as seen through the eyes of a disenchanted wife (Norma Aleandro) of an officer. *The Emerald Forest* (1985, 20th Century) examined the fate of Amazon Indians nearing extinction in light of deforestations. *Frida* (1988, New Yorker Films) documented the life story of Frida Kahlo (Ofelia Medina), the Mexican feminist painter. Robert Redford's *The Milagro Beanfield War* (1988, Universal) dealt with the efforts of a Chicano farmer (Chick Vennera) to keep his land when a conglomerate involved in agri-business encroaches on the land. *Romero* (1989, Four Seasons Entertainment/Vidmark) chronicled the efforts of Salvadorean Archbishop Romero (Raul Julia) to mediate the conflict for which he was subsequently assassinated by right-wing death squads.

Other films addressing similar concerns less effectively but with well-meaning urgency were also released. *Under Fire* (1983, Orion) depicted the emergence of the Nicaraguan Revolution, as witnessed by a trio of American journalists (Nick Nolte, Joanna Cassidy, Gene Hackman). *Salvador* (1986, Helmdale) explored the roots of the political conflict, as seen through the eyes of two down-and-out Americans (James Woods, Jim Belushi). Tony Richardson's *The Border* (1982, Universal) presented a sympathetic view of undocumented workers as victims at the hands of unscrupulous employers.

Additional films with Chicano/Hispanic backdrops included the mundane adaptation of Gabriel Garcia Marquez's short story, *Erendira* (1984, Miramex); the adaptation of Graham Greene's "The Honorary Consul," *Beyond the Limit* (1983, Paramount); *Kiss of the Spider Woman* (1985, Island Alive), which introduced the Brazilian star Sonia Braga to American audiences; the comedy *Blame It on Rio* (1984, 20th Century); the lackluster *Menudo* (1983, Embassy) and *Salsa* (1988, Vestron); and some Cheech and Chong entries: *Cheech and Chong's Next Movie* (1980, Universal), *Things Are Tough All Over* (1982, Columbia).

The following are some representative films of the decade.

Alsino and the Condor (1983, Libra Cinema 5)

Miguel Littin's *Alsino and the Condor* was Nicaragua's first feature film and an Oscar nominee for Best Foreign Film.

The film is a retelling of the Icarus myth, set in the stark realities of current-day Nicaragua. According to Greek legend, Icarus was the son of Daedalus, who, in escaping from imprisonment, falls into the sea, when, upon flying too close to the sun, his wings melt. The film is set during the waning months of the Somoza dictatorship (1979). Alsino (Alan Esquivel) is a twelve-year-old, who lives in the small town of San Telmo, with his grandmother (Carmen Bunster), whose husband had been a Dutch sailor. Alsino shares his dreams of flying like a bird with his friend Lucia (Marta Lorena Perez). The community's social fabric is destroyed when government forces led by a U.S. military adviser, Frank (Dean Stockwell), arrive in search of Sandinista guerrillas. Frank flies a helicopter named "Condor" and befriends Alsino, taking him on a ride in his flying machine. Initially, Alsino idealizes the crude but well-meaning flyer, but gradually becomes disenchanted with what he represents.

Still dreaming of flying, Alsino falls from a tree as he watches government military helicopters and cripples his back. Uprooted, he wanders through an odyssey at first, accompanying Don Nazario (Reinaldo Miravelle), an eccentric birdman. The journey becomes one of rediscovery of his country and himself.

The film was a coproduction by the Nicaraguan Film Institute, the Cuban Institute of Cinematographic Art and Industry, the Latin American Production of Mexico, and the Costa Rican Cinematographic Cooperative and was released in Spanish and English with English subtitles.

The film was directed and cowritten by Chilean exile Miguel Littin. He had attained renown with his first film, *El Chacal de Nahreltoro* (1970), based on a factual incident in Chile, in which a mass murderer was executed after society had rehabilitated him. Littin recalled the impact of that film: "It's a painful experience. I see it and I have the sensation that I'm not the director."[5] Soon after he released his second film, *La Tierra Prometida* (1973), the military overthrew the Allende government. He recalled, "Actually, I was pursued by the military junta, almost getting killed, until I found asylum in the Mexican Embassy. Then I went to Mexico where I started to reconstruct my life. . . ."[6] In Mexico, he made another internationally acclaimed film, *Actas de Marusia* (1975), which dealt with a strike in 1907 in Chile, against a European-owned mine, which resulted in the massacre of dozens of unionists by the Chilean government forces. The film was nominated for an Oscar as Best Foreign Film.

In regard to making films, he has stated, "I can accuse my colleagues. Some have to work to survive, but I survive to work and make the films I do and not any other type. Films that speak about the problems, injustices, etc. which weigh mankind down, that is important to me, that's what mobilizes me—the human condition."[7]

Alsino and the Condor received a generally enthusiastic critical response. The *Los Angeles Times* (June 2, 1983) comments were reflective of other reviewers: "A work of passionate lyricism that has been called Nicaragua's first feature. . . . Littin . . . has a wonderful way with actors, especially non-professionals like young Esquivel. Stockwell has been long overdue for such a challenging role . . . a film of raw, primitive beauty and forcefulness."

Littin's only regret about the film was: "It's unfortunate that it will only be on the art theater circuit here, because it's the kind of film Latinos here should see."[8]

The Ballad of Gregorio Cortez (1983, EM)

The Ballad of Gregorio Cortez was one of the first films to celebrate historical Mexican heroes, sadly missing in Hollywood's revisionist history.

The film was developed and funded through the auspices of Robert Redford's Sundance Institute and the Corporation for Public Broadcasting (PBS), with additional funds supplied by the National Endowment for the Arts, for the total budget of $1,300,000. Originally, it had been made to be telecast on television, under the banner of American Playhouse, but through the independent efforts of the film's star, Edward James Olmos, it was given widespread marketing and became a "sleeper," commercially and critically.

The film was based on an old corrido with the same name. Director Robert M. Young had had considerable experience in documentary filmmaking when he directed the excellent *Alambrista!* (1977), which had also featured Olmos. The film, originally shown on PBS, remains as one of the best films yet made about the plight of undocumented Mexican workers.

The film told the true story (with some liberties) of Gregorio Cortez (Edward James Olmos), a Mexican farmer living in San Antonio, Texas. On June 12, 1901, he and his brother, Romaldo Cortez (Pepe Serna), were approached by an Anglo sheriff and his deputy, who spoke only rudimentary Spanish, at best. The lawmen sought information about the sale of a stolen horse. They did not know the Spanish language makes a distinction between *caballo* (male horse) and *yegua* (mare, or female horse). Cortez responded that he had not bought a horse (what he had bought was a mare). The sheriff quickly assumed that he was lying, drew his gun, and killed Romaldo. Gregorio responded in what would legally be deemed self-defense. Racism against Mexicans being what it was in Texas motivated Gregorio to flee for his life.

Cortez was pursued by the Texas Rangers, a group notorious for its overt anti-Mexican feelings, in the biggest manhunt in Texas history. The press followed the manhunt closely, much to the dismay of the Rangers. Cortez attempted to head for the Mexican border, but decided to turn himself in when he learned his family had been imprisoned. He was put on trial, found guilty, and nearly lynched. A Chicana, Carolot Muñoz (Rosanna De Soto), organized to free him, and it was she who brought the misunderstanding to light in the denoument.

The real-life Cortez was released after several years of imprisonment. The experience, however, had all but destroyed his life, and he had run-ins with the law on several other occasions and was incarcerated yet again. A corrido developed along the border attesting to his courage and injustice and soon mixing fact and legend.

The film received glowing reviews. The *Los Angeles Times* (September 30, 1982) wrote:

What is exceptional about the film is that no matter how loud and clear the readouts from the story may be in the end, "Ballad" never plays as a heavy-gloved message picture symbolically executed in black-and-white characterizations. . . . The performances are of a uniformly very high quality, Olmos' own as Cortez and, among the many others, Barry Corbin as Cortez's defense attorney, Rosanna De Soto as the translator who, in Cortez's prison cell, evokes the truth of the tragic confrontation, and Tomy Bauer as monolingual deputies' chief pursuer. . . . The Latino audience alone is surely commercially viable at this point, and the appeals to pride, understanding and hope are considerable. . . .

The *Village Voice* (November 18, 1983) noted: "Eddie as Cortez neither speaks nor understands English. It is a remarkable performance, full of eyes, half-gestures, whispers—all without being maneuver or dull. This is what underplaying is supposed to be about, the opposite of the flamboyance El Pachuco called for. Eddie Olmos can do it all. . . . "

Playboy magazine commented:

It's a class act throughout yet Gregorio Cortez is distinguished mostly for a magnificent, low-key performance in the title role by Edward James Olmos (best known heretofore as the star of the stage and screen musical *Zoot Suit*). Olmos' wrenchingly honest underplaying stirs memories of Brando at his zenith in *Viva Zapata*. . . . Young makes it both sensitive and suspenseful—an underdog epic with plenty of bite.

Young's presentation of Gregorio Cortez is not as a romanticized hero, but as a deeply flawed and human one. Several scenes exemplify this perspective. In one scene, the fugitive Cortez comes across a cowboy by accident, and the former welcomes him eagerly to dispel his great loneliness. In another scene, in which Cortez enters "La Cantina" restaurant for refuge and food, his emaciated face contorts into anguish upon learning that his brother Romaldo has died and his family is under arrest. The final scene presents Cortez as father to his son Valeriano. It is a farewell mixed with subdued despair, pride, and pain.

The Gregorio Cortez of corrido and legend becomes imbued with mortal reality.

Born in East L.A. (1987, Universal)

Cheech Marin's *Born in East L.A.* and Luis Valdez's *La Bamba* were released within months of each other. Never before had two films about the Chicano experience been released within the same year or been as successful.

The film told the story of a Chicano, Rudy Robles (Cheech Marin), who works in an auto repair shop in East Los Angeles. His mother asks him to meet his Mexican cousin, Javier (Paul Rodriguez), who is currently working in a toy factory. Rudy hurries, forgetting his wallet, and at the factory stumbles across an immigration raid led by the notorious "Body Count" McCalister (Jan Michael Vincent). Rudy is rounded up with other workers and deported to Tijuana.

In Tijuana, Rudy is jailed for vandalizing a telephone booth. There, he meets a fallen evangelist, Feo (Tony Plana), who attempts to extort money for protection. Finally, Rudy is released with only a quarter in his pockets and is subsequently hired by Jimmy (Daniel Stern), as the doorman in a Tijuana bar. There, he meets a spirited Salvadorean refugee waitress, Dolores (Kamala Lopez) and her friend Gloria (Alma Martinez).

Rudy makes several attempts to cross the border, as a football coach and a moving bush and inside a refrigerator, but is unsuccessful. He teaches five youths from Central America and the Far East (Sal Lopez, Del Zamora, Ted Lin, Jason Scott Lee, Jee To) how to blend in as native Chicanos when they reach East Los Angeles. Hard-pressed to make a living, Rudy joins a Norteño group (Daniel Valdez, Steve Jordan, David Silva). He finally devises a plan to cross with Dolores and several thousand others.

Cheech Marin, besides playing the down-and-out Rudy, also wrote and made his directorial debut in the film. It also marked his first solo film effort, after his successful association with Tommy Chong. He stated, "The reason for the breakup was I wanted to go in a new direction and Chong wanted to stay in the same one. . . . We'll always be friends joined at the hip, but it was just time to sprout different creative wings. You can't have two drivers."[9] He wrote a parody of Bruce Springsteen's "Born in the U.S.A.," titled "Born in East L.A.," and then made a video, both of which turned out to be hits. Marin had originally been considered for the role of Joe Mondragan in Robert Redford's *The Milagro Beanfield War* (1988, Universal). His last-minute replacement encouraged him to write and star in *Born in East L.A.*

When asked about Marin's alter ego/film persona, Cheech, he commented, "Cheech (Rudy) today is more experienced, older, owns a body shop, been married, divorced, and owns his own home. He's on his own. He's a lot hipper and wiser. But he still has that same kind of younger heart. There's a bluer tinge to him now. . . . "[10] Often criticized in the past for the pot-smoking scenes in the Cheech and Chong films, he stated, "I don't write stoned, ever, because writing is a discipline. You know, you never saw anything about Cheech and Chong checking into Betty Ford. It was always the straight doctor on 'One Life to Live,' or some famous lawyer, or a 'Star Wars' actor. We were always into health. When we toured the country, we belonged to the YMCA and went to every Y in every city and worked out."[11]

The character of Rudy indeed has evolved from the *vato loco* and *la vida loca* of the 1970s and 1980s, when the Cheech persona was essentially only into self-gratification. Rudy still has a roving eye for the women, but the sense of responsibility has definitely set in. Additionally, he becomes politicized through his experience. He confronts racism and injustice and becomes aware of the mass poverty of migrating Third World peoples. In one scene, in which Rudy is selling fruit on the street, he is so moved by the hunger in the face of a little boy that he proceeds to give him and his distraught mother several bags of fruit. Later, when he finally earns enough money to pay the coyote to cross the border, he witnesses a mother separated from her husband, and, angered by the coyote's ruthlessness, gives up his seat to her.

The film also attempts to present an overdue rehabilitation of the stereotyped image of East Los Angeles, the largest barrio in the United States. The plight of undocumented workers had been dramatically effective in *El Norte* and *Alambrista!*, but *Born in East L.A.* deals with the issue in comic terms.

Born in East L.A. was released to enthusiastic reviews and was a big commercial hit.

Break of Dawn (1988, Platform)

Isaac Artenstein's *Break of Dawn* told the true story of Pedro J. Gonzalez, a Mexican singer and the first to establish a Spanish-speaking radio program in the United States. It was an important contribution in chronicling another piece of Chicano/Mexican history previously buried in oblivion.

Break of Dawn was directed and written by Isaac Artenstein, who was born in San Diego to Mexican parents and grew up in Tijuana. He had done a documentary on Pedro J. Gonzalez entitled *Ballad of an Unsung Hero* (1983), which was aired nationally on PBS stations. The documentary was honored with numerous awards: the Emmy, the Cine Golden Eagle, the Golden Mike Award, and the Blue Ribbon at the American Film Festival.

Pedro J. Gonzalez (Oscar Chavez) had served, in his youth, as Pancho Villa's personal telegraph operator. In the late 1920s, he emigrated to Los Angeles, California, with his wife, Maria (Maria Rojo). Upon their arrival, they stayed with his cousin (Pepe Serna) and his wife (Socorro Valdez).

Pedro is refused an audition at the KMPC radio station because the station's management alleges that there is no audience for Spanish-language music. He manages, however, on his own initiative, to deliver commercials in Spanish and is able finally to land a 5:00 A.M. slot on radio, quickly becoming a celebrity in the Spanish-speaking community.

The politically ambitious and corrupt Captain Rodriguez (Tony Plana) approaches Pedro to persuade him to get out the Mexican-American vote on behalf of City District Attorney Kyle Mitchell (Peter Henry Schroeder), who is based on the true-life district attorney Buron Fitts, subsequently removed from office for corruption. With the coming of the Depression, massive deportations take place, fueled by jingoism and racism. Gonzalez gives his full-hearted support to efforts to denounce and stop the deportations. Mitchell, a rabid bigot and opportunist, is angered by Gonzalez's efforts and his inability to corrupt him. Gonzalez himself is carried away with his fame and becomes involved in an extramarital affair with a seductive tango singer (Aixa Moreno). Mitchell is able to blackmail a local beauty queen, sixteen-year-old Linda (Kamala Lopez), to charge Pedro with statutory rape.

Gonzalez refuses to plead guilty and is sentenced to prison. His wife and others establish support committees, and Linda finally reveals the extortion. Rodriguez is fired by the increasingly politically besieged Mitchell, which motivates him to present material evidence of corruption. As a result, Mitchell is finally indicted and removed. Gonzalez is finally released (1940), after serving six years, and then deported to Mexico.

In 1979, he was allowed to return to the United States, and in 1985, a formal petition for pardon was denied by the California governor's office. He and his wife settled in Tijuana, where he resumed his broadcasting career on the radio station XEAU, becoming instrumental in developing radio in the border region. Later, they moved to San Ysidro, California, where they are still active in community issues.

Break of Dawn is an uncompromising film on the plight of Chicanos/Mexicanos in the 1920s and 1930s in Los Angeles. While political corruption in Los Angeles had previously been filmically documented by the novels of Raymond Chandler, and, more recently, in Roman Polanski's *Chinatown* (1974), this film was the first depicting the element of racism in city politics. The film explores an aggregation of issues affecting Chicanos/Mexicanos during the period: mass deportations in the 1930s, the political disenfranchisement, the demagoguery of red baiting and scapegoating, and cultural deprivations. It is not a romanticized or glamorized view of the era. The Chicano characters are flawed but dimensional.

Captain Rodriguez, for example, is an opportunist looking after his self-interest and is unconcerned about the Chicano/Mexican community. However, even in his relatively exalted position, he is reminded of his ethnic background. Mitchell tells him, "Don't forget where you came from, and if you don't watch your goddamned mouth, I'll have you fired!" He gets no second chance when he fails: "It's all over, Gene, I should have known better than trust a goddamned greaser like you!" Rodriguez has betrayed the interests of his own people in order to be accepted by the Anglo establishment and realizes much too late that he, too, is expendable. The tango dancer helps to frame Gonzalez rather than face charges of pandering, and Linda, a middle-class girl, is molested by her father and is willing to charge Gonzalez rather than expose how her virginity was lost.

Gonzalez himself is shown as a tarnished man, dissipated by the allure of fame. However, it is at the moment of crisis that he redeems himself and his dignity with a strength that he derives from his wife and community. His wife is in the traditional mold, but with a spark of critical thinking, initiative, and combativeness. Finally, the film pays homage to the community's solidarity and efforts to release him (some three hundred thousand signatures were delivered to the governor of California's office).

Veteran Mexican folk and protest singer Oscar Chavez was cast as Pedro Gonzalez, giving, in addition to a strong performance, several moving ballads that detailed his ordeal. Newcomer Mexican actress Maria Rojo played his wife, Maria. The actress, a veteran of Mexican telenovedas, is best known for her powerful performance as the wife in *Rojo Amanecer* (1988), the first Mexican film to deal with the 1968 Ttatelolco student massacre. Kamala Lopez played the young beauty queen, Linda. She had previously played the female lead in Cheech Marin's *Born in East L.A.* (1987) and in Jesus Treviño's *Gangs* (1989, PBS). The film was primarily shot in San Diego, California, at a budget of $850,000, but achieved a most convincing period authenticity visually.

Break of Dawn premiered at the United States Film Festival. Subsequently, it won top honors at the San Antonio Cine Festival and won two Nostoros Awards. It went on to represent the United States at the Toronto Festival of Festivals, the U.S. Film Festival in Tokyo, and the Tashkent Film Festival. Unfortunately, the film has been, for the most part, restricted to art houses and has not received the widespread marketing it merits.

The critical response was generally excellent. The *Los Angeles Times* (March 8, 1989) wrote:

Sometimes a story is so significant that it's worth trying to overlook the flaws in the way in which it is told. This is the case with "Break of Dawn," which has the awkwardness typical of some low-budget productions of a first-time director. . . . Oscar Chavez may be too old for Gonzalez, but he has a dignified presence and is a wonderful singer. . . . "Break of Dawn" evokes a sense of period with fewer anachronisms than films with much bigger budgets. . . .

The *L.A. Weekly* (March 10–16, 1989) commented:

"Break of Dawn" is an eminently bi-national film. Oscar Chavez and Maria Rojo (who play Pedro and his wife) are both stars in Mexico—and do a fine job here. Actors from El Norte and El Sur meet in a bilingual script in which the dialogue for the Spanish-speaking actors flows in and out of both languages fluidly. . . . It is also extremely timely fare. As Pedro's fame leads him into the Anglo establishment, he is confronted with the essential dilemma of the immigrant who hits the jackpot of the American Dream: does he fall for the money and women offered him in return of implicitly supporting the status quo and turn his back on the community he rose from?

The *San Diego Union* noted it was "a film with grace, guts and passion." The *Hollywood Reporter* wrote of the "sparkling lead performance by Oscar Chavez." The *San Francisco Chronicle* called it a "passionate independent film."

Crossover Dreams (1985, Crossover Films)

Crossover Dreams is an apt title for a film that explores the tribulations of a Puerto Rican musician's efforts to find fame and fortune in the mainstream music world.

The film told the story of Rudy Veloz (Ruben Blades), an ambitious Puerto Rican salsa musician, who lives in Spanish Harlem and who dreams of fame and fortune beyond the second- and third-rate nightclubs that he and his seven members play and the meager $400 they earn, minus expenses. He gets a chance to play his newest song to a sleazy record producer, Lou

Rose (Tom Signorelli), who, before a contract can be signed, is arrested for the possession of controlled substances. His mentor, veteran musician Chico Rabala (Virgilio Marti), is disenchanted with his Elvis Presley–type music and cautions him not to remove himself from his cultural and musical roots. Rabala's death on the stage of a third-rate nightclub during a performance reawakens Veloz's frustration and ambition to break out. He confides in a friend after the funeral, "I've seen our future in that church and it looks like shit! . . . If we stay, we're dead!"

Veloz meets another producer, Neil Silver (Joel Diamond), who takes a chance with him and proceeds to sign him to a contract. He meets with some initial success, which results in his considering marriage with his girlfriend of three years, Liz Garcia (Elizabeth Peña). Veloz feels he's at the break of his crossover dreams and goes on a binge of material excesses: purchasing a vintage sports car, buying trendy clothes, renting a high-rise apartment, becoming involved in loveless affairs, and using chemical substances with his schoolboy friend, horn player Orlando (Shawn Elliott).

Veloz breaks up with Liz and subsequently fires Orlando, at the advice of a "hip" producer, and then replaces him with a bland Anglo saxophone player. Totally withdrawing from his ties to Spanish Harlem, he becomes painfully more cognizant of his cultural and emotional isolation. He releases an album that receives lukewarm reviews and even less commercial response. He quickly uses up all the incoming money and more and is finally reduced to living in a down-and-out pad on Times Square. When told by his producer that he will get a second chance, he knowingly responds, "People like me don't get a second chance. . . . We don't even get answers." Sad and lonely, he returns to visit Liz, who is now married to a white, suburban dentist. He reunites with Orlando, and the two decide to build up the old band.

The film captures accurately, in the composite character of Rudy Veloz, an infinite number of gifted Hispanic musicians, as well as actors, who either had to de-Hispanicize themselves to be accepted by the mainstream or persevere in the shadows of obscurity. It explores the very real possibility that for many, especially people of color, the American Dream is just that, a dream that never comes true. It is a film that documents the contemporary experience of the Puerto Ricans, the second largest Hispanic group in the nation.

The film was directed by Leon Ichaso and cowritten by him, Marvel Arce, and Ruben Blades. Ichaso and Arce had collaborated on *El Super* (1979), about a Cuban refugee trying to adjust to life in Spanish Harlem. Panamanian-born Ruben Blades made his film debut in *Crossover Dreams,* in the role of Rudy Veloz, ironically, one that was almost autobiographical.

The film received enthusiastic reviews, and since its release, has become a key film in understanding the Puerto Rican experience. The *New York Times* (August 23, 1985) wrote:

> As it turns out, Liz isn't very lucky nor, for that matter, is Rudy, but the movie that contains them is a winner. It's "Crossover Dream," and though small and made on a modest budget, it's a sagely funny comedy, both heartfelt and sophisticated, a movie that may well realize the crossover dreams that elude Rudy. . . . In Mr. Blades, who makes him film debut as Rudy Veloz, Mr. Ichaso and Mr. Arce have discovered who's also a screen natural, the kind of actor whose presence and intelligence register without apparent effort. The members of the supporting cast are almost as good, including Miss Peña, who was very funny as the cheeky, Americanized daughter in "El Super"; Shawn Elliott, whose stage work should be familiar to New York audiences, as the best friend Rudy Veloz drops on his rocky road to stardom. . . .*

People Magazine commented, "A pointed and perceptive comedy, moving as briskly and fluently as the salsa beat itself." *Manhattan Arts* stated, "An intriguing film—imbued with a probing intelligence. An exquisitely tuned performance by Ruben Blades."

El Norte (1984, Cinecom/Island Alive)

Gregory Nava's *El Norte* and Robert W. Young's *Alambrista!* (1983) were the most important filmic contributions to understanding the plight of undocumented Mexican and Latino workers.

---

*Reprinted by permission.

El Norte was the end product of a growing number of films dealing with the exploitation of undocumented workers. Films that had previously attempted to deal with the issue in a serious way included Anthony Mann's *Border Incident* (1949), Joseph Losey's *The Lawless* (1950), William Wellman's *My Man and I* (1952), and Jesus Treviño's *Raices de Sangre* (1979).

Director and cowriter Gregory Nava was born in San Diego, California, of Mexican-American parents and was a graduate of the UCLA Film School. His thirty-minute dramatic film on the life of Garcia Lorca, titled *The Journal of Diego Rodriguez Silva,* won the Best Dramatic Film Award at the National Student Film Festival. In 1973, he won the Best First Feature Award at the Chicago International Film Festival for *The Confession of Amans,* which he wrote, produced, and directed. In 1977, he worked as a cinematographer on Anna Thomas's (coscreenwriter of *El Norte* and his wife) *The Haunting of Ms.* About the need to make *El Norte,* he said:

> When you travel anywhere in Latin America, you're immediately struck by two forces: the lush, dreamlike beauty of the land-scape—the people, colors, textiles, art, and the terrible social and political problems that are ripping these countries apart. There's an undercurrent of violence beneath this poetic beauty that can erupt at any moment, at any place. . . . [12]

Regarding his approach to the film and stricture, he commented:

> In the United States and Europe, there's a distinction made be-tween social realism, which is always very stark, and fantasy, which can be beautiful and imaginative . . . in any story dealing with Latin American culture, you cannot separate these ele-ments—they are inextricably involved. I felt that the only way to be true to that world, and to these characters, was to bring to the screen the style found in novels like *El Señor Presidente* and *One Hundred Years of Solitude.*[13]

Despite the film's numerous locales, it was shot on a limited budget. The opening sequences took place in Guatemala, but because of the nature of the content of the film and the notoriety of the right-wing regimes that ruled Guatemala, it was decided to shoot the remainder of those scenes in Chiapas, Mexico, a place similar to Guatemala. Nava recollected, "The area was fraught with social, racial and political tensions. Some of our experiences were wonderful, but others were harrowing. We found that in the tiny village where we were shooting there were eight killings a week. . . ."[14] Shooting was moved to Morelos, nearer to Mexico City, and there the film was seized. Nava recalled, "They claimed to be from the Mexican government, but it was an unofficial action. In the next forty-eight hours, we had to deal with kidnappings, threats, extortion. We really thought at that point it was all over, that we wouldn't be able to finish the film. I think that their idea was to threaten us."[15]

The film depicted the odyssey of two Guatemalan Indians, Rosa Xuncax (Zaide Silvia Gutierrez) and Enrique Xuncax (David Villalpando), to Los Angeles, California. Their father, Arturo (Ernesto Gomez Cruz), a coffee plantation worker, is murdered by the army after attempting to organize other fellow laborers. His wife, Lupe (Alicia del Lago), becomes one of the disappeared. When Enrique finds his father hanging from a tree, he and his sister decide to leave. Enraptured by the material wonders displayed in some worn-out issues of *Good Housekeeping,* they set out on their journey to El Norte.

They finally make their way to Tijuana, where they are duped into crossing the border. They eventually find a coyote, Raimundo (Abel Franco), who has them cross through an old sewage tunnel. Arriving in Los Angeles, they take an adult education course in English. Enrique obtains a job at an expensive restaurant, and Rosa, who is befriended by a wiser, older woman, Nocha (Lupe Ontiveros), gets a job as a domestic in a wealthy house. Enrique becomes so consumed with the pursuit of the materialism of the American Dream that he abandons his sister when she becomes seriously ill. Nocha tells him, "Rosa is dying, but you're already dead!"

Director Nava and Thomas went to Mexico for most of the casting, and, after dozens of auditions, selected newcomers David Villalpando to play Enrique and Zaide Silvia Gutierrez for the role of Rosa. Veteran Mexican stage actor Ernest Gomez

211

Cruz played the role of the father; Mexican film and stage actress Alicia del Lago played the role of Lupe, the mother; author-television personality Eraclio Zepeda was cast as Pedro; Guatemalan anthropoligist Stella Quan, as Josefita; and Rodrigo Pueblo, as Puma. In the United States, several well-known Hispanic performers were cast: Trinidad Silva, as the sleazy motel manager; Lupe Ontiveros, as Nacha; Abel Franco, as Raimundo; Tony Plana, as Carlos, among others.

In reference to casting the film, Nava commented:

> I kept hearing, again and again, that I should make Americans the main characters, that I'd never get it financed otherwise. I have nothing against films like "Missing" or "Under Fire," but I wanted a film where Latin American people were the protagonists. . . . Everybody told me that audiences could never be able to cross that cultural and language barrier, but I thought that even though the cultural differences were great, if the film were done right, people would be able to cross that barrier and recognize human beings on the other side.[16]

Nava's faith in his film paid off, artistically and commercially. The film has become probably the most popular and famous film on the plight of undocumented workers. It opened in limited release to excellent reviews, and word-of-mouth resulted in it being released successfully to wider audiences. The film has especially become a favorite in schools and universities. Its success, however, has not transferred to its director, as he has yet to be able to acquire funding for another film.

The *New York Times* (January 11, 1984) commented:

> A small, personal, independently made film with the sweep of "El Norte," with solid, sympathetic performances by unknown actors and a visual style of astonishing vibrancy, must be regarded as a remarkable accomplishment. . . . The film's opening portion, set in a small, remote Indian village, is so brilliantly colored and so filled with startling imagery that it approaches the "hallucinogenic realism" of modern Latin American fiction. . . . He concentrates closely on Rosa and Enrique, who are played so plainly and

touchingly (both Miss Gutierrez and Mr. Villalpando are experienced Mexican stage actors making their film debuts) that the audience cannot help but empathize. . . . Mr. Nava makes "El Norte" real and involving throughout. . . .*

The *Los Angeles Times* (March 8, 1984) wrote:

"El Norte" . . . embodies an idea whose time has come: the dramatization on screen of the plight of illegal immigrants. It is a subject that has been dealt with before in films, most notably in Robert M. Young's excellent "Alambrista!" but young independent film maker Gregory Nava has attempted no less than an epic. . . . - What ensues lays how the treacherousness of the American Dream, where, in the struggle for survival, the individual is tempted increasingly to think only to himself. . . . They are fortunate in their resourceful cinematographer James Glennon and the Folkloristas' fine score. . . . In plotting and movement . . . [the film] recalls such epics of the poor and the dispossessed as Visconti's "Rocco and His Brothers." . . . Gutierrez and Villalpando convey genuine sweetness. By the end, Enrique has come full circle, confronted with the reality that his value to the world, like his father before him, lies only in the strength of his arms. Yet, at this moment, Enrique attains universality. . . .

La Bamba (1987, Columbia)

Luis Valdez's *La Bamba* (1987, Columbia) and Cheech Marin's *Born in East L.A.* (1987, Universal) are the top-grossing films ever made about the Chicano experience. *La Bamba's* success finally put to rest Hollywood's proverbial argument that there were no viable audiences for Chicano-oriented films.

The film told the story of Ritchie (Richard) Valens (Valenzuela), Chicano rock pioneer with three Top-Ten hits: "Donna," "Come On, Let's Go," and "La Bamba." He was only seventeen when he was killed on February 3, 1959, in a plane crash, which also killed Buddy Holly and the Big Bopper. A film was overdue to celebrate an authentic cultural hero.

---

*Reprinted by permission.

The film chronicled the brief life of Ritchie Valens (Lou Diamond Philips) from his early teens when he; his mother, Connie Valenzuela (Rosana De Soto); and two younger sisters pick fruit in Northern California. Ritchie's half-brother, Bob Morales (Esai Morales), an ex-felon who drives a motorcycle and deals in drugs, arrives and contributes to Ritchie's prolonged conflict with him when he deflowers Ritchie's girlfriend, Rosie (Elizabeth Peña).

Upon his arrival at Pacoima High School, Ritchie begins in earnest to develop his guitar and singing skills while playing in numerous gigs. He also falls in love with an Anglo girl, Donna Ludwig (Danielle Von Zerneck), whose parents disapprove of the interracial romance. He rapidly rises to music stardom with three hits, tours, television appearances, and a performance in rock-and-roll pioneer disc jockey Alan Freed's (Jeffrey Alan Chandler) extravaganzas, which feature other rock legends, such as Eddie Cochran (Brian Setzer) and Jackie Wilson (Howard Huntsberry). Valens is on a winter tour with the established Buddy Holly (Marshall Crenshaw) and the Big Bopper (Stephen Lee) when he perishes.

The seeds for the film had actually begun some fourteen years prior to filming, when Luis Valdez's brother, Daniel, had approached producer Taylor Hackford, while both were employed in southern California's PBS station, KCET. Later, in 1978, when the brothers were engaged in the play *Zoot Suit,* on Broadway, and exploring the possibility of making Valens's life the subject of research, Daniel approached Hackford about a film project. By then, Hackford had made his directorial debut and had done several successful films with music as a prominent feature: *An Officer and a Gentleman* (1982), *Against All Odds* (1984), and *The Idolmaker* (1980). Hackford, who had just established his New Visions Productions, quickly accepted it, and Columbia Pictures agreed to distribute it when Hackford guaranteed it for $6.5 million. Luis Valdez wrote the script and directed, while his brother became associate producer. Permission was obtained from the Valenzuela family, and Ritchie's now-adult and married sisters, Irma and Connie, were cast in small parts as workers in the farm camp scenes. Their daughters, in turn, Gloria and Kristin, played their mothers. Ritchie's mother and his brother, Bob, also had small roles.

The film took several liberties. For example, when Valens was killed, his first album had not been released, although in the film, his manager, Bob Keene, is shown giving out the album at record shops. The album was actually released eight days after his death. Some family members had mixed feelings about the film. Ritchie's brother, Bob Morales, said, "Even though Luis Valdez . . . used his own interpretation of what happened, it couldn't have been closer for me. . . . It was almost too close."[17] His sister Irma, now a preschool teacher in Watsonville, praised the film as an inspiration for Hispanic youth: "They don't have to be macho or mean or cuss or take drugs to be a man. They will also see that it's okay to be sensitive, tender and care for their families too."[18] The film made the point that Valens made the traditional Mexican folk song, "La Bamba," the first Spanish-language song to make it to the Top-Ten pop charts. The East Los Angeles premiere band Los Lobos was hired to rerecord Valens's music, while actor Lou Diamond Phillips lip synced.

Writer-director Luis Valdez stated, "This picture is about two brothers and their mother. Our goal was to explore their reality for a couple of hours and to plug into some of the early rock-and-roll. I feel fortunate that these elements came together the way they did."[19] On a personal level, he said:

I have always felt that the '50s, as they were portrayed on film, were not the full story. . . . Rock-and-roll gave focus to the emerging youth culture, the baby boom generation. At the same time, it also became a symptom of change. And the history of rock-and-roll is parallel to the history of integration in this country, and the fusion of rhythm and blues with the country western represents, as far as I'm concerned, the coming together of black and white people in this country. It is significant that Ritchie Valens was there as an Hispanic in 1959, and with one song, internationalized rock-and-roll.[20]

In reference to Valens's death, Valdez stated, "It sort of sealed my teenage years. It ended them. I got involved in the civil rights movement and the Viva Kennedy campaign after that."[21]

La Bamba was both a commercial and critical hit. The film grossed in excess of $100 million in its initial release.. In one

215

weekend, it grossed $5.5 million, Spanish-language versions accounting for some 10 percent. Valdez commented on the unheralded success, "One of the things 'La Bamba' reveals is that there is a new, positive consensus in America about Hispanics."[22]

However, Luis Valdez came in for some criticism for some of the casting by some sectors of the Chicano community. Daniel Valdez was initially going to play Ritchie Valens, but by the time the film was made, he was too old for the part. (He settled for a small part as a family relative, Lelo.) Instead, newcomer Lou Diamond Phillips, a Filipino-Hawaiian, with strains of Cherokee, Irish, and Hispanic ancestry, was cast in the title role. Cuban-born Esai Morales and Elizabeth Peña were cast as Ritchie's brother, Bob, and former girlfriend, Rosie, respectively.

Critical response was enthusiastic. *Variety* (May 20, 1987) wrote:

> There haven't been too many people who died at age 17 who have warranted the biopic treatment, but 1950s rock n' roller Ritchie Valens proves a worthy exception in "La Bamba." . . . "La Bamba" is engrossing throughout and boasts numerous fine performances. In Lou Diamond Philips' sympathetic turn, Valens comes across a very fine young man, caring for those important to him and not overawed by his success. Rosana De Soto scores as his tireless mother, and Elizabeth Peña has numerous dramatic moments as Bob's distraught mate. Most of the fireworks are Bob's and Esai Morales makes the most of the opportunities . . . commands the screen whenever he's around, and makes the tormented brother a genuinely complex figure. Musically, Valens's tunes have been covered outstandingly by the contempo band Los Lobos. . . .

Latino (1985, Lucas Film/Latino)

Latino made an important contribution to the understanding of the common historical roots of Chicanos and Latin Americans, rather than emphasizing their dissimilar contemporary self-interests.

The film is set along the Honduran-Nicaraguan border in the early 1980s after the Nicaraguan revolution (1979) that toppled the U.S.-supported Somoza dictatorship. Eddie Guerrero

(Robert Beltran), a Chicano Special Forces Vietnam veteran and former resident of East Los Angeles (City Terrace) and a fellow Chicano, Ruben (Tony Plana), are sent to Honduras to train the Nicaraguan contras (counter-revolutionaries). Along with CIA personnel, they terrorize and recruit young Nicaraguan boys into the contra forces, who aspire to one day overthrow the Sandinistas. Eddie meets Marlena (Annette Cardona), a widowed Nicaraguan exile and agronomist with a small boy, whose family are Sandinistas. When an Anglo CIA operative calls Nicaragua another "spic country," Eddie goodnaturedly laughs it off, but the incident is the beginning of his loss of innocence. On one foray into Nicaragua, he comes upon an old woman making tortillas, whose son is abducted by the contra forces. The woman reminds him of his mother and the people of those of his own barrio.

When Marlena attempts to pry into his innermost self, he tells her, "I honestly can't say what's the truth and what's a lie anymore." Eddie has trouble relating to Ruben's gung-ho zealousness. He tells Ruben, "And that old lady who cursed me, Jesus, man, standing by her for a few minutes I thought I was in Mama's kitchen." After a trip to her father's funeral to Nicaragua, Marlena discovers about Eddie's secret mission and leaves him. Disillusioned with the moral ambiguity of the conflict, he reluctantly takes on another mission during which a Nicaraguan conscript, Luis (Luis Torrientes), who he groomed, turns against him and tells him, "Fuck you, jack!"

Noted and two-time Oscar-winning cinematographer and director Haskell Wexler made his directorial debut with *Medium Cool* (1969), about the 1968 Chicago police riots. He had lensed *Bound for Glory* (1976) and *One Flew over the Cuckoo's Nest* (1975), but had also built up prodigious output as a documentary filmmaker, including the well-known *Target Nicaragua*. When asked about his decision to make a theatrical film instead of a documentary, he stated. "I think audiences are more susceptible to drama, that we can learn through fact because we've become suspicious of what's presented to us as fact. But even with a dramatic film, I couldn't get any money anywhere to make the film so I took my own money and I borrowed from my mother."[23] Asked about the purpose of the film, he responded:

I think the ability of the American people to make a dispassionate judgment about Nicaragua is more difficult. I'm hoping that "Latino" won't just make a statement about Nicaragua and Central America, but a film against violence, against war. You might call "Latino" pacifist . . . although the word is not exactly in vogue nowadays.[24]

The principal photography on the film began in Nicaragua in February 1984, and finished in July, after another week of shooting in Los Angeles, California.

Latino was the first film to explore the moral and historical dilemma of Chicano soldiers fighting against other Latinos, who share the same language, many cultural roots, and a commonalty of poverty and an absence of political empowerment. As Eddie tells the zealous Ruben in the bar, "We're just niggers. We're the niggers of the world." Eddie has served fourteen years in combat, beginning with three tours in Vietnam, and has finally realized the emptiness of his life. He says, "It seems I've spent most of my life hiding in the bushes of countries." Eddie and Ruben are composites of the numerous other Latinos engaged or fallen anonymously on the battlefields of Third World countries, battling adversaries of similar socioeconomic status.

Critical reactions were predictably hostile and were unable to understand or appreciate the moral ambiguity of the character Eddie. *Variety* (May 22, 1985) wrote:

Although doubtlessly not intended as such, "Latino" comes off distressingly like a left-wing "The Green Berets." A nobly conceived, on-the-scene look at the battle between the Sandinistas and the U.S.-backed Contras in Nicaragua, writer-director Haskell Wexler has so woefully simplified a very complex situation that he ill serves the cause for which he feels such sympathy. . . . Dialog freely mixes English and Spanish in plausible fashion and, among the performers, Tony Plana stands out as a gung-ho U.S. Latin officer.

The *Los Angeles Times* (November 13, 1985) commented:

218

Unlike most other American films this year, Haskell Wexler's "Latino" . . . was obviously made without compromise: with passion and dedication. The movie is courageous to a fault: an indictment of U.S. involvement in Nicaragua that pulls no philosophical punches. . . . Wexler falls into an old Hollywood trap by telling the story this way, letting the sexy, fine-boned Annette Cordona be Nicaragua's soul . . . and building up Eddie, iconographically, as the classic American action-movie-star hero—handsome, bluff, boyishly cynical. . . .

The *Los Angeles Herald-Examiner* (November 13, 1985) noted:

Writer-director Haskell Wexler's "Latino" is a political film for people who like their politics ultrasalty, as in "Salt of the Earth." . . . As propaganda goes, "Latino" isn't convincing. It's shot in a semidocumentary style in actual Nicaraguan locations, but the story is rigged and acting is often awkward. . . .

The UCLA Chicano newspaper *La Gente* (November 1985) wrote a more analytical review, which stated in part (reprinted by permission):

By the general audience, the movie will be seen as a movie about United States policy towards Nicaragua but for the Chicano, for the Mexican-American who watches the movie—it will be a movie about the essence of the Chicano. The movie will have a special significance because in real life, the history of the Chicano has been one of struggle with identity. . . .

Seguin (1981, PBS)

Jesus Salvador Treviño's *Seguin* was the first film in Hollywood history to document the Mexican side of the 1836 Texas insurrection.

Seguin was initially to have been the first of a *La Historia* series, six one-hour PBS films documenting Chicano history from the Mexican-American War to the present. However, only *Seguin* was actually made and subsequently aired in American

219

Playhouse's first season. Treviño explained and commented on what had occurred:

> "Seguin" was funded by the National Endowment for the Humanities and the Corporation for Public Broadcasting during the Carter Administration. Then Reagan was elected, and he appointed William Bennett to head up the NEH. Bennett did a good job for his boss, complaining that too many NEH-funded projects were little more than propaganda for the Communists. He saw to it that there were substantial budget cuts and La Historia was one of the programs cut. . . . [25]

Seguin told the story of Juan Seguin, whose father, Don Erasmo Seguin, had supported Stephen Austin's efforts, in 1821, to bring in the first Anglo settlers into the Mexican state of Texas. Juan Seguin opposes the Anglo settlers' institution of slavery and idealistically believes that they, with time, will abandon the ignominious enterprise and incorporate themselves into the laws and culture of the Mexican Republic. Mexico had banned slavery in 1824. By 1836, Anglos outnumber Mexicans in Texas, and Seguin finds himself siding with the new immigrants and fighting against General Santa Ana, who is sent to put down the rebellion.

With Texas's independence, Seguin is elected mayor of San Antonio, but the disenfranchisement of the Mexican population, the flourishing institution of slavery, and overt racism causes Seguin a deep disillusionment. In the Mexican-American War (1846–48), Seguin sides with Mexico, and for many years thereafter, he resides in Mexico. In 1849, he is given a pardon by the U.S. government and returns to San Antonio, Texas. Today, a town in Texas is named in his honor.

The film had a uniformly and predominantly Mexican-American cast. A. Martinez played Juan Seguin; Henry Darrow was his father, Erasmo Seguin; Edward James Olmos was General Santa Ana; and Rose Portilla was Seguin's wife. Pepe Serna, Enrique Castillo, and Danny de la Paz were cast as three young firebrand friends of Juan Seguin; Lupe Ontiveros and Julio Mendina, as distraught parents; and Alma Martinez, as de la Paz's sweetheart.

Treviño was executive producer, writer, and director. He did extensive research for some four years. He would say, "We're not distorting history. This is a history that until now only a few historians were aware of. I think Seguin and his family were among the first people to experience the dual nature of bilingual-bicultural realities. Their conflicts and lives are prototypical of what all Latinos in the United States face."[26] Ironically, the film was shot in Bracketville, Texas, on the sets left behind by John Wayne while directing and starring in the one-sided and revisionist *The Alamo* (1960, United Artists). *Seguin,* budgeted at $500,000, was shot in twenty-one days.

Seguin was the first film about the Alamo and the 1836 Texas insurrection ever made in the United States that presented the Mexican side of the conflict. The film compresses a remarkable amount of history into its sixty minutes: the emigration of the first Anglo settlers, the 1836 Texas insurrection and Alamo battle, the Mexican-American War and its aftermath. It is a flawed film. Its flaws emanate mostly from its structural and historical source. It is based on the memoirs of one man, Juan Seguin. Acuña notes, "Seguin was one of a small group of wealthy Tejanos that supported the Anglo-American cause. The poor people of Tejas always remained strongly nationalistic. Juan Seguin was interested in protecting his interests, not his nationality or the rights of his people."[27]

Criticism of *Seguin* is levelled at this aspect of the film by Fregoso:

'Seguin' is a film that distorts the role of Tejanos during the Texas conflict principally by portraying Juan Seguin as an epitome. . . . In his effort to portray the Texas conflicts of the 19th century through the eyes of the protagonist, Juan Seguin, Treviño not only simplifies a historical period but also attempts to vindicate Seguin. . . . The film is critical, not of the economic structure that became the basis of human exploitation, but of the ideological force (i.e., racism) that excluded Tejano landowners from partaking in the nascent transformation of economic relations in Texas. For when Seguin says "land I fought to defend," he means "my land" in the realistic rather than the metaphoric sense.[28]

While Seguin's background is evidenced in historical fact, the film documents the consequences of Seguin's misplaced loyalties and of all Mexicans in Texas. After his wife has undergone an overt act of racism and she proceeds to inform her husband, he asks, "I'm sure that if he knew you were the mayor's wife?" At this point, she indignantly interjects, "Juan, what are you saying? Are you saying it's all right to treat any other Tejano like that?" Later, when Seguin is forced to leave Texas because of threats, he has become a man transformed. He has been corrupted and seeks redemption. He tells his wife, "I want to kill. I want to get back for all the things they've done to us." The "us" has become the entire Mexican community. He reflects, "How could I have been so blind? I thought we were fighting for Tejas, for our homeland, to make a place for our family, but it was only to make a place for the people who hate us. . . . Thank God, I'm finally too old to dream. . . ." Seguin survives and endures. Endurance and fortitude also have been important traits in director Treviño's career. Treviño said, "My approach has been to go for the opportunities that exist within the system and try to make the best of them, at times changing them, subverting them. I've been successful at doing this in certain areas."[29]

Stand and Deliver (1988, Warner Brothers)

Ramon Menendez's *Stand and Deliver,* released one year after the runaway successes of *Born in East L.A.* and *La Bamba,* concentrated on the most compelling issue in the Hispanic community: education.

Few films concentrating on education have been made by Hollywood. And of these, only a handful have been commercially or artistically successful. Among these have been *Goodbye, Mr. Chips* (1939, MGM), set in a British boarding school, with Robert Donat; *The Blackboard Jungle* (1955, MGM), set in a New York City ghetto school, with Glenn Ford; and *To Sir, with Love* (1967, Columbia), set in an impoverished London East End school, with an engineer-turned teacher played by Sidney Poitier.

Stand and Deliver told the true-life story of Bolivian-born Jaime Escalante, a math teacher at Garfield High School, in inner-city East Los Angeles. When he arrived at the school, it was ravaged by drugs, gangs, a spiraling drop-out rate, and on the point of losing its educational accreditation. In 1982, he took a group of unmotivated students whose mathematical skills were minimal and proceeded to badger them, humor them, and inspire them. Eighteen of these students took the advanced placement calculus examination (administered by the Educational Testing Service, as mandated by the College Board). The advanced placement exams earn students college credit, but are so demanding that only some 2 percent of all high school students actually take them. All of Escalante's students passed the exam, and six obtained perfect scores. However, when the Educational Testing Service determined a distinct similarity of incorrect answers among Garfield students, they were accused of cheating. Despite Escalante's adamant protest, the students were given only two choices: accept the Testing Service's decision or take the test again. When the students did subsequently retake the test, they scored even higher.

Cuban-born writer-director and cowriter-producer Melendez became intrigued about the story from a *Los Angeles Times* article. Musca stated:

> The idea of being truly innocent—and having to prove it—seemed like an intriguing premise for a film. There was an enormous probability that the students' scores would never have been questioned had they not all come from Garfield High School—with predominantly Spanish surnames. In other words, there was the distinct possibility of institutional racism.[30]

Melendez approached Escalante about a film, and it took several visits before he agreed. Melendez said, "He wasn't particularly blown away with the idea of a movie about his life and his commitment to kids and teaching them. What convinced him was my argument that if even one kid in any city across the country turned around by what we put on the screen, then we were essentially working toward the same goal."[31]

The film was funded by PBS's "American Playhouse," ARCO, the National Science Foundation, the Corporation for Public Broadcasting, and the Ford Foundation. Warner Brothers Studios distributed the movie, which was shot in Garfield High school and around East Los Angeles in a short schedule of only six weeks.

Cast in the leading role of Escalante was Edward James Olmos, who had won an Emmy Award in 1985 for his role as Lieutenant Castillo in *Miami Vice*. Olmos stated, "The concept of false accusation was a theme I had dealt with in my earlier film roles, both in 'Zoot Suit' as well as in 'The Ballad of Gregorio Cortez.'" Olmos prepared for his role meticulously, gaining forty pounds and having his hair cosmetically thinned to a few strands. He studied Escalante extensively: "Jaime and I spent extensive time together. I was lucky to have his commitment."[32] Olmos's dedication to his craft earned him an Academy Award nomination for his portrayal.

For the role of the cholo student Angel, Lou Diamond Phillips, who had played Ritchie Valens in the then-still-unreleased *La Bamba,* was cast. Rosana De Soto, who had just played Ritchie Valens' mother in *La Bamba,* was cast as Escalante's wife, Fabiola.

The film became a commercial and critical success. It did much to attract attention to Hispanics and education, heretofore nonexistent in films. While relatively a "safe film," *Stand and Deliver* stressed the virtues of self-sufficiency, self-initiative, and self-esteem as crucial factors for academic excellence. Education remains the most important issue facing the Hispanic community as statistics reveal a dismal picture across all levels: elementary, secondary, and postsecondary. As such, a film like *Stand and Deliver* was overdue.

Reviews were generally excellent. The *Los Angeles Times* (March 10, 1988) commented:

> You could remain, mesmerized, in Jaime Escalante's high school math class forever, the way you remain under the spell of Escalante himself as "Stand and Deliver" unfolds. . . . Olmos' self-effacing magnetism is at the center of a rousing true story of a man able to inspire a lethargic group of almost-dropouts at a school barely able to keep its accreditation—to galvanize them, give them pride in themselves and show them the road to earning it. . . . As the filmmakers demonstrate, pride is contagious. It has infected Garfield High, where Escalante still holds his standards

high and dares kids to follow. "Stand and Deliver" itself, with its message of the soaring rewards of learning, aims high and delivers perhaps a B+. . . .

Zoot Suit (1982, Universal)

Luis Valdez's *Zoot Suit* documented some important and recent Chicano history: the Sleepy Lagoon murder mystery of 1942 and the Zoot Suit Riots of the following year, which became an international incident.

Zoot Suit was written and directed by Luis Valdez and based on his long-running play of the same name. The play opened at the Mark Taper Forum in Los Angeles, in 1978. Thereafter, it had successful runs in other Southwest cities and ultimately ended with a short run on New York's Broadway stage. About his play, Valdez said:

> History has different levels. In reality, there are seven, from the most personal to the cosmic, all spinning around the same axis. When it came down to exploring the Sleepy Lagoon murder case, I had all this documentation and historical material. I had to work my way through the mythic. When I started out with a naturalistic approach, I lost the Pachuco. Once you're confined to reality, there's a constraint. The way to contain the character was to put him in his setting, so I framed the film around the concept of a theatrical event. I feel the film has captured a certain relevancy. We're entering a period of new initiative and patriotic self-expression. I hope "Zoot Suit" will be a reaffirmation of America as a mix of many peoples.[33]

Sleepy Lagoon was a reservoir in Los Angeles used by youths as a swimming hole and romantic hangout. A Chicano youth was found dead on August 2, 1942, and soon thereafter some six hundred Chicanos were arrested. Ultimately, twenty-two of these went on trial before an obstinate and prejudiced judge. Twelve of the defendants were sentenced to life and sent to San Quentin. The Chicano community organized a defense committee. Finally, after an appeal was won, the youths were released after serving eighteen months in prison.

In the summer of 1943, riots began in Los Angeles, after a first fight between sailors and *pachucos* (barrio gangs and/or youths who wore the stylish zoot suits). The newspapers built up a racist image of all Mexicans and Chicanos as violence-prone and uncivilized. The night after the initial fight, hundreds of servicemen invaded the East Los Angeles barrio and attacked any *pachuco* and zoot suiter they saw. The so-called "Zoot Suit Riots" went on for a week. Dozens of *pachucos* and zoot suiters were arrested, but not a single serviceman was arrested. The riots moved the Mexican government to make a formal diplomatic protest to Washington for the flagrantly unjust treatment of Mexicans/Chicanos. Ironically, while these developments were going on, thousands of Chicano servicemen were fighting and dying in a war against fascism.

The film documented the experience of Henry Reyna (Daniel Valdez), one of twelve youths sentenced to life. He undergoes two trials, a public one and a personal one. In court, he is defended by a liberal white lawyer, George (Charles Aidman), who is assisted by Alice (Tyne Daly). Reyna breaks up with his girlfriend, Della (Rose Portillo), as he becomes attracted to Alice. Reyna's second tribulation is that of himself and the mythical figure of El Pachuco (Edward James Olmos). El Pachuco represents the barrio: "I got you all figured out, Carnal; you're the one that got me here. My worst enemy and my best friend. Myself. . . ." On his release, Reyna is welcomed by his parents (Julio Medina, Lupe Ontiveros), and younger brother Rudy (Tony Plana) and sister (Alma Martinez). Although the film ends on a positive note, it mentions the fact that for the real Reyna, the future held two more prison terms, drug addiction, and a premature death in 1972. The trauma of his experience would take a terrible toll.

In reference to adapting a screenplay from his play, Valdez stated:

Actually, El Pachuco as a character emerged in one of my early plays, *Bernabe*. . . . And eventually *Zoot Suit* came along and I knew El Pachuco was going to be part of it. But the very first draft of the play concentrated on the real characters. I started out with a mound of material—6,000 pages of court transcripts, for one. . . . The hardest character to grab a hold of was Henry

Reyna. . . . I knew I didn't want to deal with the whole story from the outside looking in: I wanted to take the audience inside and then look out. And that took all the way to the screenplay to accomplish.[34]

Valdez spoke of where he obtained fragments of material for his play and film:

At the end of the play there's another famous quote, "El Pachuco, the man, the myth, still lives." . . . After Henry Leyva's death (the person, the character of Henry Reyna is based on), his family opened a small restaurant which was supposed to be a sort of gathering place for friends, family, and Chicanos. And it was called "Hank's." And in the menu it said: "Henry Leyva, the man who fought blindly for what he believed, still lives." And that's where the idea eventually fed into the play and eventually became "Henry Reyna—the man, the myth, still lives." . . . [35]

The film was made in thirteen days, most of it shot in sets in the Aquarius Theater, on the relatively modest budget of $12.5 million, by Universal. The studio was initially apprehensive about the film's success. Ned Tanen, president of Universal's Film Division, stated:

I see it as a possible breakthrough for reaching Hispanic audiences in this country. We'll market it in Hispanic centers, but we're not going to eliminate other outlets. It's colorful, it has energy, style and music. I think it's capable of broad appeal. This business is changing daily and radically. . . . I don't want to do exploitation material. I don't want to put out Spanish "Blaculas" but I think there's a major audience out there, and "Zoot Suit" will help us find it.[36]

Unfortunately, the studio did a less than effective marketing or promotional campaign for the film. Over the years, the film recouped its cost with cult and cultural audiences and its sale to television. The studio held back releasing *Zoot Suit* in the lucrative video cassette market, much to the dismay of Luis Valdez, until 1991. *Zoot Suit,* however, has a secure and lasting

227

place in the annals of Chicano cinema. It took a piece of recent and relevant Chicano history and documented it filmically, vibrantly, and powerfully.

Reviews of the film were generally positive, and the following is reflective. The *Los Angeles Times* (October 4, 1981) wrote:

> The film captures its pachuco swagger splendidly, not from the aisle seat stuck safely back in the house, but from multiple angles and distances, as if reporting a sports event, which a show with this much jitterbugging is. The aim isn't necessarily to show how "Zoot Suit" looked at the Aquarius . . . but to show how a typical performance felt. The ceremony and the story come through. Daniel Valdez and Edward James Olmos come through even more strongly than they did in the theater, which is saying something.

The Players

The fortunes of Chicano/Hispanic players in American films reflected the continued insensitivity and subtle racism in the film industry.

While more Chicano/Hispanic players appeared to be available than ever before, putting to disrepute the often-quoted Hollywood refrain that "there were no qualified" people, an extremely high turnover rate was noticeable. It indicated that Hispanic players had limited opportunities in film employment, for a limited number of years. Statistics bear this fact out:

> According to the Screen Actor's Guild, while Blacks, Latinos, Asians and American Indians account for about 22% of the nation's population, they made up 13% of the on-camera appearances in film, television and commercials in 1987. . . . According to a Screen Writer's Guild study of hiring practices from 1982 to 1985, racial discrimination accounted for minorities making up only 2% of the writers employed each year in films and T.V. . . . [37]

Predictably, too, the roles were incidental roles, hardly central to the films.

The television medium was equally negligent. It was reported that "examining more than 150 episodes of 30 network programs featuring minorities, the study found last spring's network prime-time schedule contained nine Latinos, three Asians and one Indian in regular roles. . . . "[38] The world presented was hardly reflective of the real world. "As a result, TV's world of harmony does not present viewers with a picture of an ideal society where racism has been fought and overcome. Instead, it portrays an artificial universe where racial difficulties and realities are denied."[39]

The 1980s witnessed the proliferation of a sizeable number of talented and capable Chicano/Hispanic players. A few acquired film stardom. Charlie Sheen (Carlos Estevez) and Emilio Estevez, sons of Martin Sheen (born Ramon Estevez of a Spanish immigrant father and Irish mother), came to prominence. The former was an actor in two important films: *Platoon* (1986, Orion), and *Wall Street* (1987, 20th Century). The latter came to attention in *Repo Man* (1984) and *The Breakfast Club* (1985) and developed into a credible actor, writer, and director. Chicano actor and Teatro Campesino alumnus Robert Beltran made impressive impact as a Chicano soldier assigned to train contras in *Latino* (1986, Cinecom). However, the actor that came to symbolize Chicano cinema was Edward James Olmos, a former rocker. His identification with Chicano audiences was an outgrowth of his participation in four films: as General Santa Ana in Jesus Treviño's *Seguin* (1981, PBS), as El Pachuco in both the theater and film versions of Luis Valdez's *Zoot Suit* (1982, Universal), as the luckless titled character of *The Ballad of Gregorio Cortez* (1983), and as the dedicated East Los Angeles teacher (a role for which he was nominated for an Oscar) in *Stand and Deliver* (1988, Warner Brothers).

Other notable Hispanic actors included actor-singer Daniel Valdez (Luis's brother), who played Henry Reina in *Zoot Suit* (1982, Universal); comedian Paul Rodriguez, of film and television; Puerto Rican Raul Julia, nominated for an Oscar in *Kiss of the Spider Woman* (1985, Island Alive); the Chicano character actor Trinidad Silvia, of television and film; Cuban Esai Morales, who scored as Ritchie Valens's brother in *La Bamba* (1987, Columbia); Cuban-Americans Steven Bauer and Andy Garcia; Domingo Ambriz of Robert Young's *Alambrista!* (1983); and the all-purpose Tony Plana and Rene Enriquez.

The Brazilian Sonia Braga was the only female Hispanic player to achieve stardom. She found commercial and critical success as the wealthy vamp in *Kiss of the Spider Woman* (1985, Island Alive) and as a Chicana activist in Robert Redford's *The Milagro Beanfield War* (1988, Universal). Mexican-born Elipidia Carrillo made an impressive debut in Tony Richardson's *The Border* (1982, Universal), as a young undocumented mother and scored again in Oliver Stone's *Salvador* (1986, Helmdale), as an impoverished victim of the political strife.

Other capable actresses included the stage-trained Silvana Gallardo, in *Windwalker* (1981) and *Death Wish II* (1982, Cannon); Alma Martinez, in *Seguin* (1981, PBS); Jenny Gago, in *Old Gringo* (1989); Rosana De Soto, in *La Bamba* (1987); Julie Carmen, in *The Milagro Beanfield War* (1988, Universal); Patricia Martinez, in *The Three Amigos* (1986, Orion); and the Cuban-American Elizabeth Peña, in *La Bamba* (1987, Columbia) and *Down and Out in Beverly Hills* (1986, Touchstone).

Last, but not least, the contributions of writer-actor-director Luis Valdez should not be underestimated. The founder of Teatro Campesino and writer of numerous plays, he wrote and directed the theater and film versions of *Zoot Suit* (1982, Universal) and the enormously successful *La Bamba* (1987, Columbia). He has been, and is, a dominant and creative force for the Chicano/Hispanic image coming to a more positive and truthful state.

Notes

1. Rudolfo Acuña, *Occupied America* (New York: Harper & Row, 1988).
2. Ibid.
3. Joel W. Finler, *The Hollywood Story* (London: Octopus Books Limited, 1988).
4. Chon Noriega, *What Is Hispanic Cinema?*, p. 18.
5. *Los Angeles Times,* May 1, 1983.
6. Ibid.
7. Ibid.
8. Ibid.
9. *Drama-Logue,* August 17–23, 1989.
10. *Americas 2001,* Vol. 1, No. 1, June–July 1987.
11. *L. A. Weekly,* August 28–September 3, 1987, reprinted by permission.
12. *El Norte* Press Kit (Sherman Oaks, Cal.: Cinecom International Films, 1984).

13. Ibid.
14. Ibid.
15. Ibid.
16. *Mother Jones,* February/March 1984.
17. *Los Angeles Times,* July 19, 1987.
18. Ibid.
19. *Optic Music's Film & Video Production,* September 1987.
20. *New York Times,* July 24, 1987, reprinted by permission.
21. Ibid.
22. *Newsweek,* August, 17, 1987.
23. *Latino* Press Kit, 1985.
24. Ibid.
25. *L.A. Weekly,* September 13–19, 1985, reprinted by permission.
26. *Los Angeles Times,* August 24, 1980.
27. Rodolfo Acuña, *Occupied America* (New York: Harper & Row, 1972).
28. Rosa Linda Fregoso, "Seguin: The Same Side of the Alamo," in *Chicano Cinema* (Binghamton, N.Y.: Bilingual Review/Press, 1985).
29. Barbara Zheutlin and David Talbot, *Creative Differences: Profiles of Hollywood Dissidents* (Boston: South End Press, 1978).
30. *Stand and Deliver,* Production Information Packet (Burbank: Warner Brothers, 1988).
31. Ibid.
32. Ibid.
33. *Los Angeles Times,* March 3, 1981.
34. Gary D. Keller, *Chicano Cinema* (Binghamton, N.Y.: Bilingual Review/Press, 1985).
35. Ibid.
36. *Los Angeles Times,* March 3, 1981.
37. Ron Harris, "Minorities in TV: Black/White Issue," *Los Angeles Times,* January 11, 1989.
38. Michael Ybarra, "Taking a Look at TV's Racial Picture," *Los Angeles Times,* August 23, 1989.
39. Ibid.

CHAPTER NINE
The 1990s—Crossover Dreams

The 1990s witnessed a number of remarkable international developments that, in political and economic terms, would affect history for decades to come.

The cold war's demise led to a demilitarization and improved relations between the United States and the Soviet Union. The collapse of the governments of Eastern Europe and the Soviet-backed Warsaw Pact induced smug elation in the hearts and minds of cold warriors and right-wing idealogues. However, this revelry was premature in light of the utter bankruptcy of the market economy in Latin America, from Haiti to Mexico to Brazil. After 500 hundred years, since the first European incursion into the Americas, the continent was still submerged in poverty and malnutrition, illiteracy and unemployment, and predatory and murderous military cliques.

As the 500th anniversary of Columbus's fateful voyage approached, Native Americans questioned its celebration. At the First Continental Meeting of Indigenous Peoples at Quito, Ecuador, in the summer of 1990, a Guatemalan Indian delegate stated, "These 500 years have meant nothing but misery and oppression for our people. What do we have to celebrate?"[1] This historical reassessment was taken up by others as well. Environmentalist Kirkpatrick Sale, author of the book *The Conquest of Paradise,* described "Columbus's landing and subsequent behavior as the model for later explorers who plundered the New World for gold and set in place a civilization that committed genocide and 'ecocide' against the natives and their environment."[2]

In the United States, the conservative shift continued, under the helm of George Bush. His vision of the "New Order" included gunboat diplomacy and intervention in Panama and Iraq, vetoing an extension of the Civil Rights Act, and posturing himself as the "Education President" while the trillion-dollar deficit remained unchecked. The 1990 U.S. Census revealed the undeniable fact that the Hispanic community was quickly becoming the largest minority in the nation. The Hispanic population grew from being 6.4 percent of the U.S. population in 1980 to 9 percent in 1990. In raw numbers, for example, in 1980, there were 26.5 million Blacks, compared to 14.6 million Hispanics. In 1990, Blacks were just under 20 million, while Hispanics had grown to 22.3 million. Some 70 percent of the Hispanic population was focused in four states: Texas, California, Florida, and New York.[3] Other data compiled by the American Council on Education documented a worsening situation for Hispanics:

> The study . . . showed that the proportion of Latino students completing high school slid from 60.1% in 1984 to 55.9 in 1989. . . . In 1976, Latinos represented just 2.8% of all those earning bachelor degrees. In 1989, that figure has increased only to 3%—despite the doubling of the college-age Latino population during that time. . . . [4]

The Films

The great expectations of Chicano/Hispanics for a real and sustained breakthrough in American films failed to be realized. More often than not, stereotypical images of Hispanics continued unabated on screen and television.

The prevailing images of Chicanos/Hispanics in the decade were reruns of past stereotypes and some new ones to accommodate and reflect the changing political landscape. For Hispanic males, the stereotypes were narcotraficantes/drug dealers, criminals or bandits, gang members, and undocumented workers. Latinas found themselves inevitably as prostitutes and cantineras whenever a silly summer movie required a "rites of passage" scene for some cherubic Anglo teenager or when some "good ol' boy" contingent of marines wanted some sexual frolic.

233

Television reflected a no more realistic image of American society:

> Picture an America where friendly, funky, Cub-fan-fanatic Chicano is the only inhabited spot between New York City and Twin Peaks. Imagine that this mythical U.S. has become so awash in racial sensitivity and tolerance that even drug dealers practice affirmative action, yet, strangely enough, intergalactic aliens are a far more visible minority group than Hispanics.[5]

In January 1990, the Chicano/Mexican fictional swashbuckler Zorro returned on a television series on cable's The Family Channel. Created by Johnston McCulley in 1919, the role was first dramatized on film in Douglas Fairbanks's *The Mark of Zorro* (1920). The current role was played by Ducan Regehr. It followed the well-worn proverb that the more things change, the more things stay the same. In the case of Zorro, the character has yet to be played by a Chicano/Hispanic.

In February 1990, several Chicano filmakers (directors Jesus Treviño, Luis Valdez, Gregory Nava, musician Carlos Santana, producer Mortesuma Esparza) travelled to Mexico City to attend the first week of Chicano Cinema and call for coproductions and cooperation between Mexican and Chicano filmmakers. Producer Mortesuma Esparaza noted, "To see a recent film about Vietnam like 'Born on the Fourth of July,' one does not become aware that Hispanics were one-fourth of the dead in that war and that we won more medals than any other group."[6]

In Hollywood, it was stereotyping as usual. The NBC mini-series, *Drug Wars: The Camarena Story* (1990), which purported to tell the story of DEA agent Kiki Camarena, his 1984 abduction, and murder, portrayed all Mexicans as only either corrupt government officials or drug sellers. It prompted the Mexican government to denounce the reenactment. Subsequently, NBC freely substituted news with entertainment. *La Opinion* (January 11, 1990) was moved to comment, "The recent events of the capture of General Noriega in Panama was used to promote the mini-series. Without a shred of shame, NBC promoted, 'Drug Wars' like a chapter of the so-called war against drugs, in which Noriega had just been taken prisoner." The NBC anchorman stated that "in some cases we need to invade some countries." The message was less than subtle: Latin Americans cannot manage their affairs of state and thereby the benevolent neighbor to the north must do it for them. Social Darwinism was alive and well in the 1990s.

In *The Rookie* (1990, Warner Brothers), two White cops (Clint Eastwood, Charlie Sheen) are confronted by scores of Chicano gang members running amok. The *Los Angeles Times* (December 7, 1990) noted, "The two cops' excursions into East Los Angeles are heavy on the Mexican xenophobia. . . . " Sydney Pollack's *Havana* (1990, Universal) captured some of the chaos of the last days of the Batista dictatorship but little of the Cuban people. The *Los Angeles Times* (December 12, 1990) noted, "He (Pollack) seems torn between making a great, old-style, doomed lovers' romance and a serious, politically committed epic, and he succeeds at neither. . . . " *A Show of Force* (1990), directed by Brazilian Bruno Barreto, purported to portray the real-life story of the murder of two independistas after they had been arrested by government forces in Cerro Maravilla, Puerto Rico, in 1978. The subsequent cover-up resulted in the downfall of the island's administration. The film became an exercise of typical Hollywood trivialization. The *Los Angeles Times* (May 14, 1990) wrote, ". . . a political thriller that spins giddily between fact and fancy, shocks and romance, politics and sex—and sometimes it's difficult to guess whether the sex is there to sell the politics or vice versa."

Latin Americans were on display stereotypically as *narcotraficantes,* corrupt government officials, and the proverbial hapless peasants seeking deliverance from *Delta Force II* (1990, MGM). Set in a supposedly fictional Latin American nation (a composite of Panama and Columbia), it was filmed in the Philippines and exemplified the typical Hollywood disregard for cultural or racial accuracy. It had the perennial cold warrior, Chuck Norris, as the independent-minded DEA agent in search of a drug lord (Billy Drago). The most telling line of dialogue is uttered by the dictator of the country, "If the United States accuses us of being a country of drug pushers, we accuse them of being a country of drug addicts!" The *Los Angeles Times* (August 29,

1990) noted, "Characterizations are so cardboard and stereotypical and plotting so trite that there's not enough involvement. . . ." Chicano/Mexican bandits and cantineras were in evidence in the western *Bad Jim* (1990), to be remembered perhaps only for the film debut of Clark Gable's son, John Clark Gable. Elsewhere, *Shrimp on the Barbie* (1990) chronicled the footloose adventures of a Chicano (Cheech Marin) in Australia. The *Los Angeles Times* (September 3, 1990) noted, "It's too bad that Marin didn't get to direct the film, for the gifts he displayed as a director (and writer) in 'Born in East L.A.' are just the ones needed here."

A refreshingly more accurate representation of Chicano/ Mexican reality was portrayed in *Sweet 15* (1990), an episode of the youth-oriented television series "Wonderworks," aired over PBS. The film depicted the efforts of a hard-working father (Tony Plana), trying to legalize his immigration status, while his daughter (Karia Montana) approaches the rites of passage with her *quinceñera* (fifteen-year birthday and social coming-out party).

Elsewhere, Hispanic actors/actresses were in sporadic display. Lynda Carter returned, after a long absence, to star in the NBC TV film *Daddy* (1991), based on the Danielle Steele novel. She essayed a non-Hispanic role. About her return, she stated, "I had a star attitude before. I wasn't difficult or impossible, but I bought into the attitude that being an actress makes you special. . . . I'm anxious for the industry to get to know who Lynda Carter is today. I've grown up. Hopefully, I've put my ego aside."[7] Musician-turned-actor Ruben Blades played a Mexican-American rancher moonlighting as a school custodian involved with a principal (Christine Lahti) in the TNT television film, *Crazy from the Heart* (1991). When asked about the lack of Hispanics on films and television, he commented, "They don't come to me if they are going to do a Custer movie and cast me as Custer. They say, 'He is not a North American. How can he play Custer?' But there's not a moment's hesitation that someone like William Hurt can play a Latino. . . ." He commented that it appeared that Hispanics had a better chance if they were "closer to the Anglo ideal of a leading man. . . . My position is just cast the roles in terms of talent and try to make it more representative of what it is all about."[8]

Three other television films in 1991 reverted back to the old stereotype. In *The Last Prostitute*, Sonia Braga played Leah, a legendary Hispanic prostitute who is retired from the world's oldest profession. She is pursued by two pubescent White youths in search of her sexual favors. The *Los Angeles Times* (September 11, 1991) wrote: "It's meant to be heartwarming, not loins-stirring, but generates not the slightest heat in zones erogenous or otherwise. . . ." In *Lightning Field*, a pregnant woman (Nancy McKeon) is the victim of a violent, devil-worshipping, baby-stealing Latin American cult. So blatantly racist was the Latino portrayal that the *Los Angeles Times* (September 11, 1991) was moved to comment, "The closest thing to a surprise in this stupefying walk-through of a telepic is the somewhat anachronistic portrayal of anonymously Luciferian Latinos at this late, post-multiculturalist date. . . . Needless to add, wherever the devil is set, 'Lightning Field' won't be winning any Golden Eagle Awards from Nosotros." In the NBC mini-series, *Drug Wars: The Cocaine Cartel* (1992), Alex McArthur played a DEA "good ol' boy" out to topple the Columbian drug cartel almost single-handedly, in a film reminiscent of the ridiculous *The Magnificent Seven.*

Cheech Marin produced a comedy during 1991 for Fox Television, titled "Culture Clash," about three young, aspiring Hispanic comedians (Richard Montoya, Herbert Siguenza, Ric Salinas). Marin stated, "For one thing, you've never seen that many brown faces on the tube at the same time. We'll be the only Latino show on TV."[9] Predictably, however, Fox canceled the show before its premiere.

In theatrical films, Hispanics were as rare and fared slightly better. In *Kill Me a Killer* (1991), obviously inspired by John M. Cain's *The Postman Always Rings Twice,* Julie Carmen and Robert Beltran played an unhappy wife and drifter plotting to kill her Anglo husband, the proprietor of a nightclub in East Los Angeles. The *Hollywood Reporter* (April 18, 1991) noted: "The performances are terrific, especially Carmen as the passionate wife and barmaid. Her transformation from submissive slave to fiery motivator is credible and volcanic. . . . As the soft-spoken, guitar-plucking Tony, Beltran's performance is well-calibrated and solid. . . ." *Variety* (April 9, 1991) commented, "Compensating for the film's stretch of credibility are its frequent passionate love scenes featuring Carmen and Beltran. Both performers do a fine job. . . ."

The Mambo Kings (1992, Warner Brothers), based on the Pulitzer Prize–winning novel by Oscar Híjuelos, was robbed of much credibility when, in typical Hollywood shortsightedness, the Spaniard Antonio Banderas and Italian-American Armand Assante were cast as the Cuban musicians.

The most impressive film so far in the decade to chronicle the Chicano/Mexican-American experience was *American Me* (1992), directed by and starring James Edward Olmos. Olmos played Santana, whose father (Sal Lopez) was badly beaten and whose mother (Vira Montes) was raped during the anti-Mexican Zoot Suit Riots of 1943. The film documents the evolution of Santana as a teenage gang member in East Los Angeles, his induction into juvenile and Folsom prisons, and ultimately his leadership of the Mexican Mafia. Scripted by Floyd Mutrux and Desmond Nakano (who had scripted *Boulevard Nights),* the film is the best, by far, about Chicano gangs and their subculture. Shot primarily in East Los Angeles and Folsom Prison, the film benefited from real Chicanos playing reel Chicanos and a sensitivity, and a sense of urgency not before in evidence in an American film. Olmos came in for some criticism in some quarters of the Chicano community for portraying a negative aspect of the barrio. In response, he stated:

> There are those who say, "If you can't say anything nice, then don't say it." I think it's time for us to really understand where the cancer lies. This is a healing movie. . . . It's really necessary. Sixty-five percent of the kids in the L.A. County Juvenile Hall are Hispanic. Almost half are in for murder. These are kids from ages nine to eighteen. That's a cancer we don't even want to look at. But we're going to look at it now.[10]

The *Los Angeles Times* (March 13, 1992) noted of the film, "Olmos' relentless passion is the best thing about 'American Me,' a cautionary tale that offers a chilling, oppressive look at the connections between Latino prison gangs like the Mexican Mafia and the drug traffic in the barrio. Earnest, unrelenting and violent, 'American Me' packs a considerable wallop. . . ." Films like these, however, were few and far between in a place called Hollywood.

In conclusion, the 1990s did not justify the great expectations in the 1980s that racist stereotypes of Chicanos/Hispanics would be eradicated. Neither did the decade evidence any sustained breakthrough of Hispanic performers or Hispanic-oriented films. As the 500th anniversary of the European incursion and colonization of the American continent approached, the indigenous Indian/Mestizo culture and history continued to be submerged, buried, and obliterated in real and reel life.

Notes

1. *Los Angeles Times,* April 1, 1991.
2. Ibid.
3. *Los Angeles Times,* March 11, 1981.
4. *Los Angeles Times,* January 25, 1991.
5. *Time,* May 14, 1990.
6. *Mas,* Summer 1990, Vol. 1, No. 4.
7. *TV Guide,* June 29, 1991.
8. "Television Guide," *Los Angeles Times,* August 18–24, 1991.
9. *TV Guide,* August 31, 1991.
10. *Premiere,* April 1992.

CHAPTER TEN
Chicano/Hispanic Film Stars

The 1920s

Don Alvarado. He was born Jose Paige, on November 4, 1904, in Albuquerque, New Mexico, of mixed parentage (Mexican and Anglo). He began as an extra in 1924 and reached stardom in *Loves of Carmen* (1927) opposite Dolores Del Rio. He went on to enjoy a vogue as a "Latin lover" in the twenties, and then the talkies reduced him to supporting roles. Key films: *Drums of Love* (1928), *The Bad One* (1930), *The Bridge of San Luis Rey* (1929), and *Lady with a Past* (1932). His last role was in *The Big Steal* (1949). He was father to actress Joy Paige, who enjoyed moderate success in films (e.g., *Casablanca*) at Warner's during the forties. Alvardo died of cancer in Hollywood on March 31, 1967.

Armida. She was born in 1913 in Sonora, Mexico. She was typecast as a Latina heroine in "B" films, many of them Westerns. She debuted in *La Mexicana* (1929). Key films: *General Crack* (1929) with John Barrymore, *Under a Texas Moon* (1930), *Border Cafe* (1940), and *Fiesta* (1941). She retired in 1951.

Dolores Del Rio. She was born Dolores Asunsolo y Lopez Negrete on August 3, 1905, in Durango, Mexico. She was a distant cousin to Ramon Novarro. Her Hollywood debut was in *Joanna* (1925). Stardom came with *What Price Glory?* (1926). She played exotic and sophisticated ladies in her early period. Later she played in dramas in U.S. and Mexican films and television. Her appearances in U.S. films after 1942 were infrequent. She performed in theater in the fifties and sixties. Key films: *Ramona* (1929), *Bird of Paradise* (1932), *Journey into Fear* (1942), *Maria Candelaria* (1943), *The Fugitive* (1947), *La Cucaracha* (1959),

Cheyenne Autumn (1964). She was the first Mexican Hollywood female star. She died of natural causes on April 11, 1983.

Mona Maris. She was born Maria Capdevielle in 1903 in Buenos Aires, Argentina. She enjoyed brief success in the late twenties and early thirties, usually typecast as a sultry and exotic señorita. Debuted in *The Little People* (1926, UK). Key films: *Under the Texas Moon* (1929), *The Arizona Kid* (1930), *One Mad Kiss* (1930), with Jose Mojica. She retired from films after an Argentinian film and went to live in Lima, Peru.

Jose Mojica. He was born in San Gabriel, Jalisco, Mexico, in 1896. He arrived in the U.S. in 1921 and was recruited by the Chicago Opera, where he spent nine years. The young tenor was brought to Hollywood in the late 1920s as a rival to Ramon Novarro and stayed on to star in fourteen films, most of them with Fox. Debuted in *One Mad Kiss* (1930). Key films: *Ladron de Amor* (1930, Mexico), *When Love Laughs* (1933), *The Cross and the Sword* (1934), *Un Capitan de Cosarios* (1935). After *Melodias de America* (1942), he retired and joined the priesthood. He died of hepatitis on September 20, 1974, in Lima, Peru.

Antonio Moreno. He was born Antonio Garride Monteagudo on September 26, 1887, in Madrid, Spain. He was the first Hispanic film star in Hollywood and competed with Valentino and Novarro for the mantle of "Latin lover" in the 1920s and then was relegated to character roles with the coming of the talkies. He began as an extra in 1912 and reached prominence in *The Latin Quarter* (1914). Key films: *The Spanish Dancer* (1923) with Pola Negri, *The Torrent* (1926) with Greta Garbo, and *It* (1927) with Clara Bow. His last role was in *The Searchers* (1956). He died in 1967.

Barry Norton. He was born Alfredo Biraben on June 16, 1905, in Buenos Aires, Argentina. He enjoyed a brief vogue in the late 1920's and early 1930s as a Latin lover and romantic leading man. He also starred in Hollywood Spanish language films and directed several himself. Some film credits: *The Lily* (1926) *What Price Glory?* (1926), *Sunrise* (1927), *Dishonored* (1931), *El Diablo Del Mar* (1936), *Around the World in 80 Days* (1956). He died in 1936.

Ramon Novarro. He was born Jose Gil Samaniegos on February 6, 1899, in Durango, Mexico. He was a distant cousin to Dolores Del Rio. He was the first Mexican Hollywood star. He was employed as a Hollywood extra during 1917–21. Stardom came with *The Prisoner of Zenda* in 1923. Often typed as a "Latin lover" in the twenties, he was a versatile actor of drama and light comedy and also wrote an opera and directed in film, theater, and television. Key films: *Scaramouche* (1923), *The Arab* (1924), *The Midshipman* (1925), *The Student Prince* (1927), *Ben-Hur* (1927), *The Pagan* (1929), *Mata Hari* (1932), *The Cat and the Fiddle* (1934), *Contra La Covriente* (dir., prod., sc.—1936), *La Comedie de Bonheur* (1940), *La Virgen que Forjo una Patria* (1942), *The Big Steal* (1949), *Heller in Pink Tights* (1960). He was murdered in his Hollywood Hills home on October 31, 1968.

Duncan Renaldo. He was born on April 23, 1904, in Spain. He played Latino heroes for three decades, mostly in Westerns (among them the Cisco Kid character on screen and television). Key films: *The Bridge of San Luis Rey* (1929), *Trader Horn* (1931). He replaced Cesar Romero as the Cisco Kid in *The Cisco Kid Returns* (1945) and played the role in three more films and in the 1950s TV series. He died on September 3, 1980, of heart failure.

Gilbert Roland. He was born Luis Antonio Damaso Alonso in Chihuahua, Mexico, on December 11, 1905. He began as a Hollywood extra in 1925. Stardom came in *Camille* (1927). He played romantic heroes in the twenties and thirties, the Cisco Kid (six films) in the forties, and character roles in the fifties and sixties. Key films: *The Dove* (1927), *She Done Him Wrong* (1933), *The Sea Hawk* (1940), *Robin Hood of Monterey* (1947), *The Bad and the Beautiful* (1952), *The Bullfighter and the Lady* (1952), *Cheyenne Autumn* (1964). He died of cancer on May 16, 1994.

Raquel Torres. She was born Paula Osterman on November 11, 1908, in Hermosillo, Mexico. A dark-haired beauty, she was among the first of the Mexican-born stars in the 1920s. Often wasted, she scored strongly in three important films: *White Shadows of the South Seas* (1928), *The Bridge of San Luis Rey* (1929), and *Duck Soup* (1933) with the Marx brothers. She retired after her ninth film, in 1934. She died of a heart attack on August 10, 1987.

Lupita Tovar. She was born in Oaxaca, Mexico, in 1911 of a Mexican father and a U.S.-born mother. She was typecast as a Latina heroine mostly in "B" films. Debuted in John Ford's *The Black Watch* (1928). She starred in Mexico's first talkie, *Santa* (1931). Key films: *Vidas Rotas* (1935, Spain), *An Old Spanish Custom* (1935, UK). She retired after *The Crime Doctor's Courage* (1945). She married agent Paul Kohner, and their daughter, Susan Kohner, achieved some film fame in the 1950s. In 1981, Lupita received the Diosa de Plata award from the Mexican Association of Film Critics and Unions for Mexico's first talking film.

Lupe Velez. She was born Maria Velez de Villalobos on July 18, 1908, in San Luis Potosi, Mexico. She began as a dancer and contracted to costar with Douglas Fairbanks, Sr., in *The Gaucho* (1927), which brought her stardom. A versatile talent in drama and comedy, she was also an accomplished singer. Key films: *The Half-Naked Truth* (1932); *The Girl from Mexico* (1939), which began the Mexican Spitfire films; *Playmates* (1941). She committed suicide on December 14, 1944.

The 1930s

Leo Carrillo. He was born on August 6, 1880, in Los Angeles, California. Essentially a character actor, he played cheerful Hispanic second leads or villains. Debuted in *The Dove* (1928). Key films: *Viva Villa!* (1934), *Blockade* (1938), *The Fugitive* (1947). He played the Cisco Kid's sidekick in the 1950s TV series. He died in 1961.

Tito Guizar. He was born Francisco Tito Guizar on April 8, 1908, in Guadalajara, Mexico. A singer and actor in Mexico, he was brought to Hollywood in the 1930s to replace Jose Mojica. Debuted in *Under the Pampas Moon* (1935). Key films: *The Big Broadcast of 1938* (1938), *St. Louis Blues* (1939), *The Llano Kid* (1940), *Mexicana* (1945). He retired to Mexico in the 1950s.

Rita Hayworth. She was born Marguerita Carmen Cansino, in New York City, on October 17, 1918. Began dancing professionally as a child and then became a Hollywood extra in 1935. She reached film stardom in *Only Angels Have Wings* (1939). She was typecast as the forties sex symbol. Key films:

Blood and Sand (1940), *Cover Girl* (1944), *Gilda* (1946), *The Lady from Shanghai* (1948), *Pal Joey* (1957), *Separate Tables* (1958), *The Money Trap* (1966). Married to Orson Welles, 1943–47, and Dick Haymes, 1953–54. She died of Alzheimer's disease on May 14, 1987.

Margo. She was born Marie Marguerita Guadalupe Teresa Bolado Castilla y O'Donnel on May 10, 1917, in Mexico City. A dancer, singer, and actress, she made an impressive debut in *Crime without Passion* (1934). Key films: *Robin Hood of El Dorado* (1936), *Winterset* (1936), *The Lost Horizon* (1937), *Viva Zapata!* (1953). Married to actor Eddie Albert, she cofounded Los Angeles's Plaza De La Raza. She died of cancer on July 17, 1985.

Chris-Pin Martin. Rotund Mexican-American character actor (1893–1953). Films: *Bordertown* (1935), *Stagecoach* (1939), *The Mark of Zorro* (1940), *The Ox-Bow Incident* (1943), *San Antonio* (1945).

Conchita Montenegro. She was born on September 11, 1912, in San Sebastian, Spain. Typecast as an exotic Hispanic heroine: *The Cisco Kid* (1931), *Never the Twain Shall Meet* (1931), *Handy Andy* (1934). She left Hollywood for French and Spanish films.

Rosita Moreno. She was born in Pachuca, Mexico. A singer and dancer, she played Latina heroines: *The Santa Fe Trail* (1930), *King of the Gypsies* and *Love's Frontier* (1934), with Jose Mojica.

Movita. She was born Movita Castaneda in 1917 in Mexico. She played the female lead opposite Clark Gable in *Mutiny on the Bounty* (1935) but thereafter was reduced to "B" films: *Rose of the Rio Grande* (1938), *The Girl from Rio* (1939), *Viva Zapata!* (1953). Married to Marlon Brando, 1960–68.

Anthony Quinn. He was born Antonio Rodolfo Oaxaca Quinn in Chihuahua, Mexico, on April 21, 1915. He began as an extra in 1936. Film stardom came in *Black Gold* (1947). Versatile actor of screen, stage, and television. Key films: *The Brave Bulls* (1951); *Viva Zapata!* (1953), which won him a Best Supporting Actor Oscar; *La Strada* (1954); *Lust for Life* (1956), which earned him a second Best Supporting Actor Oscar; *Requiem for a Heavyweight* (1962); *Lawrence of Arabia* (1962);

Zorba the Greek (1964); *Revenge* (1990). TV series: "The Man and the City," 1971–72.

Nita Rey. She was born Nancy Torres in Guadalajara, Mexico, in 1911. She played second female leads in Hollywood beginning in 1929: *Oklahoma Cycle* (1930), a "B" Western with Bob Steele, among others.

Cesar Romero. He was born on February 15, 1907, in New York City of Cuban parentage. He began as a dancer and then played leads and second leads as Latin lovers and suave villains. Debuted in *The Shadow Laughs* (1933). He was the second Cisco Kid in six films, *The Cisco Kid and the Lady* (1939), etc. Other films: *Tall, Dark and Handsome* (1941), *Coney Island* (1943), *Captain from Castille* (1947). He performed on stage and television. He died of complications of a blood clot on January 1, 1994.

The 1940s

Rodolfo Acosta. He was born in Chihuahua, Mexico, in 1920. Established as a villain in Mexican films, he debuted in Hollywood in *The Fugitive* (1947). Others: *The Bullfighter and the Lady* (1951), *One-Eyed Jacks* (1961). He died on November 7, 1974.

Pedro Armendariz. He was born on May 9, 1912, in Mexico City. A charismatic and gifted actor, he debuted in Mexican cinema in *Maria Elena* (1935) and quickly achieved stardom: *Maria Candelaria* (1943), *El Bruto* (1952), *Lucrecia Borgia* (1953). He went on to become an international film star: *Lucretia Borgia* (1953, France), *Uomini e Lupi* (1956, Italy), etc. Starred in fifteen U.S. films: *Fort Apache* (1948), *The Three Godfathers* (1948), *The Big Boodle* (1957), *Captain Sinbad* (1962), *From Russia, with Love* (1963). Ill with terminal cancer, he shot himself on June 18, 1963.

Desi Arnaz. He was born Desiderio Alberto Arnaz y de Acha III on March 2, 1917, in Santiago, Cuba. In the United States since the age of sixteen, he formed his own band and then established himself as a singing bongo player. His film debut was in *Too Many Girls* (1940) and in the same year married his leading lady, Lucille Ball. Other films: *Bataan* (1943), *Holiday in Havana* (1949), *Forever Darling* (1956). He starred with Miss

Ball (whom he divorced in 1960) in TV's "I Love Lucy," 1957–67. He died on December 2, 1986.

Alfonso Bedoya. Mexican character actor (1904–57), usually as a villain: *The Pearl* (1945), *The Treasure of Sierra Madre* (1948), *Border Incident* (1949), *The Big Country* (1958). He died in 1958.

Linda Christian. She was born Blanca Rosa Welter on November 13, 1923, in Tampico, Mexico. A stunning beauty, she enjoyed moderate success as a Latina leading lady, mostly in "B" films. Debuted in *Holiday in Mexico* (1946). Other films: *Tarzan and the Mermaids* (1948), *House of the Seven Hawks* (1959), etc. Married to Tyrone Power (1949–54) and mothered two actress daughters, Romina and Taryn Power.

Arturo de Cordova. He was born Arturo Garcia Rodriguez on May 7, 1908, in Mérida, Yucatán, Mexico. He began as a journalist and radio broadcaster and reached stardom in Mexican films with *Celos* (1935), as a romantic and dramatic matinee idol. He was brought to Hollywood to star in ten films of varying quality, usually typed as a swashbucking Latin lover: *For Whom the Bell Tolls* (1943) and *A Medal for Benny* (1945) being the exceptions. Key films: *Frenchmen's Creek* (1944), *New Orleans* (1947), *El* (1952), *Reportaje* (1953), etc. Won numerous Ariels, Mexico's Oscar, when he left the United States in the early fifties. He died of a heart attack on November 3, 1973.

Dona Drake. She was born Rita Novella in 1920 in Mexico City. She played decorative second leads: *Aloma of the South Seas* (1941), *Let's Face It* (1943), *Without Reservations* (1946), *Princess of the Nile* (1954). She is retired.

Esther Fenandez. She was born in Mascota, Jalisco, Mexico, on August 23, 1920. A former model and dancer, she achieved major Mexican cinema stardom with *Alla en el Rancho Grande* (1936). She won Mexico's Oscar, the Ariel, for *Santa* (1943) as Best Actress. She was ill-used in two U.S. films: *Two Years before the Mast* (1946) opposite Alan Ladd and *Pancho Villa Returns* (1950). She retired in the 1950s.

Jose Ferrer. He was born Jose Vicente Ferrer de Otero y Clintron on January 8, 1912, in Santurre, Puerto Rico. A gifted and versatile actor, he gained prominence in the Broadway theater before films: *Joan of Arc* (1948); *Crisis* (1950); *Cyrano de*

Bergerac (1950), which earned him an Oscar for best actor (the first Latino to receive one); *Moulin Rouge* (1952); *Sadie Thompson* (1953); *Lawrence of Arabia* (1962), etc. Also directed films and performed on TV. He died on January 26, 1992.

Gabriel Figueroa. He was born on April 24, 1907, in Mexico. He is one of the greatest cinematographers of world cinema, especially in twenty-four films with director Emilio Fernandez, including such films as *Maria Candelaria* (1943) and five films with Luis Buñuel, *Los Olvidados* (1950) among others. He has worked in the United States often, in John Huston's *The Night of the Iguana* (1964) and Clint Eastwood's *Kelly's Heroes* (1970) and *Two Mules for Sister Sara*.

Roberto Gavaldon. He was born on June 7, 1909, in Jimenez, Mexico, He served as an assistant director in the 1930s in Hollywood, and in the 1940s he became a director in Mexican films. He directed two U.S. films: *The Adventures of Casanova* (1948) with Arturo De Cordova and *The Littlest Outlaw* (1955) with Pedro Armendariz. His masterpiece remains *Macario* (1960), a powerful tale of man's latent obsession with death and immortality.

Dick Haymes. He was born Richard Benjamin Haymes on September 13, 1916, in Buenos Aires, Argentina. Upon his U.S. arrival he became in rapid succession a radio announcer and band vocalist with Harry James' band. Enjoyed film success with *Dramatic School* (1938), *State Fair* (1945). *One Touch of Venus* (1948). Married to actress Joanne Dru, 1941–49, and Rita Hayworth, 1953–54. Bankrupted by 1960, he attempted a comeback in the mid sixties. He died of lung cancer on March 28, 1980.

Estela Inda. A gifted Mexican actress since the 1930s: *La Noche de los Mayas* (1938), *Bugambilia* (1944), etc. She made one U.S. film playing "Malinche" in *Captain from Castille* (1947). Her greatest role remains that of the working-class mother in Luis Buñuel's *Los Olvidados* (1950).

Adela Mara. She was born Adelaida Delgado on April 28, 1923, in Highland, Michigan, of Spanish parentage. An attractive and vivacious blonde, she played exotic heroines in "B" films: *Navy Blues* (1941), *You Were Never Lovelier* (1942), *Wake of the Red Witch* (1949), *The Sands of Iwo Jima* (1949), *The Big Circus* (1959). She was active in television. She is now retired.

Carmen Miranda. She was born Maria do Carmo Miranda da Cunha on February 9, 1909, near Lisbon, Portugal. She grew up in Rio de Janeiro, Brazil, and became a popular recording star and film star. U.S. debut in *Down Argentina Way* (1940). Typecast as temperamental and one-dimensional Latina, mostly in musicals: *Weekend in Havana* (1941), *Copacabana* (1947), *Scared Stiff* (1953). She died of a heart attack on August 4, 1955.

Ricardo Montalban. He was born in Mexico City on November 25, 1920. He made his Mexican film debut in *Los Tres Mosqueteros* (1941). His Hollywood film debut was in *Fiesta* (1947). Initially typecast as a "Latin lover." Versatility came with experience in film, theater, and television. Key films: *Neptune's Daughter* (1949), *Battleground* (1949), *Right Cross* (1950), *My Man and I* (1952), *The Money Trap* (1966), *The Naked Gun* (1988). TV series: "Fantasy Island," 1976–83.

Maria Montez. She was born Maria Africa Vidal del Santo Silas on June 6, 1920, in Barahona, Domincan Republic. An attractive brunette, she was typecast as an exotic leading lady in very popular adventure films for Universal: *The Invisible Woman* (1940), *Arabian Nights* (1942), *Ali Baba and the Forty Thieves* (1944), *Sudan* (1945), *The Exile* (1948), *Siren of Atlantis* (1948). She left Hollywood for European films in the late forties. She died prematurely of a heart attack in 1951.

Estelita Rodriguez. She was born on July 2, 1915, in Juanara, Cuba. Typed as an exotic Latina mostly in "B" films: *Mexicana* (1945), *Old Los Angeles* (1948), *Belle of Old Mexico* (1950), *Rio Bravo* (1959). She died on March 12, 1966.

Elena Verdugo. She was born in 1926 in Hollywood, on land that her Spanish descendants had received as land grants from the king of Spain. A striking brunette, she played female leads in "B" films and supporting roles in big-budget films: *The Moon and the Sixpence* (1950), *The Marksman* (1953). She played in two TV series, "Meet Millie" and "Marcus Welby, M.D.," 1969–75.

The 1950s

Rafael Campos. He was born in 1936 in the Dominican Republic. He played character roles most of his career and in his two first films juvenile leads: *The Blackboard Jungle* (1955),

The Trial (1955), *Oklahoma Crude* (1973). He died of cancer on July 9, 1985.

Cantinflas. He was born Mario Moreno Reyes in Mexico City on August 12, 1911. Born in dire poverty, he first entered show business as a circus acrobat before his Mexican film debut in 1936. Stardom came in *Asi es Mi Tierra* (1937). He personified Mexico's "Everyman" in dozens of satirical comedies that ridiculed authority, man's vanity, and greed. Key films: *Ahi Esta el Detalle* (1940), *El Bombero Atomico* (1950), *El Extra* (1962), *Un Quijote sin Mancha* (1969), and his last, *El Barrendero* (1983). He starred in two U.S. films: *Around the World in Eighty Days* (1956) and *Pepe* (1960). He died of cancer on April 20, 1993.

Elsa Cardenas. She was born on August 3, 1938, in Tijuana, Mexico. Debuted in Mexican films and then in U.S. films: *The Brave One* (1955), *Giant* (1956), *Fun in Acapulco* (1963), *The Wild Bunch* (1969). She is semiretired.

Linda Cristal. She was born Victoria Moya in 1935 in Buenos Aires, Argentina. She debuted in Mexican cinema in *Cuando Levanta la Niebla* (1951) and in the United States in *Commanche* (1956). She was quickly typed as an all-purpose exotic, usually as an Indian maiden or Mexican señorita: *Cry Tough* (1959), *The Alamo* (1960), *Two Rode Together* (1961), *Mr. Majestyk* (1974). She starred in the TV series "The High Chaparral" in the 1970s.

Mel Ferrer. He was born Melchior Gaston Ferrer on August 25, 1917 in Eberton, N.J., the son of a Cuban surgeon and Manhattan socialite. This tall leading man began acting on Broadway and film debuted in *The Girl of Limberlost* (1945) and went on to enjoy a modest stardom in the 1950s. Key films: *Lost Boundaries* (1949), *The Brave Bulls* (1951), *Scaramouche* (1952), *War and Peace* (1956), *The Sun Also Rises* (1957), *A Time for Loving* (1972), etc. He has also produced, directed and scripted. He was married to Audrey Hepburn (1954-68).

Pedro Gonzalez Gonzalez. Diminutive Mexican-American character actor (1926–71) born in San Antonio, Texas. Typecast often as amiable comedy relief: *Wings of the Hawk* (1953), *Rio Bravo* (1959), *Support Your Local Gunslinger* (1971).

Katy Jurado. She was born Maria Christina Jurado Garcia in 1927 in Guadalajara, Mexico. She debuted in Mexican films in 1943. She specialized in streetwise and independent-minded Latinas: *Bullfighter and the Lady* (1951); *High Noon* (1952); *Broken Lance* (1954), for which she was nominated for an Oscar as Best Supporting Actress; *One-Eyed Jacks* (1961); *Pat Garrett and Billy the Kid* (1973). She won Mexico's Ariel for Buñuel's *El Bruto* (1952). She was married and divorced from actor Ernest Borgnine.

Susan Kohner. She was born on November 11, 1939, in Los Angeles, California. She was the daughter of Lupita Tovar and agent Paul Kohner. After winning acclaim in the Broadway theater, she made her film debut in *To Hell and Back* (1956). Key films: *Dino* (1957), *The Big Fisherman* (1959), *Freud* (1962). She was the first Mexican-American actress to be nominated for an oscar for *Imitation of Life* (1959). She retired in 1964 and published a book, *Silhouettes 1937–1938*.

Rita Macedo. A gifted Mexican actress, she debuted in Mexican cinema in *Las Cinco Noches* (1942). She played the second female lead in one U.S. film, *Stronghold* (1952), opposite Arturo de Cordova and Veronica Lake. She married and divorced actor-director Emilio Fernandez. She gave memorable performances in Buñuel's *Ensayo de un Crimen* (1955) and *Nazarin* (1959). She committed suicide in November 1993 in Mexico City.

Maria Elena Marquez. An acclaimed Mexican actress since the early 1940s: *La Perla* (1945), *Cuando Levanta la Niebla* (1952), *Reportaje* (1953), etc. She starred in two U.S. films, the superior *Across the Wide Missouri* (1951) with Clark Gable and the inferior *Ambush at Tomahawk Gap* (1953).

Miroslava. She was born Miroslava Stern on March 10, 1926, in Prague, Czechoslovakia. She went to Mexico as a war refugee in 1940 and became a popular and versatile star in Mexican films: *Bodas Tragicas* (1946), *Ensayo de un Crimen* (1954), *Escuela de Vagabundos* (1956). She made an impressive U.S. debut in *The Brave Bulls* (1951) and was ill-used in the inferior *Stranger on Horseback* (1955). The melancholy blonde died of an overdose of sleeping pills on March 10, 1955.

Rosenda Monteros. A pretty Mexican actress who found moderate popularity in U.S. films in the fifties and sixties: *A Woman's Devotion* (1956), *Villa!* (1958), *The Magnificent Seven* (1960), *Savage Pampas* (1967).

Sarita Montiel. She was born Maria Antonia Fernandez Abad in 1928 in Campo de Criptana, Spain. A striking beauty and popular singer, she gained stardom in Spanish and Mexican films beginning with *Te Quiero para mi* (1944). She was courted by Hollywood for four films: *That Man from Tangier* (1953), *Vera Cruz* (1954) with Gary Cooper and Burt Lancaster, *Run of the Arrow* (1957) with Rod Steiger, and *Serenade* (1957) with Mario Lanza. She returned to Spanish and Mexican films such as *El Ultimo Cuple* (1957) and *La Violetera* (1958). She married and divorced director Anthony Mann.

Rita Moreno. She was born Rosita Dolores Alverio on December 11, 1931, in Humacao, Puerto Rico. She debuted on Broadway stage at the age of thirteen and in films at fourteen, in *A Medal for Benny* (1945). Typecast as a Latina sexpot in the fifties in mostly inferior roles, she acquired accolades thereafter. Key films: *The Ring* (1952); *The King and I* (1956); *West Side Story* (1961), for which she became the first Latina to win an Oscar as Best Supporting Actress; *The Night of the Following Day* (1969); *Carnal Knowledge* (1971). She won a Tony for her Broadway role in *The Ritz* in 1976.

Rosaura Revueltas. She was born in 1919 in Mexico to a family of artistic distinction. Her brothers were Jose, a writer; Fermin, a painter; and Silvestre, a composer. Initially a dancer, the gifted and uncommonly beautiful actress debuted in Emilio Fernandez's *Un Dia de Vida* (1950) and followed with *Las Islas Marias* (1950) opposite Pedro Infante. She made her U.S. debut in *Sombrero* (1953). Her lead role in *Salt of the Earth* (1954) resulted in world acclaim and Hollywood and Mexican film blacklisting. Thereafter she toured the world with Berlolt Brecht's German troupe, Berliner Ensemble. She is retired.

Lalo Rios. He was born in San Miguelita, Mexico, in 1927 and grew up in the Lincoln Heights barrio in East Los Angeles. As a gifted and sensitive actor, he found his opportunities restricted by Hollywood prejudice and exclusion. He was memorable as a Chicano youth in *The Lawless* (1950) and as the boxer in *The Ring* (1952). Thereafter, he was relegated to small parts and television: *City beneath the Sea* (1953), *The Big Leaguer* (1953), *Touch of Evil* (1958). He died on March 14, 1973.

251

Carmen Sevilla. She was born in 1930 in Sevilla, Spain. An attractive singer, she graced continental and Mexican films. She made three U.S. films: *Spanish Affair* (1958), *King of Kings* (1961), and *Anthony and Cleopatra* (1972).

Armando Silvestre. A muscular Mexican actor (born 1926) has enjoyed moderate popularity in Mexican cinema. He has played mostly Indian villains in U.S. films: *Wyoming Mail* (1950), *Geronimo* (1962), *The Scalphunters* (1968).

Valentin de Vargas. Latino leading man of "B" films: *Touch of Evil* (1957), *Hatari* (1962), *The Firebrand* (1962) as Joaquin Murieta.

The 1960s

Antonio Aguilar. A popular singer/actor star of Mexican films since the late 1950s. He made one U.S. film, *The Undefeated* (1969), with John Wayne.

Alfonso Arau. He was born on January 11, 1932, in Mexico City. A dancer, actor, and director, he established himself in Mexican films: *En Este Pueblo no hay Ladrones* (1964), *Calzonzin Inspector* (1973), *Mojado Power* (1979). He was impressive in *The Wild Bunch* (1969), but his other U.S. roles have been routine. He scored a surprise hit directing *Like Water for Chocolate* (1992). His most recent directorial effort was *A Walk in the Clouds* (1995) with Anthony Quinn.

Pedro Armendariz, Jr. He was born on March 9, 1947, in Mexico, son of the famous Mexican film star. He has had moderate success: *Guns for San Sebastion (1968), The Undefeated* (1969), *Chisum* (1970), the latter two with his father's close friend, John Wayne.

Aurora Clavel. A talented dark-haired Mexican actress, she has played an assortment of supporting Indian and alluring camp follower roles in Mexican and U.S. films: *Tarahumara* (1964), *Major Dundee* (1964), *The Wild Bunch* (1969), *Soldier Blue* (1970).

Ana Martin. Pretty and petite Mexican actress, she made one impressive U.S. film appearance in the underestimated *Return of the Gunfighter* (1968) opposite Robert Taylor. She has been a top star in Mexican films and television since the late sixties: *El Gangster* (1964), etc.

Pilar Pellicer. A distinguished Mexican actress of screen, stage, and television and sister of the late Pina Pellicer, she was born in Mexico City, began as a dancer, and made her film debut in *El Gangster* (1964). Key films: *Tajimara* (1965), *La Choca* (1973), etc. Ill-used in two U.S. films: *Day of the Evil Gun* (1968) with Glenn Ford and *Love at First Bite* (1979).

Pina Pellicer. She was born on April 3, 1935, in Mexico City, younger sister of Pilar Pellicer. A gifted and sensitive actress, she made a memorable U.S. film debut in Marlon Brando's evocative *One-Eyed Jacks* (1961), which won her the Best Actress award at the San Sebastian Film Festival. She won more international awards for her portrayal of the peasant wife in the Mexican classic *Macario* (1961). Three more films followed: *Rogelia* (1961), *Dias de Otoño* (1961), *El Gran Pecador* (1961), and an appearance in "Alfred Hitchcock Presents": *Juan Diego*. Her brief, turbulent life came to an end by suicide on December 10, 1964.

Silvia Pinal. She was born in 1929 in Sonora, Mexico. She is the most versatile of all Mexican actresses in Mexican cinema, stage, radio, and television. Key films: *Puerto Joven* (1949), *El Inocente* (1955), *Divinas Palabras* (1977). Starred in a trio of Buñuel classics, *Viridinia* (1961), *The Exterminating Angel* (1962), and *Simon of the Desert* (1965). Hollywood wasted her in two films, *Guns for San Sebastian* (1968) with Anthony Quinn and *Sharks* (1970) with Burt Reynolds.

David Reynosa. He was born January 29, 1926, in Aguascalientes, Mexico. A brawny and rugged leading man and singer in Mexican films: *Aqui Esta Herarlio Bernal* (1957), *Viento Negro* (1964). He was impressive in two U.S. films: *The Rage* (1966) and *Stick* (1985). He died of cancer on June 9, 1994 in Mexico.

Jaime Sanchez. Stage-trained Puerto Rican actor, memorable in *The Wild Bunch* (1969), ill-used thereafter. Other films: *David and Lisa* (1962), *The Pawnbroker* (1965), *Beach Red* (1967).

Raquel Welch. She was born Raquel Tejado in Chicago, Illinois, of Bolivian parents. Typed as a sex symbol in the sixties, she developed into a formidable actress in Broadway theater, television, and films: *A House Is Not a Home* (1964), *Fantastic*

Voyage (1966), *Kansas City Bomber* (1967), *The Three Musketeers* (1974), *The Legend of Walks Far Woman* (1978).

The 1970s

Barbara Carrera. She was born on December 1, 1945, in Managua, Nicaragua. A bronzed beauty, she was typecast as a Latina vamp early by Hollywood. Key films: *The Master Gunfighter* (1975), *The Island of Dr. Moreau* (1977), *Never Say Never Again* (1983). She was impressive in the TV miniseries "Centennial" (1979).

Lynda Carter. She was born in 1952 in Phoenix, Arizona, of a Mexican-American mother and Anglo father. A beauty contest winner, she won the lead in TV's top-rated "Wonder Woman" (1976–79). Other than *Bobbie Joe and the Outlaw* (1976), her film appearances have been on television.

Henry Darrow. He was born on September 15, 1933, in New York City. This amiable and easygoing actor won accolades for a series of leading roles on television: "The High Chaparral" (1967-71); "The New Dick Van Dyke Show" (1973-74); "Harry O" (1974-75); "Zorro and Son" (1983); and "Me and Mom" (1985). His best film role remains that of the patriarch in *Seguin* (1982). Other films: *Badge 373* (1973), *Attica* (1980), *L.A. Bounty* (1989), *The Last of the Finest* (1990).

Moctezuma Esparza. Chicano film producer and graduate of Abraham Lincoln High School, who began in documentary and educational documentaries in 1973. His production company Esparza/Katz has been active in producing Latino-themed projects. Films include: *Once in a Liftime* (1978), *The Ballad of Gregorio Cortez* (1983), *The Milagro Beanfield War* (1988), *Gettysburgh* (1993).

Stella Garcia. A Latina actress who disappeared after two impressive film roles, in *The Last Movie* (1971) with Dennis Hopper and *Joe Kidd* (1972) with Clint Eastwood.

Jorge Luke. Minor Mexican lead (born 1943) in several U.S. films: *The Revengers* (1972), *Ulzana's Raid* (1972), etc.

Cheech Marin. He was born in Los Angeles, California, on July 13, 1946. He and Tommy Chong comprised a comedy team that did nightclubs, record albums, and films. Film debut in *Up* *in Smoke* (1978). Other films: *Cheech and Chong's Nice Dreams* (1981); *Things Are Bad All Over* (1982); *Born In East L.A.* (1987), which he also directed; *Rude Awakening* (1989). He played the sidekick in Luis Valdez's *The Cisco Kid* (1994).

A. Martinez. A Chicano leading man, born in 1948, in Los Angeles, California. Scored a success in TV soap opera "Santa Barbara" in 1984. His best performance, however, remains as the title character in *Seguin* (1980). Other films: *The Cowboys* (1972), *Pow Wow Highway* (1989).

Ofelia Medina. A gifted actress, memorable in *Frida* (1988). Made one U.S. film, *The Big Fix* (1978), with Richard Dreyfuss. More recently, she has been an activist for political reform in Mexico, especially in behalf of Indian human rights.

Taryn Power. Daughter of Tyrone Power and Mexican actress Linda Christian, she was born on September 13, 1953, in San Francisco, California. A talented beauty, she scored a hit in the Mexican Film *Maria* (1970) and followed it with some successful U.S. films: *The Count of Monte Cristo* (1975), *Tracks* (1977), *The Eye of the Tiger* (1977). She became semiretired when she married.

Maria Richwine. A Columbian-born actress best known for her role of "Maria," the Puerto Rican wife of rocker Buddy Holly, in *The Buddy Holly Story* (1978). Ill-used thereafter: *Vengeance* (1989), etc.

Jorge Rivero. A muscle-bound Mexican action star (born 1944) in Mexican films since 1964. Has met with moderate success in U.S. films: *Soldier Blue* (1970), *Rio Lobo* (1970), *The Last Hard Man* (1976), *Fist Fighter* (1989).

Pepe Serna. A versatile Chicano actor of stage, screen, and television. He was born in 1944 in Corpus Christi, Texas. Key films: *Johnny Got His Gun* (1971), *Red Sky in the Morning* (1970), *Raices de Sangre* (1979), *Seguin* (1980), *The Ballad of Gregorio Cortez* (1983), *Break of Dawn* (1988), *American Me* (1992).

Martin Sheen. He was born Ramon Estevez on August 3, 1940, in Dayton, Ohio, of a Spanish father and Irish mother. He won accolades on the stage before heading for Hollywood. Key films: *The Incident* (1967), *The Subject Was Roses* (1968), *Apocalypse Now* (1979), *The Believers* (1987), *Wall Street* (1987). On television: *The Execution of Private Slovik* (1974), *Blind Ambition* (1981), *Kennedy* (1983). He is active in social causes. He is father to Emilio Estevez and Charlie Sheen.

Jesus Salvador Treviño. A director-writer who holds an honored place in the annals of Chicano cinema. He has served both as a pioneer and as a vanguard of the Chicano experience. He was born in East Los Angeles, graduated to public television in the late sixties, and directed a milestone documentary, *Yo Soy Chicano* (1972). His first feature was the impressive *Raices de Sangre* (1979), the first Mexican film to be written and directed by a Chicano. Among his most important television work is *Seguin* (1980).

Daniel Valdez. A Chicano actor/musician writer, the younger brother of Luis Valdez, he was born in 1949 in Delano, California, to a family of Mexican farm workers. While members of the United Farm Workers Union, he and his brother founded El Teatro Campesino in the mid sixties. Daniel's best screen role was as "Henry Reina" in *Zoot Suit* (1981). Other films: *Which Way Is Up?* (1977), *The China Syndrome* (1979), *La Bamba* (1987).

Isela Vega. A statuesque Mexican actress born in Sonora, Mexico, and typecast as a sexpot: *Don Juan 67* (1966), *El Festin de la Loba, La Pacadoras,* etc. She later became a producer and evolved into a good actress when given the opportunity, as in Sam Peckinpah's *Bring Me the Head of Alfredo Garcia* (1974). Other U.S. films: *The Deadly Trackers* (1973), *Drum* (1976), *Barbarosa* (1982). She retired from films in the mid eighties.

Richard Yniguez. A promising Chicano leading man, especially impressive in *The Deadly Tower* (1975) and *Raices de Sangre* (1979). Ill-used by Hollywood thereafter: *Together Brothers (1974), Boulevard Nights* (1979) etc. He has done extensive work on stage and television.

The 1980s

Maria Conchita Alonse. She was born in 1957 in Cienfuegos, Cuba. She became established as a television and film star in Venezuela before entering U.S. films. Often typed as a Latina sexpot: *Fear City* (1984), *Moscow on the Hudson* (1984),

Extreme Prejudice (1987), *Colors* (1988), *Predator 2* (1990), *Roosters* (1994).

Steven Bauer. He was born Esteban Echevarria on December 2, 1956, in Havana, Cuba. He has met with moderate success as a romantic leading man: *She's in the Army* (1981), *Scarface* (1983), *Thief of Hearts* (1984), *Gleaming the Cube* (1989), *Drug Wars: The Caramena Story* (1990).

Robert Beltran. He was born in Bakersfield, California. A talented Chicano leading man deserving of better opportunities, he was most impressive as the troubled Chicano military adviser in *Latino* (1986). Other films: *Zoot Suit* (1980), *Eating Raoul* (1982), *Lone Wolf McQuade* (1983), *Calendar Girl Murders* (1984), *Scenes from the Class Struggle in Beverly Hills* (1989). More recently, he is a co-star in TV's "Star Trek: The New Generation," beginning in 1995.

Ruben Blades. He was born on July 16, 1948, in Panama City. He has managed two successful careers in music and films. His best film role remains that of "Rudy Veloz," an East Harlem salsa singer attempting to break into the mainstream music industry, in *Crossover Dreams* (1985). Other films: *Critical Condition* (1986), *Fatal Beauty* (1987), *The Milagro Beanfield War* (1988).

Sonia Braga. She was born in 1951 in Maringa, Brazil. Typed as a Latina sex symbol in Brazilian and U.S. films: *Doña Flor and Her Two Husbands* (1977), *I Love You* (1982), *Lady in the Bus* (1982), *Gabriela* (1984), *The Kiss of the Spider Woman* (1985), *The Milagro Beanfield War* (1988), *Moon over Parador* (1988), *The Rookie* (1990), and *The Burning Season* (1994—TV).

Julie Carmen. A Latina leading lady with extensive theater background: *Night of the Juggler* (1980), *Gloria* (1980), *The Milagro Beanfield War* (1989), *The Penitent* (1987), *Neon Empire* (1991).

Elipidia Carrillo. She was born on August 16, 1961, in Paracuara, Michoacan, Mexico. A sensitive and talented beauty often typed as an uprooted Latina, victim of contemporary economic and political upheavals in Latin America: *El Mundo Nuevo* (1975), *A Filo del Agua* (1976), *The Border* (1982), *Salvador* (1986), *Predator* (1987).

Miriam Colon. A durable Puerto Rican actress (born in 1949) of stage, screen, television: *Crowded Paradise* (1956), *One-Eyed Jacks* (1961), *Scarface* (1983), *Back Roads* (1981).

Rosana De Soto. An amiable and versatile Chicana actress born in San Jose, California. Prominent on film and television: *The In-Laws* (1979), *The Ballad of Gregorio Cortez* (1983), *American Justice* (1985), *La Bamba* (1987), *Stand and Deliver* (1988), *Family Business* (1989).

Rene Enriquez. A character actor of Nicaraguan ancestry (1933–90) better known as "Lt. Ray Calletano" in TV's "Hill Street Blues." Films: *Girl of the Night* (1960), *Bananas* (1971), *Serpico* (1973), *Under Fire* (1983).

Emilio Estevez. He was born on May 12, 1962, in New York City, son of Martin Sheen. Emilio is an actor, director, and writer, and has appeared in *Apocalypse Now* (1979), *Tex* (1982), *Stakeout* (1987), *Young Guns* (1988), *Young Guns II* (1990), *Men at Work* (1990).

Jenny Gago. She was born in Peru in 1953. Statuesque actress has attempted to break Latina sexpot typecasting: *Under Fire* (1983), *Best Seller* (1983), *Old Gringo* (1989), *Sweet 16* (1990).

Silvana Gallardo. An accomplished and versatile actress born in New York City's South Bronx of Venezuelan ancestry. She did mostly Broadway and off-Broadway theater through the sixties and in 1977 made an impressive TV debut in the PBS Special "The People vs. Inez Garcia." Films: *Windwalker* (1980), *Death Wish II* (1982), *The Calendar Girl Murders* (1984), *Silence of the Heart* (1984), *Copacabana* (1985), *Out of the Dark* (1989), *Solar Crisis* (1990), *Women in Prison* (1991).

Andy Garcia. Cuban-born (April 12, 1956) leading man: *Blue Skies Again* (1983), *The Untouchables* (1987), *Stand and Deliver* (1988), *Black Rain* (1988), *Godfather III* (1990) for which he was nominated for an Oscar for Best Supporting Actor.

Bianca Jagger. She was born on May 2, 1945, in Managua, Nicaragua. Socialite turned actress and social activist: *Couleor Chair* (1978), *The American Success Company* (1980), *The Cannonball Run* (1981). Once married to rock star Mick Jagger, 1970–79.

Raul Julia. He was born on March 9, 1940, in San Juan, Puerto Rico. Gifted stage, screen, and television actor: *The Organization Man* (1979); *Kiss of the Spider Woman* (1985), for which he was nominated for an Oscar as Best Actor; *Moon over Parador* (1988); *Tequila Sunrise* (1988); *Romero* (1989), *The Addams Family* (1992). While filming *El Mariachi II* in Mexico, he suffered a massive cerebral hemorrhage. After eight days in a coma, he died on October 24, 1994. His last film was *The Burning Season* (1994—HBO).

Alma Martinez. A talented Chicana actress, born in Coahuila, Mexico. She has done extensive film, theater, and television ("The New Adam 12" [1990]) and worked with El Teatro Campesino. Films: *Zoot Suit* (1982), *Barbarosa* (1982), *Under Fire* (1983), *Trial by Terror* (1984), *Born in East L.A.* (1987), *The Novice* (1995).

Esai Morales. Aspiring leading man born in 1963 in New York City of Cuban parentage: *Forty-Deuce* (1982), *Bad Boys* (1983), *La Bamba* (1987), *Bloodhound of Broadway* (1989).

Edward James Olmos. He was born on February 24, 1947, in the Boyle Heights neighborhood of East Los Angeles, California. This Chicano leading man began as a rock musician and by the late 1960s gravitated to theater, television, and film. Key films: *Alambrista!* (1977); *Seguin* (1981); *Blade Runner* (1982); *Zoot Suit* (1982); *The Ballad of Gregorio Cortez* (1983); *Stand and Deliver*, for which he was nominated for an Oscar for Best Actor (1987); *Triumph of the Spirit* (1989); *Talent for the Game* (1991); *American Me* (1992) (starred-directed-coscripted); *Roosters* (1993); *The Burning Season* (1994–HBO).

Elizabeth Peña. She was born in 1961 in New Jersey, of Cuban ancestry. Active in theater, television, and film: *El Super* (1977), *Crossover Dreams* (1985), *Down and Out in Beverly Hills* (1986), *La Bamba* (1987), *Vibes* (1989).

Tony Plana. Versatile all-purpose actor of Cuban ancestry: *Zoot Suit* (1982), *An Officer and a Gentleman* (1982), *Salvador* (1986), *Latino* (1986), *Born in East L.A.* (1987), *Break of Dawn* (1988), *J.F.K.* (1991).

Paul Rodriguez. He was born in 1955 in Mazatlan, Mexico. He began as stand-up comedian and has been active on screen and television: *D.C. Cab* (1987), *Born in East L.A.* (1987), *Made in America* (1993).

Charlie Sheen. He was born Carlos Irwin Estevez on September 3, 1965, in Santa Monica, California, son of Martin Sheen. Prominent leading man in some important films: *The Execution of Private Slovick* (1974), *Platoon* (1986), *Wall Street* (1987), *Young Guns* (1988), *Major League* (1989), *Cadence* (1991), *Hot Shots Part Deux* (1993).

Trinida Silva. Colorful Chicano actor who died in a car accident (1950–88). Films include: *Alambrista!* (1976), *Walk Proud* (1979), *The Milagro Beanfield War* (1988), *Colors* (1988).

Jimmy Smits. The tall leading man of Puerto Rican ancestry was born in Brooklyn, New York, on July 9, 1955. A stage-trained actor, he came to wide prominence in two popular TV series, *L.A. Law* and later on *N.Y.P.D.* His films include: *Running Scared* (1986), *True Believers* (1987), and *The Old Gringo* (1989). His best role was the embittered younger brother in *My Family* (1995).

Rachel Ticotin. She was born on November 1, 1958, in the Bronx, New York. A gifted and sensitive Puerto Rican actress, she has often been missed by Hollywood. Films include: *The Wanderer* (1979), *Fort Apache, the Bronx* (1981), *Total Recall* (1990), *F / X II* (1991), *Falling Down* (1993).

Luis Valdez. He was born in 1940 in Delano, California, to a family of Mexican migrant workers. Cofounded with his brother, Daniel, El Teatro Campesino in 1965, while a member of the United Farm Workers Union. Primarily a playright and director, he has also acted. Credits: *I Am Joaquin* (1967) as narrator, *Zoot Suit* (1983) as director and writer, *Which Way Is Up?* (1977), *La Bamba* (1987) as director and writer. He has done extensive television. His most recent directorial effort was *The Cisco Kid* (1994), and he is working to make a film about Cesar Chavez.

The 1990s

Interview with Silvana Gallardo (April 5, 1991)

Q. Which have been your favorite roles?

A. I have had many wonderful roles. . . . I did an episode of Lou Grant [*Prisoner*] which I liked very much. I played a first lady of a fictitious South American country run by a

Versatile Venezuelan-American Silvano Gallardo, star of film, stage, and television. Here in *Death Wish II* (1982). Courtesy of Hoening & Baxter.

dictator. It was controversial and important. I enjoyed my role in *Copacabana* because I got to sing and dance and be outrageous. I loved playing Inez Garcia. I actually met her. I like roles that have a social significance.

Q. What would you recommend to young Hispanic actors who hope to break into television and film?

A. All young actors should study their craft and be very patient. It's a long distance run and there are no real shortcuts. Do plays . . . be seen . . . get good photos that represent them . . . live a real life.

Q. How have you been able to escape stereotypical roles?

A. At first I didn't escape the stereotype. My first role, I was dressed in blue and yellow and orange, etc., and was very pregnant. I have turned down roles now that I feel are demeaning to Latins. I have turned down many maid roles . . . not all . . . but most.

Q. Do you feel that the Hollywood film industry has changed their perceptions of Hispanics?

A. No, I do not feel that Hollywood has changed much in their perception. Most of the roles are still as maids and gang members, etc. I have been luckier than most, but it still bothers me when my agent calls with an interview for a great part . . . even though she is a maid.

Q. Who were your acting role models?

A. My favorite role models . . . Vivica Lindfors, Katharine Hepburn, Montgomery Clift, Marlon Brando.

Q. Do you think things are improving for Hispanics in the film industry?

A. Yes and no. At one Golden Eagle Awards ceremony, they had mostly Anglo presenters . . . non-Hispanic. . . . I feel they were doing the same thing . . . keeping Latins out.

Q. What control have you been able to acquire to alter sexist roles offered?

A. None of my roles have been sexist.

Q. Who are your favorite film directors?
A. My favorite director . . . Elia Kazan. Ones that I've worked with and really liked . . . Gregory Hoblit, Curtis Hanson, John Gray, Leo Penn, Larry Elikann and Joan Micklin Silver . . . to name a few.

Q. Do you see Hollywood continuing to make films like *El Norte, La Bamba,* and *Stand and Deliver?*
A. As long as there is money in it for them, they will do features such as *Stand and Deliver.*

Q. Do you have some favorite and future project that you would like to make?
A. I have written a manuscript called *The Winning,* which I very much want produced and want to star in.

Q. Would you like to direct in the future?
A. Yes, I would like to direct and produce. I did that in my video *The Acting Class* . . . next time a feature.

Q. Would you like to produce in the future?
A. Yes, but only as the star. My brother, Edward, is a fine playwright and has a project I want to do . . . *Waltz on a Merry-Go-Round.*

Q. Have you thought of doing a film version of your PBS Special on Inez Garcia?
A. I would like to do a film version of Inez Garcia, as that was one of my most favorite works.

Q. Do you feel there is a difference between acting in the theatre and on film?
A. Not really. Good acting is good acting. Many people think they can get away with bad acting on stage . . . but you really can't. It's all the same . . . only you have to be heard, project on stage.

Q. Do you prefer comedy or drama?

A. I love drama, but if it is really funny . . . not stupid but real funny, then I love doing comedy.

Q. Who have been the favorite actors you have worked with?

A. My husband, Billy Drago. I also loved working with Robert Loggia and Trevor Howard.

Q. Did you find difficult to play your role in *Death Wish II?* Especially, in the sense that it involved violence against women and not glorify or sensationalize it?

A. *Death Wish II* was a very hard film to do. I did the role because I wanted to show people the reality of rape. Not a glorified, pretty, rape, but a hard and disgusting and painful experience. I went to a crowded movie house to see it . . . No one laughed . . . No one said ugly things . . . they watched a woman being victimized, brutalized. I think it was real and made a difference.

Q. Being an accomplished actress, did you find doing the nude scenes in *Death Wish II* very hard to do?

A. It was very difficult to do, but it was a closed set. Only those directly involved were there, and I was covered until the director screamed "action." And then I was in the scene.

Q. Do you have other vocations besides acting?

A. I'm a wonderful teacher. I believe that is an art form. I'm also a wonderful cook.

Q. What would you like to say to your fans and public?

A. This is a very hard business. You have to be willing to invest from your heart and soul with no guarantee of a pay off. If you can do anything else, you should. I love the work. I care about the art of acting. I care about every student that stays with me. I love my husband and my home and my life.

Interview with Alma Martinez (May 11, 1991)

Q. Who were the role models that inspired you to become an actress?

A. Maria Felix, Errol Flynn, Katharine Hepburn.

Q. How have you been able to avoid being cast in stereotypical or sexist roles?
A. By refusing such roles and my training myself as an actress and expanding my life experiences and knowledge of people.

Q. Which have been your favorite roles on television and films?
A. *La Rielera/Corridos*; the rest is on the stage.

Q. Would you like to teach acting or direct in the future?
A. Yes. Definitely.

Q. Is there some favorite project that you would like to bring to television or screen?
A. Yes. Novels: *Mexican Village, Famous All over Town, Barrio Boy.*

Q. What would you recommend to young Chicanos/Latinos who would like to pursue a career in acting?
A. Approach as a career-train, do it, be tenacious and dedicated. Don't take, "Are you crazy?," for an answer.

Q. How prevalent is prejudice or racism in the Hollywood film industry? In theatre?
A. Very, very prevalent. SAG [Screen Actor's Guild] is doing the best job in fighting it but AFTRA and especially AEA (theatre union) are the worst.

Q. Do you think that more films like *El Norte, Zoot Suit,* or *Stand and Deliver* will continue to be made by Hollywood or do you think this was only a brief infatuation by Hollywood with us?
A. Hollywood didn't make the films, Chicanos did. Hollywood doesn't realize yet that it needs us.

Q. Do you see as viable any Mexican-Chicano co-production like *Raices de Sangre* in the future in order to offset lack of Hollywood financial backing for Hispanic-oriented films?

A. Yes. Two projects are now in preproduction stages. Directors Alex Cox, Rafael Portillo.

Q. Do you think that one area of conflict with Hollywood and Hispanics is that perhaps we tend to perceive ourselves differently from what they perceive us to be?
A. Most definitely. Most of Hollywood relate to Hispanics via their domestic help.

Q. Other than in Nosotros, is there other concrete unity by Hispanic actors and actresses? What role do you think the community can play to improve the opportunities for Hispanics in television and film?
A. Nosotros is not concrete. HAMAS is a much better organization and more far-reaching. Boycotting product sponsors who misrepresent or fail to represent Hispanics in the media. Sponsors buy air time.

Q. Who are your favorite Mexican, Chicano or American directors?
A. Directors: Luis Valdez, Sidney Lumet, Jonathan Demme, Coppola, Scorsese, Luis Barretto.

Q. What are some of your favorite Mexican or Chicano-oriented films?
A. *Zoot Suit, El Norte,* all of Indio Fernandez, all Mexican (Golden Age Period).

Q. Do you prefer to play comedy or drama?
A. Either—a good script is the element.

Q. Which medium has been more artistically satisfying to you: theatre, television or film?
A. Theatre.

Q. If there are Hispanic screenwriters out there who would like to interest you in a script, should they contact a studio or yourself?
A. Me!

Q. Is there anything you would like to say to the Hispanic community and fans?

A. Be more demanding of television. It is a subversive, covert teacher. Media has the power to transform all.

An Interview with Rosaura Revueltas (February 14, 1992, Cuernavaca, Mexico)

"No, I wouldn't change nothing. I wouldn't change any-thing . . . !" stated the Mexican ex-actress Rosaura Revueltas, whose brilliant film career was destroyed as a consequence of her participation in a film banned politically in the United States in 1954.

The actress, who was blacklisted in both the U.S. and Mexi-can film industry after her lead role in the famous *Salt of the Earth,* commented on a variety of issues in an exclusive inter-view with her at her home in Cuernavaca, Mexico. "What type of human rights deprives a woman at the pinnacle of her youth and career, destroys her career so that she may not be able to do anything? But that is what that film cost me. That film cost me my career . . . ," stated the former actress. She said this with a tinge of sadness and resignation, but with an affirmation of the maturity of her political principles.

In the early 1950s, Rosaura Revueltas was one of the most brilliant Mexican actresses. Her family was prominent in the artistic and political circles of the era. Originally from Durango, her family produced three brothers who distinguished them-selves in the arts: Jose, in literature; Silvestre, a composer; and Fermin, a painter. For her part, Rosaura distinguished herself in theatre and film.

She obtained stardom after two lead roles in a pair of films directed by the reknowned Emilio "Indio" Fernandez. In *Un Dia de Vida* (1950), for her role of Mama Juanita she won the Ariel, Mexico's version of the Academy Award. In her second film, *Las Islas Marias* (1950), she played a mother of three wayward off-spring trapped in the despair of perpetual poverty. The film gave her an opportunity to share starring honors with Mexico's great film idol Pedro Infante. Due to these successes, she was contracted by Metro-Goldwyn-Mayer for their Mexico-lensed film *Sombrero* (1953), with a cast that included Ricardo Montalban, Yvonne De Carlo, Pier Angeli, and Vittorio Gassman.

In the United States, it was the era of Sen. Joseph McCarthy and the anticommunist hysteria, which was characterized by gross violations of civil liberties. In 1953, the well-known screenwriter Michael Wilson (he had been an Oscar winner for *A Place in the Sun*) and director Herbert Biberman offered Rosaura the lead role of Esperanza in their film *Salt of the Earth*. The character Esperanza was the Mexican-American wife of a mine union leader involved in a strike in New Mexico. Ironically, the union leader, the workers, and the labor struggle were based on fact. For example, Juan Chacon, who enacted the role of the union leader, played himself.

In any case, already at the start of the film Wilson, Biberman, and producer Paul Jarrico had been blacklisted by the House Un-American Activities Committee (HUAC). As a consequence, the powers that be in the U.S. film industry and government circles attempted to prevent the making and distribution of the film. Rosaura recollected why she made the film. ". . . I don't know if, if out of sentiment, but my father, my grandfather had been miners and I wanted to do something in favor of the miners. And when I read the screenplay it was a work of art, a work of literature . . . magnificent! A language, a sensitivity to know the Mexican, and Wilson was a complete gringo! . . ."

Rosaura was arrested, jailed, and subsequently deported from the United States. I asked her what assistance the Mexican government or the ANDA (the Mexican Actors' Guild) provided. She responded with a resigned rancor, "Frankly, they gave me no assistance over there, not the consul, not the ambassador over there, nothing, nothing, because I am a Revueltas . . ." In relation to the Mexican Actors' Guild she stated, "Yes, there was a lot of polemics at the beginning . . . But, but as they were filming several U.S. films in Mexico, everybody was afraid to say a word. At the beginning, yes, there were voices of support, and later nobody spoke up, not a word. Everyone forgot about the issue . . ."

She was effectively blacklisted in both countries. Later she traveled as an actress with Bertolt Brecht's famous Berliner Ensemble throughout Europe. Years later, she established a dance school in Cuernavaca. She had been a dancer before entering the acting profession.

While *Salt of the Earth* was banned in the United States until the late 1960s, in the rest of the world the film acquired unanimous acclaim and earned a cult status. Rosaura won numerous acting awards and praise. In reality, it was the first "Chicano" film. It was the first time in the history of the U.S. cinema that the world was perceived through the eyes of a working-class Mexican-American woman. Additionally, the film tackles issues rare in any cinema: sexism, racism, culture, community, and labor struggle. Nevertheless, it was all acquired at a heavy price in human terms. Miss Revueltas affirmed emphatically, ". . . this film cost me my career . . . But it won me many friends and the admiration of many. . . ."

The ex-actress commented on other concerns with ardor and conviction. On the subject of racial discrimination in Mexico she stated, "They say there isn't . . . but yes, discrimination, of course there is discrimination! The same as in all the *telenovelas* [Mexican soap operas]. All the ones who have Mexican characteristics are servants, all the others with blond hair, artificial blond hair . . . are the ladies of the house . . ."

She lamented the mediocre state of Mexican cinema, and I asked her who was the best exponent of Mexican film. ". . . Emilio Fernandez was the best. He really created a great cinema which made Mexico renowned abroad in a positive way, because he had a talented crew, because he had actors and Gabriel Figueroa as a cinematographer . . . ," she commented. I asked her if she had seen any Chicano films. "No, I have seen none! . . . Yes, I've heard of all of them, but they don't come to Cuernavaca," she said.

Finally, I asked her if she wanted to say something for the new Chicano generation, who have seen *Salt of the Earth* and consider her an authentic heroine. Her eyes sparkled brightly with hope and understanding. ". . . that we must struggle and master everything. . . . To have dignity above everything, to

The author and Rosaura Revueltas during an interview in January 1992 in Cuernavaca, Mexico.

maintain their dignity, the dignity of identity. Because to go to the United States is to lose your identity."

Note: Two of Rosaura Revueltas's films are available on video: *Las Islas Marias* and *Salt of the Earth*.